Moral Understandings

Moral Understandings

A Feminist Study in Ethics

Margaret Urban Walker

ROUTLEDGE

New York and London

Published in 1998 by
Routledge
29 West 35th Street
New York, NY 10001

Published in Great Britain in 1998 by
Routledge
11 New Fetter Lane
London EC4P 4EE

Printed in the United States of America on acid-free paper
Design: Jack Donner

Library of Congress Cataloging-in-Publication Data

Walker, Margaret Urban, 1948–
    Moral understandings : a feminist study in ethics / Margaret Urban Walker
        p.   cm.
    Includes bibliographical references and index.
    ISBN 0–415–91420–5. — ISBN 0-415-91421-3 (pbk.)
    1. Feminist ethics. I. Title.
    BJ1395.W33 1998
    170'.82—dc21   97–2449
                                                                          CIP

For My Mother
Virginia Sullivan Urban
With Love

contents

preface

I'm awfully relieved this book is past, but find with some regret that it is mostly prologue. I began in moral philosophy some fifteen years ago in perplexity and irritation. I did not see in much moral theory depictions of agency, judgment, and responsibility that I could recognize in my own experience. Moral theory seemed to me far out of joint with moral phenomenology. Ten years later feminist theory had given me a new and exciting slant on why I might have found it so. Feminist work in ethics brought immediately to the fore the question of whose experience theories speak for and to, and the importance of seeing theory as both an expression of a theorist's position to know and a claim of authority for that position. Perhaps, then, my perplexity resulted from my own position and its different sight lines, and my irritation from the presumption of authority for a position I did not share. Some other women's work supported the hunch that one aspect of positions determining lines of sight was gender. But then it turned out that gender is not the only such aspect, and that gender isn't one self-same component of points of view. So, what point of view *was* I, or were others writing on ethics or its feminist versions, inhabiting? What could be said from, and for, these points of view? And what claims to authority were not destined to be embarrassed in due course?

Excitement was followed by more perplexity and downright discouragement. I don't know if reflection destroys moral knowledge, but this much reflexivity torpedoed my sense of professional entitlement to speak about, or for, "the" moral agent or "our" intuitions and concepts of morality. I felt myself deskilled. After a year or two in an acute metamoral funk, I found ways to do what I guess philosophers always do: I made topics of my problems. I took as my topics the problems of reflexivity in moral theorizing. The problems include appreciating the complexity and tracing the shifting outlines of the different positions, morally and socially, that there are to be spoken about, for, and to, in that theorizing. What resulted is a sort of prolegomenon to any future work of my own. I hope some others may share my sense that moral philosophy becomes freshly interesting, and appropriately daunting, seen as I have rendered it here.

Inevitably, if unwisely, I have certain hopes for the audience to whom I might speak with this book. I want to address readers more than casually familiar with feminist and other politically critical or postmodern discourses who may be confused about what there is to say about ethics, or skeptical that there is anything to say about ethics, given what these bodies of work reveal. I try to show that a great deal of what we have learned in the last twenty years from these inquiries about subject positions, power, and social constructions is not opposed to ethics, but is instead part of an ethics that talks about how human beings actually live and judge.

I want to show the same to some moral philosophers who may be baffled by or hostile to these same critical discussions, if they know about them, or who may like to think either that these critical discussions are beside the point of ethics, or are an anti-ethics, which is then a good reason not to have to know about them. To these readers I have tried to indicate what this critical thinking has to offer ethics, and why.

I assume many philosophers and others are committed to views about the nature of morality that are different from or incompatible with the expressive-collaborative, culturally situated, and practice-based picture of morality I present here. I do not suppose I will persuade these readers to my view. I do hope that they will be challenged by my examinations of ways moral theories end up encoding specific social positions and cultural assumptions in highly idealized forms, and will feel a need to say more about how their theories meet, descriptively and prescriptively, the phenomenon of differentiated social-moral identities and statuses that are the rule rather than the exception in human societies. They might explain how a theory that holds that "there is" a uniform position of agency, judgment, or responsibility is supposed to map onto, or be seated in, moral-social worlds that are differentiated. My hope is that they might be struck differently by what is familiar.

Finally, I hope that if this book makes its way into classrooms or seminars, students will find a framework that helps them ask questions about their experiences of authority in morality and in social life, especially questions about who defines the moral problems and responsibilities that there are, and the perspectives that are necessary and admissible in discussions of them. I hope those students who go on to teach and write about moral philosophy will keep on asking these questions, and keep them alive and central to ethics as a philosophical discipline.

Such are my hopes. Now for my debts.

Although this book was written in the past three years, some of its ideas have long roots. Speaking of narratives, as I do below, I believe this book began life in a cafe in Belgium a long time ago, and came to a finish quite a bit later under the palm trees of Florida. I thank Herman DeDijn and Arnold Burms of the Catholic University of Leuven for a cafe conversation while I was a Guest Professor at the Higher Institute of Philosophy in 1981–82 about why consistency is important in morality. Robert Audi's National Endowment for the Humanities Summer Institute on Action Theory in 1984 at the University of Nebraska helped me think at length about the structure of actions and lives, a topic that has made its way into this book differently than I could have imagined then.

Fordham University provided me with Faculty Fellowships at every point of eligibility, in 1982, 1986–87, 1992, 1996–97, without which I could never have moved forward with my research. I thank graduate students at Fordham in seminars on moral theory (Spring 1990), moral agency (Spring 1995), and feminist theory (Spring 1992 and Fall 1995) for being responsive and challenging audiences for many of the ideas that grew into this book. A seminar with Carol Gilligan, holder of the Laurie Chair in Women's Studies at Rutgers University in Spring 1986, was a turning point for me; I am grateful to Carol Gilligan for her intellectual support of my earliest efforts to bring moral philosophy together with feminism. A week as instructor at an NEH Summer Seminar on Ethics and the Liberal Arts at Bethany College in West Virginia in July, 1991, was a useful and agreeable rehearsal for my ideas about an expressive-collaborative model for ethics; I thank Nancy Blackford for the invitation, the group for its probing discussions, and Wally Martin for challenging follow-up conversation. A visiting semester at Washington University in St. Louis in Spring, 1994, cleared the space in which my vision of this book finally jelled. Thanks to Marilyn Friedman, Larry May, and Roger Gibson for the invitation, and to them and other department members for congenial company. I completed this book during the 1996–97 academic year as a Frances Elvidge Fellow at The Ethics Center of the University of South Florida in St. Petersburg, with additional generous support of a Faculty Fellowship from Fordham University that made a full year's leave possible. Thanks to Peter French, Director of the Ethics Center, for the opportunity to share in the development of that new venture.

Many people have been friends, colleagues, and interlocutors in ways that helped me to write this book. Most of these people are ones I know, but I owe a deep debt to the work of Bernard Williams and Stanley Cavell, whom I do not. I am very glad to know as many feminist philosophers as I do, and to have shared the unique adventure in our lifetimes of women's unprecedented entry in significant numbers into positions of intellectual authority in our culture and profession. I thank all those women from whom I learned to do feminist philosophy; they are found in my bibliography.

My projects have been enriched for many years by Christopher Gowans's work in ethics and by his friendship. John Greco's insightful comments on my recent work, and his tutoring on some points of epistemology have been much appreciated. Several years of conversations in a shifting but resilient feminist reading group have taught me much, and I thank Patricia Mann, Kate Mehuron, Lee Quinby, and Elaine Rapping for what I have learned. My colleagues for several years in an interdisciplinary Fordham Faculty Ethics Seminar have shown me kinds of thinking about ethics that philosophers often just don't do; a special thank you to psychologist Celia Fisher for building the group, and to Dean Joseph McShane, S. J. for funding it. My colleagues at The Ethics Center of the University of South Florida helped me fine-tune some things in the final stages of this book: thanks to Peter French, Peggy DesAutels, Michael Byron, Mitch Haney, and Mark Woods. Fond thanks to Peggy for intellectual and practical support at the Center.

Many people have at some points offered comment, support, counsel, conversation, or their own philosophical work for which I was glad or grateful in writing this book. I mention people in the endnotes to chapters, but I want to thank Alison Jaggar, Sally Ruddick, Virginia Held, Simon Blackburn, Cheshire Calhoun, Diana Meyers, Marilyn Friedman, Larry May, Michael Stocker, Elizabeth Hegeman, Sissela Bok, Vincent Colapietro, and Walter Sinnott-Armstrong. Judith Bradford thinks like greased lightning; our rounds of intellectual leapfrog over the past several years have driven and indelibly stamped this book. I am grateful to James Lindemann Nelson and Hilde Lindemann Nelson in special ways. Jim's responses to my work have been models of pointed philosophical criticism gently bestowed. Hilde has read every word of this book more than once and provided throughout insightful philosophical prods, expert editorial advice, a fine sense of style, and unstinting encouragement.

Special fond thanks to two friends, Susan Walsh and Caroline Kalina, M.D., who have shared with me a lifetime's study of lives, fates, and character. My sister, Linda McCarthy, took the photo of me that appears on the book jacket; more important, I thank her for assisting our mother to continue her own life day by day.

This book might never have been attempted without the enthusiastic support of Maureen MacGrogan. My sadness that we did not finally publish this together is as deep as my gratitude to her. I thank Laska Jimsen for sensitively and conscientiously seeing the manuscript most of the way home with me, and Colin Jones and Bill Germano for seeing it into production. Managing Editor T. J. Mancini's calm good cheer was much appreciated in the final stages. I am grateful to Lorraine Code and Iris Young who speedily read the manuscript for Routledge. The changes I have been able to make in response to their insights have significantly improved the book.

Chapter 2 of this book appeared previously in almost identical form as "Where Do Moral Theories Come From?" *Philosophical Forum* 26 (1995): 242–57. It is used by permission of the journal.

A different version of chapter 3 appeared as "Feminist Skepticism, Transparency, and Authority," in *Moral Knowledge? New Readings in Moral Epistemology*, edited by Walter Sinnott-Armstrong and Mark Timmons, copyright © 1996 by Walter Sinnott-Armstrong. It is used by permission of Oxford University Press, Inc.

A shorter version of chapter 5 was published as "Picking Up Pieces: Lives, Stories, and Integrity," 23 pages in *Feminists Rethink The Self*, edited by Diana Tietjens Meyers, copyright © 1997 by Westview Press. The material is reprinted by permission of Westview Press.

I thank the publishers for permission to reprint these pieces.

For what remains incomplete, overstated, underargued, or just peculiar in this book, I have only myself to blame.

St. Petersburg, 1997

part one

The Mise-en-scène

Moral Philosophy Now

one

The Subject of Moral Philosophy

I believe that a "we" is often made by giving some knowers authority over others, as adults have authority over children. In this case, the others' knowledge does not disappear, it is hidden.

—Kathryn Pyne Addelson, *Moral Passages*

If I am inclined to suppose that a mouse has come into being by spontaneous generation out of grey rags and dust, I shall do well to examine those rags very closely to see how a mouse may have hidden in them, how it may have got there and so on. But if I am convinced that a mouse cannot come into being from these things, then this investigation will perhaps be superfluous. But first we must learn to understand what it is that opposes such an examination of details in philosophy.

—Ludwig Wittgenstein, *Philosophical Investigations*

Morality, many of us think, tells us something deep and central about how to live. Ethics, moral philosophers might say, is a reflective and normative study of morality. This much does not yet tell us what kind of thing "morality" is and so what is the subject matter of ethics. Nor does it tell what kinds of reflection on that subject matter are characteristic or constitutive of ethics. The idea that ethics is a "normative" study could mean that ethics studies norms or that ethics sets them. This difference is clearly an important one for ethics, bearing not only on the kind of study it is but on the epistemological position of the ethicist, for example, the moral philosopher. In assuming any of these matters to stand a certain way, one will have picked out a particular conception of ethics that, inevitably, has already selected some particular view of morality.

This book is as much about ethics, the philosophical study of morality, as it is about morality. It is mainly about moral epistemology, that is, about the nature, source, and justification of moral knowledge. A point of this book is to put in question, and hopefully to change, some views common at least among philosophers about what moral knowledge is like, where to look for it, and how to tell when you've found some. I defend a view of morality that makes knowledge in and of morality thoroughly enmeshed with social knowledge, both articulate and implicit. Further, I count among the concerns of moral epistemology questions about the epistemology of moral theorizing, and more specifically, the epistemic positions of moral philosophers.

Contrary to what I learned in becoming a professional philosopher, I now see moral philosophers and the study they undertake as *within* the plane of morality, not outside it or above it. Moral philosophers reflect on morality, moral judgment, and moral responsibility as they are familiar with it, and they are familiar with it from their own moral training, formed character, and social experience. The discourse of moral philosophy, with its claims that certain judgments are moral ones, that certain beings are moral persons, that certain conditions of responsibility are true and others incoherent, is not outside the social discourse of morality in which these very same matters are at issue.

Moral philosophers speak from *within* a moral form of life to others within it; but what they say tends to carry the weight of a learned or expert discourse. When they say certain features of morality are true ones or certain interpretations of moral life important, or when they mention them at all, they give these features or interpretations visibility and legitimacy. This situation raises questions about the epistemological situation of moral philosophy. What are philosophers doing in entering these claims in the context of "ethics," and what is a moral philosopher's standing to enter claims about the nature of morality, to *represent* it within and to a particular society? Are moral philosophers, in being this and in being trained for it, in a particularly good position to represent what morality is like? Are they, for example, representative of the moral communities that have provided their materials for reflection? Or do they possess a particularly clear vantage point for selecting these materials?

Moral philosophers often pass over these questions in silence, or implicitly assume a representative position in invoking "our" intuitions or habits of speaking. Some philosophers identify themselves or their representative claims with those who are "educated" or "enlightened." Others lay claim to a kind of "expertise" or "freedom" based on superior (i.e. systematic or theoretical) insight or skill.[1] Contemporary moral philosophers usually do not want their writing and teaching to be seen as "moralizing," that is, wading into moral life in defense of particular convictions. We learn to position ourselves as observers or analysts of, not actors or participants in, morality.

Many moral philosophers will say that in their philosophical reflections they are not "merely" reflecting on their own moral experience (much less mirroring it), but are tapping into moral reality, or the moral realm, or the structure of practical reason, or the nature of the right or the good. But this assumes two things. It assumes that the moral reality, realm, nature, or structure is something accessible and determinate quite apart from anyone's acquired experience of them, and that the moral philosopher can tell when she or he has grasped these things as they really are apart from his or her thoroughly tutored and cultured experience of them.

One way to confront or rebut these assumptions is to try to show that there is no such determinate thing or realm independent of people's experiences of it. This makes one some kind of "anti-realist," in contemporary philosophical terms. Another way is to try to show that no one is ever justified in claims made about what morality (really) is or what it (really) demands. This makes one some kind of "moral skeptic," in philosophical terms. Yet another is to announce oneself a "relativist," by using the claim that the reality of morality is not something apart from the culture that harbors it to draw the conclusion that as it seems to each (or each culture) within its experience, so it is.

Because I believe morality consists in interpersonal acknowledgment and constraint, from which people learn that they are responsible for things and to others, I cannot think of it as something that could obtain outside human relations and humans' experiences of them. Morality arises and goes on between people, recruiting human capacities for self-awareness and awareness of others' awareness; for feeling and learning to feel particular things in response to what one is aware of; for expressing judgment and feeling in the responses appropriate to them. This means I do not recognize something that sets morality's terms and standards anterior or exterior to human life and human beings' awareness and judgment, such as a divine moral authority or a natural law of morality, or a world without human awareness but nonetheless containing moral facts. But I do not give up the right to talk about moral reality, because I think morality is a strikingly real dimension of every human group's social life.

Because I believe that many claims about morality (as well as within it) are false (for example, that moral judgments serve only to express individuals' feelings, or that women are lesser kinds of moral persons than men, deserving less or more restricted consideration) and that one can present substantial evidence in support of the denials of these claims, I am not a moral skeptic. I regard the debate about whether one has to be some kind of realist to be able to say moral claims are true or false as ongoing; I do not take a side in that (see Blackburn 1993).

I believe many claims made about and within morality, including those of many moral philosophers, are made from positions startlingly unexamined or inadequate to know those matters judged about. Feminist and other critical analyses of social hierarchies that ascribe inferior positions to some people have taught me to be skeptical about people's positions to know their and others' social and moral worlds. This is not because nobody knows anything morally, but because differently placed people know different things in fact. What some people know hides or obscures what is known by others, and differences between people in what they can get away with claiming they know are among the most important differences in moral and social places. Social orders differentiated by power and status, the rule rather than the exception in human societies, are morally complex and usually problematically so. Their moral structures are epistemically orchestrated in elaborate, self-preserving ways; both how they are orchestrated and the results of their being so are often part of what is morally problematic about them. The theme of "epistemic rigging" in actual social-moral orders is central to the studies in part three of the book.

Because I believe that moral and social life are thoroughly enmeshed, and that moral knowledge like other knowledge is situated (that is, it is made possible and is limited by where it comes from and how it is achieved), I will no doubt be seen by some people as some kind of relativist. I don't mind being some kind of relativist, as long as I am not the kind that renders individuals' or societies' moral self-criticism incoherent, or that declares intergroup or intercultural moral evaluation and criticism impossible or forbidden. I do not think there are too few (or no) facts pertinent to moral beliefs and their assessment, but that there are often too many. I certainly do not think "anything goes" at home or elsewhere.

I do think we must recognize that our moral claims have at a time whatever justifications we can give them, and that the force of our justifications to those like "us" does not predict their force to others. Since morality is about mutual understanding and habitable ways of life, situations of inadequately shared epistemic ground present more than epistemological problems. They pose moral questions. What should we do for, or what may we do to, others when we and they are not parties to the same understandings? I do not believe there is a general answer to this question. Ultimately, I think the justification of the moral understandings that are woven through a particular lifeway rests on the goods to be found in living it. A profound complication is that for many forms of moral-social life, there is no one thing that it is to live them. Even the shared understandings that roughly demarcate communities are not *simply* shared in the ways we are tempted to think. When moral understandings are "shared" their force in defining responsibilities and prerogatives is recognized in common; this need not mean that they are endorsed by all or exist by the consent of those who live them, nor that all understand the same things about how they are maintained, and who bears their costs or reaps their benefits. My concluding chapter tries to make clearer the implications of a fully socially situated view of moral knowledge both within and between moral communities.

In this book I try to avoid wholesale metaphysical and epistemological positions—especially "standard brand" ones with familiar labels—as well as attempts to refute them. And I do not, it will be obvious, propound a moral theory, either in the restricted sense of "theory" I repeatedly criticize below, or in the sense of a substantive conception of a good or rightly organized life. The matters I take up here are on the level of a *conception of morality*, a view about the nature and point of morality, the kind of thing (or arrangement or institution) morality is. These matters create tests and implications for what moral philosophy can be like, and for what its burdens and possibilities are.

Two Pictures of Morality

I aim first to raise doubts about a certain view of moral theorizing and its allied conception of morality. I call the view a *theoretical-juridical model* of morality and moral theory. This is not a moral theory; it is a kind of template for organizing moral inquiry into the pursuit of a certain kind of moral theory. It has prevailed as the template for "serious" or "important" moral theorizing in ethics, especially in America in the twentieth century. Many utilitarian, contract, neo-Kantian, or rights-based theories that are otherwise diverse and contradict each other can be seen to realize or approximate the theoretical-juridical model. It prescribes the representation of morality as a compact, propositionally codifiable, impersonally action-guiding code within an agent, or as a compact set of law-like propositions that "explain" the moral behavior of a well-formed moral agent (not, however, in the sense of predicting what will happen or revealing the causal mechanisms underlying what does happen, but rather by "explaining" what should happen). The doubts I want to raise are about the adequacy of this model as a kind of characterization of morality.

It represents morality itself as if it were, primarily or in its most important part, a surprisingly compact kind of theory or some kind of internal guidance system of an agent that could be modelled by that kind of theory. It makes morality look as if it consists in, or could be represented by, a compact cluster of beliefs. I claim this view of morality as consisting largely or essentially in something we think or know is implausible. It is also a distorting view of the kinds of understanding that are at work in the parts of morality that do consist in knowledge or thought. It demotes a great deal of what is known, felt, and acted out in moral relations to "nonmoral"—merely factual or collateral—information. It shrinks morality "proper" down to a kind of purified core of purely moral knowledge.

The assumption of a pure core of moral knowledge fits conveniently with the idea that moral philosophers can gain access to morality by mostly or entirely nonempirical reflection on conceptual and logical relations or on the deliverances of "intuition." Immediate availability to reflection will seem dubious if morality is not only about what is thought but about what is perceived, felt, and acted out; and not only what is perceived and felt and enacted by individual persons but what is constructed and reproduced *between* them. Chapter 2 examines the constellation of that special project and its theory-model in the pivotal work of Henry Sidgwick. Chapter 3 looks at the nature of this model and its epistemology in more detail (compare Schneewind 1984; Williams 1985; Taylor 1995.)

The project of codifying a compact core of unsituated, purely moral knowledge fuses a number of tendencies in twentieth-century moral philosophy. It tends to be intellectualist in seating morality primarily in some central, specifically moral, beliefs, and rationalist in assuming that the central moral beliefs are to be understood and tested primarily by reflection on concepts and logical analysis of the relations of evidential support among moral beliefs. The project is individualist in its assumption that the central moral concepts and premises are to equip each moral agent with a guidance system he or she can use to decide upon a life or its parts (or to equip them with the criteria for assessing the guidance of individual lives, however selected). At the same time, this approach is impersonal: The right equipment tells one what is right to do (or explains why something is right to do) no matter who one might happen to be and what individual life one is living, no matter what form of social life one inhabits and one's station within it. This unilateral individual, yet impersonal, action-guidance is believed possible because morality is seen as socially modular: If there is a timeless, contextless, pure core of moral knowledge, differences between forms of social life and differences among the positions one may occupy within them can only provide occasions for different applications of core or essential moral knowledge which itself remains the same. But it could only be the same, modular with respect to the rest of social life, if it is the nature of core moral knowledge to transcend culture, history, and material conditions, both individual and shared.

The intellectualism, rationalism, individualism, modularity, and transcendence of a certain picture of morality reinforce each other. I try to make clear some of the ways they do so in the chapters that follow. As an alternative to this still influential picture, which persists both in robust and in piecemeal forms, I offer a different model at the same level of generality. It is not a moral theory, but a template and interpretive grid for moral inquiry. Like the theoretical-juridical conception, this alternative model suggests normal forms for moral inquiry. It directs us, however, to look at more and other things than the theoretical-juridical model picks out and to ask different questions about them. I call my alternative an *expressive-collaborative model*. Chapter 3 presents its view of moral justification as a kind of equilibrium among people that can survive the transparency that reflection produces. Chapter 4 proposes its way to get at morality's content: Track responsibilities. This view prescribes an investigation of morality as a socially embodied medium of mutual understanding and negotiation between people over their responsibility for things open to human care and response.

Morality allows and requires people to understand themselves as bearers of particular identities and actors in various relationships that are defined by certain values. People learn to understand each other this way and to express their understandings through *practices of responsibility* in which they assign, accept, or deflect responsibilities for different things. Moral accounting invokes the evaluative language, exemplary judgments, deliberative formats, and distributions of responsibility that are recognized as authoritative—"shared"—in its social setting. By using these resources in giving accounts, moral actors sustain this "medium" of moral self-expression and mutual recognition. Yet some of their uses may alter the medium itself. Practices of responsibility are constructive; they may reproduce existing terms of recognition or they may shift them.

In other words, morality consists in a family of practices that show what is valued by making people accountable to each other for it. Practices of making morally evaluative judgments are prominent among moral practices, but they do not exhaust them. There are also habits and practices of paying attention, imputing states of affairs to people's agency, interpreting and redescribing human actions, visiting blame, offering excuses, inflicting punishment, making amends, refining and inhibiting the experience or expression of feelings, and responding in thought, act, and feeling to any of the foregoing. In all of these ways we express our senses of responsibility. It is only in the case of some of them that we may be articulate about what we do and how we do it, and relations between articulate moral thought and inarticulate know-how are not transparent.[2] Moral competence enlists the diverse skills needed to learn to do and appreciate all these expressions of our agency and what we value.

In all of its expressions, morality is fundamentally *interpersonal*; it arises out of and is reproduced or modified in what goes on between or among people. In this way, morality is collaborative; we construct and sustain it together (although, as will be seen, not by any means on equitable or voluntarily chosen terms). What goes on morally between people is constrained and made intelligible by a background of understandings about what people are supposed to do, expect, and understand. These are the "moral understandings" of my title. Self-direction, responsiveness to others, and mutual accountability are constant tasks in human social life, but the ways that human societies shape these vary. Particular understandings are revealed in the daily rounds of interaction that show how people make sense of their own and others' responsibilities in terms of their identities, relationships, and values. But we have to *look* in order to see them. When we look it is also plain to see that not everyone is comparably situated or advantaged in the encounters that reproduce or reconfigure moral orders and lives.

An expressive-collaborative view sees the reflective and normative tasks of ethics in a particular way. One kind of reflection appropriate to moral philosophy is *reflective analysis* of forms of moral life. The task is to examine those parts of social life that reveal which understandings sustain practices of responsibility, and how those understandings work. The aim is to find out what moral norms are actually like, how they inhere in and are reproduced by interactions between people, and how moral orders are concretely embodied in social ones. This analysis can only operate on information about the flow of interactions in daily life. In order to discern what distinguishes particular lifeways, this reflection needs objects of comparison, both contrasting cases of practices of responsibility between societies, as well as contrasting cases within them. Objects of comparison are important because moral philosophers inevitably reflect on morality from within lifeways embodying particular forms of morality, and from a particular position within those lifeways. They may thus find salient only some kinds of understandings and practices and may be completely unaware of others. They may also find interactions intelligible in certain terms from social positions they are familiar with, without knowing that these interactions make different sense to others differently placed, if they make sense to those others at all.

An empirically saturated reflective analysis of what is going on in actual moral orders needs to be supplied by many kinds of factual researches, including documentary, historical, psychological, ethnographic, and sociological ones. These researches are not themselves moral philosophy, but without them ethics has nothing to reflect on but moral philosophers' own assumptions and experiences. Giving up on the pure core of moral knowledge, and trying to make the best and most complete sense of all the information we can get about the real forms morality takes in diverse human lives, is no small task for moral philosophy. A lot of this book is about the necessity and difficulty of that task.[3]

Another task for moral philosophy is *critical reflection* on features and conditions of specific forms of moral life. Critical reflection tests whether moral understandings really are intelligible and coherent to those who enact them, whether they are similarly so from diverse points of view within them, and whether they are the kinds of understandings that can be so. This has to do with the nature of these understandings— principally, understandings about who gets to do what to whom and who must do what for whom, as well as who has standing to give or to demand accounts. It has also to do with the candor of the parties to these understandings with each other and with themselves. Critical reflection looks for relations of earned trust that allow understandings to continue as such; it looks out for places where only or primarily coercive power, or duplicity, or manipulation, even force, sustains arrangements that (try to) present or justify themselves, to at least some of their parties, as interpersonal understandings.

Critical reflection presses toward transparency; this is discussed in chapters 3 and 9 below. This reflection aims to test whether moral forms of life can account for themselves morally, at least in some terms those forms of life themselves embody.[4] This kind of criticism is intimately linked to the task of rich description and analysis already mentioned. Critical reflection needs insight into both actual practices of responsibility and the participants' conceptions of them. In a social order of even slight complexity, this insight into different practices from different positions within them is not spontaneously available to individuals at arbitrarily chosen positions. It requires not only empirical observation but report and testimony from many different places. Critical reflection asks whether what is going on in actual moral orders makes the right kinds of sense to the participants in those ways of life.

This reflection is normative in that it holds particular moral relations and understandings (that are themselves normative) to some standards of shared intelligibility. The idea is that moral relations, which recruit human capacities for conscious self-direction and mutual suasion based on mutually recognizable values, ought to be something like what they appear to be. One part of this thought is that if interactions are in reality based on something else entirely, like main force or some forms of manipulation, they are not to that extent moral ones, although they may (in fact typically do) take place in some broader social context of moral relations. Another part of the thought is that self-directed behavior for which people are accountable ought to be able to make sense *in fact* in ways that at the same time make sense *to them*. If it does not or cannot, then there is at least confusion, if not something worse, afoot.

Often, I think, there is something worse. This involves deception and suppression of kinds that are commonly backed up in the end by coercive pressure and force, sometimes implemented through enforced deprivation of material means as well as social recognition. I refer repeatedly in this book to social arrangements—slavery, patriarchy, white supremacy, class or professional privilege—in which this is in reality what is happening. I am not prepared to make an argument here that no one should ever live with or through lies. I am not even sure that conclusion is unconditionally true. I am reasonably satisfied that in the kind of social arrangements I return to over and over here, the people who have been forced to live with, and live out, others' lies about them have not found these terms of common life acceptable, and have accepted them under coerced or manipulated conditions that imposed grave, even catastrophic, losses.

There is, finally, *fully normative reflection* in ethics, the attempt to see whether a particular way to live is, indeed, "how to live" at least for human beings in a particular set of historical, cultural, and material circumstances, which already include some legacy of moral understandings and practices of responsibility. In fact, philosophers in the canonical "Western" tradition have characteristically identified ethics with a still more ambitious project of defending a view about how to live for human beings as such. What is justice (virtue, piety, etc.) itself, as Socrates kept asking? I confess to deep skepticism about that more ambitious project with its ancient Platonic root; I am no longer certain that I understand what is described by it. That project seems to me committed to the *ideality* of morality, according to which morality is never what any group of people is doing in a place at a time, but something that transcends all places and times at which human beings work out ways to live.

In rejecting the ideality of morality, however, I do not surrender this fully normative dimension of moral philosophy. Ethics tries to find out whether certain things are really right or good, and whether some ways to live are really better than others. I see the task of fully normative reflection as intrinsically comparative; in other words, when we ask ourselves what can be said for some way of life, we are asking whether it is better or worse than some other way we know or imagine. Objects of effective comparison are found either in different extant ways of life, where we can at least see something about what lifeways actually come to, or in differences between a particular way of living and imaginable and accessible variations on that way. However, projects of global justification—even comparative ones between whole determinate lifeways in given circumstances—are epistemologically staggering. I have come to wonder, or rather to worry about, why it is so important to know whether "we" are right and "they" are wrong, *tout court*. At the same time, it may be essential morally and politically to know which particular features of our lives we are fully prepared to stand on, and when there are features of others' ways of living we can justify not standing for. So I conclude in chapter 9 with some discussion of moral criticism and objectivity, within and "across" moral cultures.

It will be obvious now that I am maintaining that moral philosophy bears a far greater *descriptive* and *empirical* burden, in pursuing details of actual moral arrangements, than is commonly thought. I will also argue for a distinctive and unfamiliar *moral* and *political* burden of taking seriously the many knowledges about responsibility and value that inhere in different social roles and positions. To fail to seek out and entertain many distinct moral understandings that supply a going social-moral order is to fail to honor people at those many different locations with the status of moral subject. Simply, moral philosophy should not arbitrarily select or presumptively disqualify some moral experiences; for those neglected are too experiences of human beings who are fully parties to the moral understandings that furnish their ways of life. To ignore some or privilege others without explicit rationale is derelict both descriptively and morally.

It is not necessary in order to represent more than one's own experience in moral philosophy to claim that morality obtains or arises from somewhere outside all human experiences. The surest way not to represent merely one's own experience in moral philosophy is to open the way for the experiences of many others. This is to envision a research program for ethics that situates its analytic, critical, and fully normative reflections within an awareness that writing and teaching ethics is itself conduct and practice, with its own moral and political situation to account for. This book is a sketch of, and a plea for, such a program.

My Working Hypotheses

The first four chapters of this book aim to show the possibility and desirability of retiring a theoretical-juridical view of ethics in favor of an expressive-collaborative one that focuses on understandings of responsibility. The next four examine ways these understandings can define different moral positions in actual orders, and the complexity of what it means for moral understandings to be "shared." The final chapter explores some of the moral and epistemic problems that arise when they are not. Each chapter is meant to stand on its own, but all were written for this book. I doubt that each makes quite the sense I intend it to make without the support and illumination of the others. Together they put forward a research program for ethics that embodies several working hypotheses about morality and so about ethics. In the following chapters I argue sometimes from, and sometimes to, these views, hoping to render them clearer and more plausible.

1. Morality itself consists in practices, not theories.

In saying morality itself is not plausibly thought of as consisting in theory, or as possessing some minimal core that might be abstracted in a compact theoretical representation, I by no means imply that it is impossible or unnecessary to theorize about morality. Instead, I mean to underscore that theories of morality should not be confused with morality, the human social phenomenon the theories are about. In many investigations there is no chance of confusing theory with its object. In the case of ethics, systematic and very general thinking about morality is often presented as if it were the discovery or uncovering of what morality itself actually is. Chapters 2 and 3 try to show how a conception of morality as itself theory-like or apt for compact propositional codification is installed by excluding most of what morality might consist in as a socially and psychologically real dimension of human life.

If morality is not theory but certain kinds of practices, the theory *of* morality is an attempt to understand these practices. Even if simplicity and elegance are desiderata of some kinds of theory (e.g. scientific explanatory ones), it does not follow that these are features, much less desiderata, of the practices that the theory of morality is about. Whether they are depends on the nature and point of these practices. It also does not follow that moral philosophy requires or permits the kind of theory for which these desiderata are appropriate. If moral philosophy has the reflective and normative jobs I have outlined for it above, for example, then we have no reason to think theories of morality ought to look like scientific explanatory ones, for they are not attempts to formulate generalizations or to expose causal mechanisms that predict or explain what in fact is going to happen between human beings. Rather, theories of morality are attempts to find out what people are doing in bringing moral evaluation to bear (in judgment, feeling, and response) on what they and others do and care about, and whether some ways of doing what they are doing are better ways than others.

It is not obvious in advance, not to me at any rate, exactly what such a theory has to look like. My own theories about morality in what follows look as they do partly because I take morality to consist in complex practices of certain kinds in complexly differentiated social orders and individually varied lives. They also look as they do because of some specific interests I have in theorizing moral practice. I want to highlight what I believe is excluded and distorted in a theoretical-juridical approach. I want to do this in turn so I can show how moral theorizing, differently understood, can directly interrogate some of the most morally troubling aspects of human social life: domination, oppression, exclusion, coercion, and basic disregard of some people by others. The fact is that morality as actual human practice has more often supplied understandings that legitimate such human relations than ones that condemn them. If we know such things are deeply wrong, it is because we have found our way to another actual human practice of responsibility that condemns these others. Or at least some of us have found our way to the bare image, or specific fragments, of such a practice. It is that practice in this world we need to know how to defend and make real.

2. The practices characteristic of morality are practices of responsibility.

If morality consists in practices, moral theorizing needs to ask what is characteristic of moral practices, what is done in them and by means of them? I propose that it is fruitful to locate morality in *practices of responsibility* that implement commonly shared understandings about who gets to do what to whom and who is supposed to do what for whom.[5] In making each other accountable to certain people for certain states of affairs, we define the scope and limits of our agency, affirm who in particular we are, show what we care about, and reveal who has standing to judge and blame us. In the ways we assign, accept, or deflect responsibilities, we express our understandings of our own and others' identities, relationships, and values. At the same time, as we do so, we reproduce or modify the very practices that allow and require us to do this. We keep our practices of responsibility going, in accustomed or amended forms. Changes in the distribution of responsibilities and the measures of their fulfillment are fundamental changes in the structure of moral life, affecting not only who is likely to do certain things but how people will be regarded in light of their performance or failure to perform.[6]

An expressive-collaborative model of practices of responsibility invites detailed and situated descriptions of the expectations and negotiations surrounding assignments of responsibility. It emphasizes that it is in the nature of morality to work by means of interpersonal understandings, so that what is to be described includes the participants' grasp of what the understandings are. Close description and critical analysis can expose misfits among what happens, what participants think is going on, and what some parties think that others think. There is also the question whether everyone who participates in practices of responsibility is in the same sense a party to them. It is typical in human societies for some people to enjoy advantages over others in the ways responsibilities are distributed and enforced. Some enjoy freedom from unwanted responsibilities or the prerogative of requiring answerability from people who are not entitled to ask for it in return. One of the most effective ways to find out what is valued and who is who in social orders is to follow the

trail of responsibilities. Chapters 3 and 4 explore the nature and epistemology of practices of responsibility.

3. Morality is not socially modular.

How do moral practices relate to other practices in social life? Are moral
practices relatively autonomous with respect to other social ones, or
implicated in them? Moral practices, in fact, cannot be extricated from
other social practices, nor moral identities from social roles and institutions in particular lifeways. This fact, and the consequent impossibility
of "purifying" morality or moral knowledge or practical reason, are at
the heart of this book.[7] It is not only that moral understandings intertwine with social ones, but that moral understandings are typically
effected *through* social ones. One clear example is the way moral
accountability is constructed through divisions of labor that define distributions of responsibility (chapter 4). Other examples consist in ways
people's social station and situation, whether of privilege, subordination,
oppression, or marginality, permit them different forms of moral self-
description, define for them distinct ranges of accountability, and expose
them to blame for different things or by different judges (chapters 5, 6,
7, and 8). Thus are different moral positions constituted. Not everyone
is equally burdened or esteemed morally, and not everyone is in the same
position to give or to demand moral accounts. Because social segmenta-
tion and hierarchical power-relations are the rule, rather than the exception, in human societies, the commonplace reality is *different moral
identities in differentiated moral-social worlds.*

Moral theorizing within the theoretical-juridical approach typically
universalizes and homogenizes "the" moral point of view or position of
"the" moral agent, and traffics in claims about "our" concept of responsibility, sense of justice, intuitions, or obligations. In differentiated
moral-social worlds, however, "we" may be participants in different
practices supporting different moral concepts, or may participate in
practices whose differences give the same moral terms different meanings. "We" may also participate in the same moral practices differently,
that is, occupying positions with different responsibilities, authority, and
accountability. Consider, say, the "honor" of slaveholding patriarchs,
the "honor" of their women, the oxymoron (to them) of "honor" of or
among their slaves. Not just what there is to judge about, but the sense
there is to be made of it, may differ profoundly among those sharing a
country, a community, an institution, a household, or a bed. People are

measured in different contexts by the same measures, or by different measures in the same situations, and some people set without appeal the measures by which others are going to be judged, even by themselves.

Theories that do not acknowledge this not only fail to describe a basic and pervasive feature of human moral life, but effectively erase the majority of human beings in depicting a moral persona or identity dominant in some form of social life as if it were the only one. A dominant identity is, in fact, a norm, but not in the sense of being typical. Dominant identities are normative for the enjoyment of full or premier or privileged moral status, and where there are full or premier or privileged moral positions there are also diminished, subordinate, or disqualified ones. Chapters 5 through 8 explore these problems.

4. Moral theorizing and moral epistemology need to be freed from the impoverishing legacies of ideality and purity that make most of most people's moral lives disappear, or render those lives unintelligible.

I take this to be a consequence of the first three assumptions. Morality needs to be seen as something existing, however imperfectly, in real human social spaces in real time, not something ideal or noumenal in character. And both the understandings of morality within societies and the understandings of morality in moral philosophy need to encompass many kinds of information about human social worlds and many forms of interpersonal recognition in thought, feeling, and response. Chapter 9, in conclusion, takes up some questions about moral objectivity, intelligibility, and criticism both within and "across" moral worlds.

Feminist Ethics and Its Difference

To say theories struck from the theoretical-juridical mold have been dominant in twentieth-century Anglo-American ethics is to say that theories of this type have enjoyed special visibility and prestige in academic philosophy. It does not mean they have been the only theories around or that their premier position has gone unchallenged. The dominance of a disciplinary paradigm shows in its prevalence in shaping professional work and training, its embodiment in the structures of courses and texts, its secure seating in prestigious institutions, and its conspicuous presentation in central venues of publication and discussion (see also chapter 2). It is almost inevitable that work at odds with a regnant paradigm will present itself as challenging or attacking the paradigm, or as an attractive alternative to it. A measure of the dominance of a paradigm is its success in making work done within its discipline but done in other ways struggle against it, thereby acknowledging and reproducing its importance. Not to address the paradigm or the work it informs is simply to appear ill-trained or professionally out of it.

A lot of work in recent decades has testified to the power of theoretical-juridical moral philosophy by setting itself against that approach. This has produced odd bedfellows and superficial similarities among very different projects in ethics that have in common for the most part what they reject. At the close of the century, it seems that the idea of compact, code-like theory has lost altitude, perhaps because there have been so many challenges to this idea from so many different, indeed conflicting, perspectives.[8]

Many criticisms of neo-Kantian, utilitarian, contractarian, or other types of theory that fit the theoretical-juridical form attack the epistemological or psychological adequacy of those theories. "Particularist" moral epistemologies rooted in views as old as Aristotle's or as contemporary as those within cognitive science question whether mature and sensitive capacities of moral judgment could be acquired by or explained as the application of a small core of very general principles.[9] Bernard Williams (1973 and 1981), Michael Stocker (1976 and 1990), and Larry Blum (1980 and 1994) argue against the psychological tenability of impartialist "modern" moral theories. Even as the theories tell us how to live they defeat or defy motives of attachment to particular people that give us reasons to live or allow us to live well.

Charles Taylor and Alasdair MacIntyre deplore contemporary moral philosophy's lack of historical and sociological insight or grounding. Code-like theories bypass the specific ways goods and selves are understood in continuing and evolving traditions within communities (MacIntyre 1981 and 1988; Taylor 1989; see also Walzer 1983). Communitarians like Michael Sandel find the social nature of persons either missing altogether or ideologically distorted in the modern individualist frame that contains these theories (Sandel 1982). Stanley Cavell and Richard Rorty emphasize the personally expressive or communally strategic powers of moral discourses which allow us both to find and define who we are (Cavell 1979; Rorty 1989 and 1991).

I owe many debts to these thinkers and discussions. Yet I have found in feminist ethics something I did not find elsewhere. The essays in this book are "feminist" not because they are about women, or because I am a feminist, or because I call them "feminist." They are feminist because they are imbued with insights, commitments, and critical and interpretive techniques of feminist theories made by many women in the past several decades. I would not have known how to look at things this way had I not studied for many years this creative, cooperative, and willful body of women's work animated by love and anger. Although I return to it repeatedly, especially in chapter 3, I want to foreground here what I have taken up as the transforming insight of feminist ethics. I need to make this clear at the outset as much for those familiar with feminist ethics (who may view its importance or point differently) as for those who are not familiar with it (and so may either have no ideas or strange ones about what feminist philosophers have done).

Feminist ethics is the outgrowth of contemporary feminist political movements in the United States and other Western European democracies from the 1960s onward.[10] It is part of a larger project of feminist theory that "attempts to account for gender inequality in the socially constructed relationship between power—the political—on the one hand and the knowledge of truth and reality—the epistemological—on the other" (MacKinnon 1987, 147).[11] The tradition of Western Anglo-European philosophical ethics has been until just recently almost entirely a product of some men's—and almost no women's—thinking. The societies producing this ethics have typically excluded women (and many men) from political offices, religious hierarchies, policy institutions, higher education, and mass media, where moral values and ideals are authoritatively endorsed. Almost every canonized philosopher up to the twentieth century has explicitly held that women are lesser or incompetent moral (and epistemic) agents. These social and historical facts raise questions about representations in ethics of "our" moral life. Are these representations really representative? Of all, even most, of "us"? Studies of the form and content of academically dominant theories confirm the suspicion that while these theories represent something, they do not represent positions or experiences of most women, or many men.

In examining contemporary moral theories and their modern antecedents feminists find kindred preoccupations, assumptions, and points of view. These theories idealize relations of nonintimate, mutually independent peers seeking to preserve autonomy or enhance self-interest in rule- (or role-) bound voluntary interactions. They mirror spheres of activity, social roles, and character ideals associated with socially advantaged men. They reflect norms of masculinity that apply at least to men so privileged, if not to men generally (Baier 1987 and 1995; Benhabib 1987; Friedman 1993; Held 1987 and 1993; Whitbeck 1983).

This image of normal moral agents and their contexts of choice ignores or distorts a great deal that *women* in Western societies, even across class and racial groups, have historically been expected and required to do. Women are typically assigned discretionary responsibilities to care (in physically and often emotionally intimate ways) for others, either as paid or unpaid labor. Often, the others to be cared for are dependent and vulnerable, and women are expected to care for them with dedication and restraint. Women are expected to perform in subordinate or dependent economic, social, and political roles obediently and loyally, if not selflessly. Women are pressed or forced to accept domestic, reproductive, and sexual arrangements set and enforced by male authorities; many of these arrangements offer limited possibilities for individual choice or negotiation of terms (Okin 1989; Mann 1994). Dominant moral theories thus seem to see a moral world from typical situations and familiar positions of some men, but (even now) few women; this shows something about what theory-makers have been able or likely to know about "our" moral world.

The canonical form of moral judgment in dominant theories tracks gendered social positions and prerogatives as well. Moral judgment or justification is rendered as the uniform application of law-like, impersonally action-guiding principles to cases relevantly similar from an impartial point of view. In this "theoretical-juridical" picture "the" moral agent in action resembles a judge, manager, bureaucrat, or gamesman, exercising patterns of judgment appropriate to legal, institutional, or administrative contexts, or games (Walker 1992). The picture suggests either the reciprocal social positions of participants or competitors in a rule-structured practice, or the positions of those with authority to apply law or policy impartially to cases. Since positions and operations like this characterize roles, offices, and activities that were historically reserved to men in Western societies, again it seems that theory-makers know what some men (are supposed to) know.

So feminist critique of ethics finds *gender bias* in dominant theories of Anglo-American ethics that embody the theoretical-juridical approach. The pervasive imagery of a fraternity of independent peers invoking laws to deliver verdicts with authority is not just exclusive of women, however. The normative subject thus conjured up is not (typically) a woman; but he or she is also not a child, a person of disadvantaged economic, educational, or professional position, or someone of despised racial, caste, ethnic, sexual, or religious identity. It is not someone with temporary, chronic, or progressive disabilities. This moral agent is none of us at all times, and many of us at no times. Gender bias, then, is one facet of a highly restrictive and broadly exclusive discourse that fails to speak for or to many, perhaps most, of us.

What feminists show is not that moral philosophy is simply mistaken in its claims to represent moral life. Rather, feminist critiques show how moral philosophers have in fact represented, in abstract and idealized theoretical forms, aspects of the *actual* positions and relations of *some* people in a certain kind of social order. This social order is the kind where the availability of these positions depends on gender, age, economic status, race, and other factors that distribute powers and forms of recognition differentially and hierarchically. Dominant moral theories depict the self-images, prerogatives of choice, required patterns of moral reasoning, and anticipated forms of accountability of *some* people in societies like ours; those placed in certain ways, not just in any or every way.

It is the moral agency of people "like that" that is dignified and "normalized" by its portrayal in culturally authoritative philosophical accounts. What is portrayed is put forward as a representation of real, or full, or unproblematic moral agency. Anyone who isn't or can't be "like that" is either left unrepresented in such accounts, or is effectively represented as different, problematic, less than fully fledged from a moral point of view. Yet such moral theories are invariably put forward as accounts of "the" moral agent exhibiting the intuitions, sense of justice, practical wisdom, or patterns of rational choice characterizing "our" moral life (Calhoun 1988). Academic moral theories both mirror and reinforce publicly authoritative discourses of justice, rights, and obligations in Western countries.

Feminist criticism leans on a fault line in these theories and discourses. If they derive authority from their supposed representation of a moral life common to all (or even most, adult ones) of us, they are in trouble; they depict some aspects of the lives of the few, rather than most of the lives of the many. If the credibility of claims to represent is saved by admitting that what is depicted is representative of rather little of the moral lives of most of us, then these views lose their authority as representative of "our" (much less "human") moral life. This is the difference in feminist ethics: it puts the *authority* and *credibility* of representative claims about moral life under harsh light, and challenges epistemic and moral authority that is politically engineered and self-reinforcing.

This is not the most familiar view about feminist ethics (see Walker 1989b and 1992). Many people now associate feminist ethics with (and sometimes solely with) an ethic of care. Care ethics are some of the most visible creations of feminist ethics, along with maternal and friendship paradigms of moral relations, and conceptions of responsibility in situations of interdependency, vulnerability, and trust (Baier 1995; Bowden 1997; Cole and Coultrap-McQuin 1992; Held 1993 and 1995; Manning 1992; Noddings 1984; Ruddick 1989; Tronto 1993; Whitbeck 1983). This work aims to remedy the exclusion or distortion of women's lives in moral theory by representing understandings of value, agency, and responsibility embedded in practices that have been and still are "women's work." It has resulted in new ethical visions from standpoints within some women's experiences that provide challenging objects of comparison for nonfeminist moral theories as well as for ways we actually live.

Most of these projects were catalyzed, if not suggested, by Carol Gilligan's now well-known and widely debated claims about a "different moral voice" more characteristic of women than of men (Gilligan 1982). Gilligan claimed her empirical research on moral development revealed two distinct, comparably mature and integrated moral orientations, "justice" and "care." Each of these moral perspectives includes a view of selves and their relations to others, a picture of the structure of moral thinking, and a commitment to certain values. Care reasoning, she further claimed, was significantly more likely to be used, especially as a predominant approach to moral thinking, by female subjects in her socially advantaged samples (see Friedman 1993; Walker 1989a).

The first claim challenged Lawrence Kohlberg's theory of moral development, powerfully influential in the 1970s, that held justice reasoning to represent, for all cultures and times, the highest, because most mature and integrated, stage of development possible in human moral reasoning. The second claim identifies the "consistent observational and evaluative bias" (Gilligan 1982, 6) that marred Kohlberg's and other studies of human and moral development in Gilligan's discipline of psychology: the exclusive or predominant use of men and boys to establish norms, measured against which women's moral thinking would later be found wanting.

While hot debate and giddy jubilation swirled around Gilligan's different voice and gender difference claims, Gilligan's own statement at the outset of her book about the "problem of interpretation" (Gilligan 1982, 2) went largely unremarked. She denied that her purpose was to generalize about either sex. Gilligan said her point was to identify "a problem in the representation, a limitation in the conception of human condition, an omission of certain truths about life" (Gilligan 1982, 2) that results from systematic research bias that presents some people's moral thinking as representative of all people's. This is precisely the problem of the authority and credibility of representative claims about morality that is at the root of feminist criticism.

While Gilligan's book sparked care ethics, her point about a "problem in the representation" was not, ironically, consistently taken by women eager to confront the mainstream gender bias in ethics by—at long last— representing "women." In a society traversed by differences of power within gender, and by other differences (especially differences due to race and class) as deep and pervasive as gender, do all and only women speak with the same "voice" to moral and other issues of social life? Do brown or yellow women, or poor or illiterate women, see daily life with the same eyes as their white, or well-educated, or economically secure "sisters"? Reaction to care ethics and to claims about women's moral voices shows that many of the same questions Gilligan and other feminists raised about the authority of some men to represent "people" can be raised about the authority of some women to represent "women" (See hooks 1984; see also chapter 3 in this volume for additional references.)

Maria Lugones and Elizabeth Spelman analyzed and indelibly underscored the problem of theorizing for and about women in their superb and troubling "Have We Got a Theory for You: Feminist Theory, Cultural Imperialism, and the Demand for "The Woman's Voice":

> [T]he prescription that life for women will be better when we're in workforce rather than at home, when we are completely free of religious beliefs with patriarchal origins, when we live in complete separation from men, etc. are seen as slaps in the face to women whose life would be better if they could spend more time at home, whose identity is inseparable from their religious beliefs and cultural practices . . . , who have ties to men—whether erotic or not—such that to have them severed in the name of some vision of what is "better" is . . . absurd. (Lugones and Spelman 1983, 579)

The moral here is not that women's experiences do not need representing. It is rather that: "The deck is stacked when one group takes it upon itself to develop the theory and then have others criticize it. Categories are quick to congeal, and the experiences of women whose lives do not fit the categories will appear as anomalous when in fact the theory should have grown out of them as much as others from the beginning" (Lugones and Spelman 1983, 579). Many different experiences of our shared moral-social life, experiences of many women and many men, are produced by the same distributions of power and credibility that insure that most of these experiences will not be heard or heeded in places of authority.

Despite her demurrals about generalization, Gilligan herself was criticized for overgeneralizing about what women think; for doing so on a basis of small homogenous samples of economically and educationally advantaged North American white men and women; for attributing to "gender" what might be due to gender only within certain class and cultural milieu, or might be due more to these other factors than to gender at all; and for canonizing an ethical viewpoint that reflects the attitude of responsiveness and accommodation of people accustomed to subordinate roles. She, like Kohlberg, has been criticized for crediting too readily what people say in interviews about their moral views, including ones involving hypothetical situations, rather than looking at moral behavior.

Conceding that these criticisms have merit, I believe Gilligan's work matters for ethics, and not just for care ethics. Suppose that Gilligan erred in the precise moral differences or magnitude of difference she attributed to gender, or was mistaken in attributing certain differences in moral thinking to gender differences independently of other social ones. Even so, her claims set off intense discussion revealing more socially linked differences in moral view and more complex ones than she had claimed. Additional research and analysis have tended to confirm her larger point about representative claims deployed as norms of humanity or maturity. Social and cultural differences do seem to figure in appreciating and reasoning about moral problems (see Harding 1987, Stack 1993, Baumrind 1993 on Gilligan; Geertz 1983, Shweder 1991, Miller and Bersoff 1995, and Wainryb and Turiel 1995 on culture and morality).

Gilligan's depiction of a "care" perspective undeniably struck a chord of recognition in many women. Suppose that women who recognized their own voice in Gilligan's different one were preponderantly white, middle-class, well-educated North American women like her subjects. Suppose many of these women found Gilligan's claim of gender difference plausible because they recognized the difference between their own evaluative perspective and that typical of the men with whom they were most familiar: white, middle-class, well-educated North American men. It is very important indeed to have marked off a particular kind moral outlook among *these* men, even by defining it in contrast only to similarly situated women. For it is these men who make moral theory in

America. Even now, our most reknowned and celebrated moral philosophers and their European counterparts are almost all of them men
socially like these. And if Gilligan's interview methods do not necessarily
reliably reveal on-line moral behavior, they do reveal how subjects
objectify their self-images and reflectively reconstruct the train of moral
decision and justification when entertaining moral problems in thought.
Is this not what our moral philosophers do when they take the path of
largely reflective insight into moral knowledge, unconstrained by many
kinds of empirical information and uninformed by testimonies from
many kinds of moral lives?

Feminists, at least, have been forced to confront, and continue to
remind each other of, problems of socially loaded theoretical representation in their work on ethics and on gender (Jaggar 1995). Gilligan's
"problem in the representation," however, is still not lodged in the
working methods of moral philosophers. Moral philosophers' surprising
confidence or alarming insouciance about the richness or representative-
ness of their own reflective resources or repertories has been long with
us and is handed down the generations. When moral philosophers do
not learn to query and situate their own specifically cultured social and
moral experience, they are rendered liable to misrepresent what they
reflect on in several ways.

Moral philosophers are liable to misrepresent contingent forms of
self-awareness and relationship as timeless, contextless, universal facts
about "human" nature or life. They may analyze concepts without
noticing the contingent and complex practices that give these particular
concepts sense. They are apt to reproduce visible and valued cultural
identities as universal facts or necessary conceptual truths about "persons," "agents," or "lives," when they are really depicting social norms,
and historically and culturally local ones, at that. They may not notice
that dominant identities require other, subordinate or marginal ones, for
their material support as well as their conceptual definition. Thus, they
are liable to reinforce or confer legitimacy prematurely on forms of life
they have uncritically reproduced in their "objective" and "critical"
accounts. In all this they are subject to illusions of placelessness or scientific rigor. They are apt, that is, to parade fact as necessity, historical contingency as eternal condition, norm as nature, social construction as
nature's way, endorsement as disinterested depiction, concordance
among peers as objectivity, and their own often questionable positions
to know as positions of expertise, even "scientific" ones (see, for example, Brink 1989, 95–99). There is no reason to feel sure moral philoso-

phy is free of these pitfalls, if moral philosophers have not worked out critical methods and reflexive techniques designed precisely to spot and avoid them.

Feminist writers have criticized theoretical-juridical views on many of the same grounds as nonfeminist writers mentioned above. They have promoted particularist epistemologies, the importance of connection and attachment, the historical contingency of social forms and roles, the depth at which these social forms are sunk in the identities of individuals, and the power of shared discourses and rhetorics to shape our social worlds and our places in them. But while those nonfeminist philosophers above mentioned tend to emphasize the diversity of goods, relations, particular situations, historical traditions and communities, or individual attachments and commitments, feminists draw attention to diversities of social positions, stations, or identities constituted by unshared and unequal powers within communities. This is the case with gender and other hierarchies in our society (see also Skillen 1978 and Wilson 1993). Feminists ask what the consequences are of such social arrangements for people's moral standings, for the moral understandings that keep those standings in place, *and* for the reflective study of those moral understandings that is ethics. Feminist opposition to mainstream moral theory is disloyal to the disciplinary convention within moral philosophy of not noticing that ethics comes from somewhere and someone in particular, and that what or who ends up represented is nonaccidentally related to who gets to represent "us."

Where Am I?

This is a book in moral philosophy, and it begins by claiming that moral philosophers are in the plane of morality, not hovering above it or perched outside it. So there I must be, too. I can only write from a particular social place at this time, already cultured and experienced in particular ways, some no doubt characteristic of some groups of people, some perhaps (slightly) idiosyncratic. Only still-powerful conventions in moral philosophy make it necessary for me to say: You must remember this.

If it is not obvious already, it will be obvious to readers of this book by its finish that a sustained challenge to the epistemic hubris of moral philosophers leaves the moral philosopher who poses it in a very uncomfortable position. I am in the essentially embarrassing position of writing ethics on the topic of the questionable authority of moral philosophers to write ethics. When I first arrived at this position, a few years ago, I was silenced and paralyzed.

I do not think now that silence and paralysis are permissible responses to this problem. If there is a problem about authoritative definitions of morality and formulations of moral problems in our actual divided and stratified social worlds, the last thing one who notices that problem should be is silent, at least about *it*. These divisions and inequities are after all not only problems for ethics but are among the deepest and most humanly costly problems that ethics has to confront. Given that others will go on authoritatively representing our moral lives who either do not notice this problem or do not find themselves taxed by it, I suppose it is worthwhile to try to draw attention to the problem. I have attempted to construct some parts of a theory of it and some parts of a method in response to it. One has to believe there are at least better, less officious or dubious, ways to position oneself in ethics, whether or not I have done so.

But I won't say I "leave others to judge" how much and in what ways I have embarrassed myself, tripping over my own complacently unnoticed positions. That is misleading. For one thing, I don't have to leave it to anybody; it's not mine to control. More importantly, I don't put this study forward as a take-it-or-leave-it set piece. I offer it as an object of comparison, for better or worse, in moral philosophy. I hope that it will spur imagination about new practices of teaching, writing, and debating about ethics. I hope to prompt collaborations in and experiments with moral inquiry as much by my failures here as by anything I have gotten right. There is no reason to think that anyone individually could imagine the full gamut of representational techniques for mapping and of critical devices for testing our differentiated and multilingual moral-social worlds.

two

Where Do Moral Theories Come From?

Henry Sidgwick and Twentieth-Century Ethics

[T]he self-representers have in truthfulness to represent themselves *as* self-representers, have to paint themselves in the act of painting themselves.

—Annette Baier, *Moral Prejudices*

Much of his writing met this fate. It was set down, depersonalized, and then erased. Much of his time was spent deciding whether or not to erase things. He usually did.

—A. S. Byatt, *Possession*

The question of my title is at once conceptual and historical. It is really several questions. How have certain propositional formulations, especially those authored by professional academic moral philosophers out of a certain set of (professionally and academically informed) interests, come to be seen as proper "moral theories," exemplifying a form canonical for philosophical accounts of morality? What is that canonical form? Why have many of us come to (and learned and been taught to) see *that* particular kind of account as authoritative? What kind of authority do we take it to have? What kind of authority do we assume *we* have in plying this kind of account, and with what interests and what effects do we do so? These are questions about how we know what to do (and what we are doing) in doing ethics.

One reason moral philosophers might ask these things is to remind themselves that they are participants in a particular set of institutional arrangements and social practices in which they have come to know "what to do." One reason they might remind themselves of this is that they may otherwise be unaware in important ways of the specificity of what they do, whether there are alternatives to it, and what the alternatives are. Another reason is that moral philosophizing is itself conduct and practice. Moral philosophers are morally responsible for it.

A genealogy of the contemporary idea of moral theory would be an important part of answering these questions. By a "genealogy" I mean, at a minimum, (1) a history which accounts for how a certain kind of knowledge claim and its object emerge out of certain authoritative discourses and practices. Having this might allow us to consider (2) whether theoretical moral knowledge, which comes to be viewed as the object to which moral theory approximates, may in fact be an *effect* of discourses, practices, and institutions that support and authorize its construction. If theoretical moral knowledge (or the claim to it) might itself have political and social effects, this in turn raises the issue (3) what the political and social stakes are in this, and whose they are. Here I make an incomplete gesture at (1). I offer only a small fragment of a discursive "history of the present" (Foucault 1979, 31) of twentieth-century Anglophone moral philosophy. Still, it suggests moral theories really do come from specific places at certain times.

This fragment takes a shortcut through the work of one philosopher, and mixes historical and conceptual points about what is found there. I examine the work and the role of the work of Henry Sidgwick, the eminent late nineteenth-century philosopher now most associated with the continuation of the tradition of English utilitarianism. I am not alone in viewing Sidgwick as, more than an important utilitarian theorist, a kind of progenitor of the form of moral theorizing that was not a matter of course in Sidgwick's time but has since become so in professionalized Anglo-American academic ethics. Sidgwick's influential treatise *The Methods of Ethics* (1874) is not just a classic of moral philosophy and of utilitarian philosophy, but a pivot in the course of the emergence of the dominant twentieth-century notion of a certain type of moral theory as "what to do" in moral philosophy.

That Sidgwick did what he did is a matter of history, and the precise mechanisms through which what Sidgwick did has exerted its influence is matter for factual research and debate. But an analysis of Sidgwick's conceptualization of morality and ethics in *Methods*, with attention to Sidgwick's historical placement, his institutional role, and consequent intellectual authority, may serve as a reminder that a certain kind of moral theorizing emerges from assumptions and choices which, having a history, are ones that might not have been, and might even now not be, made. I will follow Sidgwick's construction of moral philosophy in *The Methods of Ethics*, extracting from it a schematic model of moral theory that I call the *theoretical-juridical model*. It is my claim that this is the template (with variations and modifications) of "what to do" as ethics in much of, and often in the most prestigious venues of, twentieth-century Anglophone academic philosophy.

"Systematic and Precise General Knowledge of What Ought to Be"

J. B. Schneewind, one of the most illuminating analysts of the contours of modern moral philosophy, considers Sidgwick to have "succeeded at least in creating the prototype of the modern treatment of moral philosophy" (Schneewind 1977, 1). John Rawls, who (fittingly) provides the foreword to the contemporary Hackett edition of Sidgwick's *Methods* (Sidgwick [1907] 1981), concurs that it is "the first truly academic work in moral philosophy which undertakes to provide a systematic comparative study of moral conceptions" (v) and commends the study of *Methods* not only for its extraordinarily searching treatment of classical utilitarianism, but for the "originality" of Sidgwick's "conception of moral philosophy" (vi).[1] What the prototypical conception looks like, and the selections and exclusions involved in Sidgwick's construction of it, we will soon see.

Schneewind places Sidgwick, who assumed the position of Knightsbridge Professor of Moral Philosophy at Cambridge in 1883 (nine years after the first edition of *Methods*) and remained in it until his death in 1900, in the third of three generations of Victorian moral philosophers. The turn of the nineteenth century saw the influence of Paley, Reid, and Bentham, and midcentury of John Stuart Mill and William Whewell. The 1870s and following were the era of Sidgwick, Bradley, and Spencer, but also of a decisive shift toward academic specialization and the professionalization of philosophy and other "disciplines" in the universities. Schneewind remarks that by 1876, the year the journal *Mind* was established, the professionalization of philosophy was under way: "Bain in Scotland, Green at Oxford, Sidgwick at Cambridge were among the first of a new breed of philosopher. Unclerical, independent of formal allegiance to any set creed, they saw philosophy as an academic discipline dealing with problems defined and transmitted by a group of experts who were the best available judges of proposed solutions. . . . Philosophy . . . came, in both Scotland and England, to be practiced essentially as it is now . . . increasingly detached from practical affairs" (6). Sidgwick was a later successor of Whewell, whose title had been (tellingly) Knightsbridge Professor of Casuistical Divinity, and whose approach to moral philosophy enshrined the "intuitional" view treated with such care by Sidgwick, who believed such a view embodied the "common sense morality" of his time (see Jonsen and Toulmin 1981).

Sidgwick enters his brief for detachment in moral philosophy early, in the preface to the First Edition (1874): "I have thought that the predominance in the minds of moralists of a desire to edify has impeded the real progress of ethical science: and that this would be benefited by an application to it of the same disinterested curiosity to which we chiefly owe the great discoveries of physics" (viii). That there is, as in the case with physics, something free of human artifice already there to be discovered is the "simple assumption" that frees Sidgwick's inquiry from psychological, sociological, historical, and practical burdens: "there is something under any given circumstances which it is right or reasonable to do, and . . . this may be known" (vii). Sidgwick, however, does not identify his task with the search for *particular* right and reasonable things to do under some given circumstances. It is, as stated on the first page of the introductory chapter, the job of Ethics (the philosophical study of morality) to "attain systematic and precise *general* knowledge of what ought to be" (emphasis mine) by critically comparing as to "certainty and precision" (Preface, viii) the different *methods*—"rational procedure[s] by which we determine what individual human beings 'ought' . . . to do or to seek . . . " (1). A main task of the brief introductory chapter is to urge upon the reader two distinctions. One is the difference between "science" and "Ethics," or between the sense in which he does want to claim the project of Ethics is "scientific" and the sense in which he does not want to claim this (1–2). The other is about a difference between, as he puts it, "the plan and purpose of the present treatise" and "the nature and boundaries of the subject of Ethics as generally understood" (11–12).

Ethics may properly be called "scientific" insofar as it aims at "systematic and precise general knowledge," but not, as is the case with science (simpliciter), knowledge of "some department of actual existence," such as, in the case of morality, actual "varieties of human conduct, and of men's sentiments and judgments respecting conduct" (2). Ethics seeks systematic and precise general knowledge of what is right, and what makes judgments valid. Even while Sidgwick avers that Ethics must make a "careful study of actual phenomena," its task is not to aim at explanatory laws or uniformities, but at regulative ones (2). It is, then, the *form* of "science," not its explanatory or predictive role with respect to a body of fact or phenomena, that "scientific Ethics" takes over.

The canonical form for "science" has long roots reaching back to classical philosophy, and shorter ones reaching back to the Newtonian synthesis in physics. The common thread is unification and illumination of diverse particular facts or truths by exhibiting them as derivable (and perhaps deducible, with adequate collateral information) from a small collection of extremely general laws or axiomatic principles. Yet, if Ethics (and Politics) have as "their special and primary object to determine what ought to be, and not to ascertain what merely is, has been, or will be," (1) one might wonder why the fittedness of the form of science to Ethics is not itself in question. It is a question Sidgwick does not broach in the book's 528 pages. He does, however, in the first few pages prize off Ethics from "other" genuinely empirical sciences, such as psychology and sociology, and so from its obligations to consider actual psychological capacities and actual forms of group life (2).

Neither is Sidgwick's project quite like "the subject of Ethics generally understood," either in content or approach. For it eschews consideration of the historical situations, relations, and succession of "systems" (12) and firmly disowns the "hortatory" aim (13) of "supplying a set of practical directions for conduct" (14). These are among the "recognized ways" of treating the subject of Ethics which Sidgwick did not find "desirable" to adopt. Sidgwick does not just put to one side these recognized ways of doing Ethics, but finds them irrelevant or inimical to what he has in mind in *Methods* to do. Sidgwick emphasizes that there are "different views of the ultimate reasonableness of conduct, implicit in the thought of ordinary men, though not brought into clear relation to each other" (6). Contemporary readers will agree, as no doubt many did in Sidgwick's time, with this point: People are apt to make different moral judgments in many cases, especially complex or unfamiliar cases. Just following, Sidgwick stresses the importance of what he apparently thinks comes to the same, that there is "a diversity of methods applied in ordinary practical thought" (6).

Whether one should see divergence in moral judgment necessarily or exclusively in terms of subscription to different "methods"—rational procedures of decision for individual cases—is far less obvious. Less obvious still is the claim that these "methods" (which Sidgwick curiously points out are "not here studied historically, as methods that have actually been used or proposed for the regulation of practice" (12)) are (the?) "alternatives between which—so far as they cannot be reconciled—the human mind seems to me necessarily forced to choose, when it attempts to frame a complete synthesis of practical maxims and to act in a perfectly consistent manner" (12). The choice is forced by "a fundamental postulate of Ethics," that "so far as two methods conflict, one or other of them must be modified and rejected" (6) because we can't "regard as valid reasonings that lead to conflicting conclusions" (6). Moral disagreement or diversity is already rendered as application of different rational procedures. Application is already rendered as something like deduction of the particular from the general. Bases or reference points of moral reasoning are already rendered as "methods" or assumptions at a high level of generality. And the "fundamental postulate" (that precludes, apparently, diversity as well as actual inconsistency) already assumes that there is some unitary and unified perspective from which the right action-guiding conclusions (logically) directly descend, and so from which they must inherit their own required internal coherence.

In concluding his introduction, Sidgwick once more articulates his "object": "to expound as clearly and as fully as my limits will allow the different methods of Ethics that I find implicit in our common moral reasoning; to point out their mutual relations; and where they seem to conflict, to define the issue as much as possible" (14). *Methods* sculpts its object out of the history and present of a particular moral climate, out of a wide field of facts constituting and impinging on human moral behavior, thought, and practice, and out of an already formed tradition of speculation, criticism, and exhortation on moral matters in English letters and life.

Two sorts of things are cut away—detached—in hewing out the object of *Methods*. On the one hand, empirical contributions from such areas as we call social sciences, and considerations of the historical and cultural placement of "our" moral views, are set aside. On the other, *Methods* exempts itself from finally establishing some method as the right one, and hence of urging on its audience the practical direction and specific applications that method requires. Thereby two sets of questions are put aside and two powerful assumptions teetering between the descriptive and the prescriptive are set in play. One posits a compact core of purely moral knowledge; the other claims that moral philosophy is not only free of significant empirical burdens, but innocent of practical commitments.

The relevance of concrete historical and cultural circumstance, and of constraints on human psychological function and social organization (as well as the interrelations among these), to what and how moral concepts mean, and to whom, is excluded. Sidgwick assumes there is a "morality of common sense" not fractured by class, gender, race, or educational divisions and stratifications (see also Schneewind 1977, 193). A footnote far into the text admits that he "ought certainly to have discussed further how we are to ascertain the 'experts' on whose 'consensus' we are to rely" (343), whom earlier he identified with "at least . . . that portion of mankind which combines adequate intellectual enlightenment with a serious concern for morality" (215). Up front in the preface to the Second Edition, however, common sense morality is said simply to be "my own morality as much as it is any man's" (xii). Aside from whether there is extant consensus, Sidgwick, in bypassing the factual records of moral life, entitles himself to the assumption that morality, or something essential or central to it, is the kind of thing that will yield to complete systematization in the form of a compact theory. He assumes that there is something thought or believed that is central to morality, and that he can extricate it from all the welter of fact comprised by moral and social life. Finally, in place of the perhaps various interpersonal and social interests that morality may embody or allow expression to, Sidgwick puts certain epistemological interests and demands of philosophical theorizing. In these ways Sidgwick defines the idea of a *pure core of knowledge* at the heart of morality.

At the same time, abstaining from claims to final validation and the directive heft they may have defines the position of the moral philosopher in distinction to the moralist. Sidgwick as moral philosopher conducts a disinterested search for true moral knowledge guided by disinterested demands of precision, clarity, and consistency. The cloak of scientific objectivity signifies the promise and ensuing prestige of scientific accomplishment. It also shields from view the historical, cultural, and social location of the moral philosopher, and that of moral philosophy itself as a practice of intellectual and social authority. This practice and the authority of its practitioners are sustained by particular institutions and social arrangements, and possibly influence these institutions and social arrangements in turn. By these excisions Sidgwick constructs the *purity of moral philosophy*, a principled abstention from interest and practical commitments that enables its proper work. While Kant is the locus classicus for a principled claim that moral philosophy is grounded in its "pure part," in Sidgwick's moral philosophy, purity is effected by stipulation with no obvious rationale.

A Theoretical-Juridical Model for Ethics

Significant tensions, ambiguities, and inconsistencies traverse Sidgwick's masterwork, but its modelling of its own moral philosophy—the prototypical and original conception—is fairly clear. It is, I claim, also

extremely familiar to anyone acquainted with twentieth-century Anglophone academic ethics as it predominantly is done, especially in America. I call the prototype that Sidgwick limns self-consciously by a series
of deliberate distinctions and detachments the *theoretical-juridical
model* (TJM) for the doing of ethics. I call it this because I believe it is
the template, the master form, of much twentieth-century ethics. Its
dominance consists in the prestige of work that follows its prescriptive
contours. Its dominance is further reflected in its disappearance from
view as a distinct project within a larger and varied tradition of moral
philosophy, a project committed to a specific conception of morality,
moral philosophy, and the relations between them.

A staple of the contemporary organization of ethics texts, moral problems anthologies, discussions in philosophical journals and colloquia,
and a prevalent understanding of "applied ethics" is the assumption that
philosophical ethics is "about" a contest among different moral theories,
and about the conflicting moral judgments that may be reached by
applying the theories to the issues or cases. The refinement and critique
of these theories and their applications is a great deal of "what is done"
in philosophy books, journals, colloquia, and classrooms. Philosophers
already know what the "main" moral theories are. They are always at
least Kantian and utilitarian theories in various versions, and often
rights theories or social contract theories, or in particular Rawls's theory.
Sometimes traditions of moral thought with premodern roots are
included, as with natural law theory or (unhappily named) "virtue
theory." These latter already strain the frame of organization, because
they developed long before that frame was invented. The frame is a certain historically emergent idea of moral theory and moral philosophy
that I am calling the TJM. It may now be easier to see what it is, and
how it is produced.

The idea of moral theory that organizes the field of twentieth-century
academic ethics is:

> A *moral theory* is a consistent (and usually very compact) set of law-
> like moral principles or procedures for decision that is intended to
> yield by deduction or instantiation (with the support of adequate col-
> lateral information) some determinate judgment for an agent in a given
> situation about what it is right, or at least morally justifiable, to do.

Moral theories try to "represent" the ideal capacity of the well-equipped moral agent, or to justify its issue, in a *codifiable, compact, consistent* (set of) *procedure(s)* for generating or justifying action-guiding judgments.

Anyone steeped or schooled in the conventions of standard contemporary moral philosophy might well remark, "Well, yes. Of course. What else could (or should) moral philosophy do?" This reveals the underlying theoretical-juridical model that shapes contemporary ethics:

> (TJM): *Moral philosophy* has as its central aim the discovery/construction, testing, comparison, and refinement of moral theories (as above defined), which exhibit the essential core of pure or proper moral knowledge, in distinction from merely collateral practical, psychological, sociological, anthropological, historical, etc. (i.e. merely factual, nonmoral) information.

The way this conception is "theoretical" is clear: Moral capacity is pictured as itself a kind of theory within an agent, or at least as something the agent knows that can be represented in that form. The conception is "juridical" twice over: Moral theories are themselves seen as delivering or justifying verdicts on cases (jury or judge, as it were); and moral philosophy is a tribunal under which competing moral theories are scrutinized and judged for (especially their logical and epistemological) adequacy.

This is, of course, Sidgwick's scheme of organization of his *Methods*. Moral judgments issue from methods, which are general procedures of rational decision-making, and the original conception of moral philosophy in Sidgwick's treatise is that of impartially adjudicating the precise scope, worth, and limits of the (competing) methods in the disinterested pursuit of moral truth. As the preface to the First Edition promised, "all the different methods developed in it are expounded and criticized from a neutral position" (viii). *Methods*, which at once instances, articulates, and partially defends this original conception, constructs it by a variety of assumptions and exclusions.

This conception is no longer original; it is now, for many professional philosophers, just what moral philosophy "is." But it is easier to see now that it involves, conceptually, three increasingly strong and specific constraints:

> (TJM 1) *Restriction of morality to knowledge:* The task of moral philosophy is to discover and validate the knowledge in which moral capacity or the justification of its results (essentially) consists.

(TJM 2) *Restriction of moral knowledge to moral theory:* Moral knowledge consists in a completely general theory which explains (the derivation of) and so justifies all true moral judgments.

(TJM 3) *Restriction of moral theory to the "scientific" model:* An adequate moral theory will be structurally and functionally similar (or analogous) to a "scientific one."[2]

Several features specify the structure and function of theoretical-juridical moral theories. It almost goes without saying that essential moral knowledge is assumed to be propositionally expressible, so explicitly stateable and teachable (the *codifiability assumption*). It is assumed that what the propositions of the theory express are law-like generalizations (typically over acts in situations) corresponding to the particular moral judgments we make about what to do (the *nomological assumption*). Particular moral judgments are viewed as derivative (by deduction or instantiation) from the generalizations which generate or justify them; the generalizations are more primitive, so embody more fundamental or essential moral knowledge. (Call this the *logical priority assumption.*) Finally, *systematic unity* requires these moral covering laws, following Sidgwick's "fundamental postulate," to form a set consistent in itself, usually ordered or weighted so as to eliminate incompatible applications, and to be few (if even more than one) in number.

Every one of these standard features is included in Sidgwick's original. Sidgwick demands that rules of duty admit of "precise definition in universal form" (228), allowing them to serve as "scientific axioms" for use in "clear and cogent demonstrations" (215) that proceed from "as explicit, exact, coherent" statements (216) of the directive rules of conduct as are possible. These characteristics define a specific kind of moral theory that might naturally be called a "code."[3]

The conviction that a proper moral theory will be a code-like theory is not incompatible with relativism about such theories. One might imagine, for example, various agents or communities arriving by a method of reflective equilibrium at various codes that fit their (perhaps divergent) well-considered judgments or nonmoral background theories. But the project of code-like moral theory is widely viewed as Sidgwick viewed it, as the search for the instrument that allows to be known that "something under any given circumstances which it is right or reasonable to do" (vii), i.e. right or reasonable for anyone in the given circumstances to do. Call this widely held belief the assumption of *impersonality*; it entails that there is just one uniform codification of morality, which if true is true for everyone.[4] While logical priority of a code of principles goes a long way toward cordoning off a core of "proper" or "essential" moral knowledge, the common addition of impersonality effects the complete *purity* of the knowledge code-like theories seek to embody. Facts individuating persons and their social situations or cultural environments are always "collateral," i.e. merely factual nonmoral information. These facts are to the side of what moral philosophy needs to and should be concerned with; they are without special interest or importance for the moral philosopher.

But the actual historically and culturally shaped moral environment, its characteristic institutions, relations, and roles, and facts of many kinds about people's relationships, histories, and circumstances are central to human beings' "common sense" attempts to determine or defend the scope and limits of their moral responsibilities (see chapter 4 of this book). Is it for these people (often referred to from within the TJM impersonally as "the" moral agent) that code-like moral theories are sought? Is the search for system, and more specifically for theory, driven by some practical or moral need of unphilosophical people? Is moral theory for the sake of morality, or in morality's interest? Or is the search for moral theory propelled by the interests of philosophers in the elegance and legibility of unity and system, and in cravings for the epistemological security of firm foundations that a system of moral laws might be thought to provide?

The claim that reflective systematization of moral beliefs and ideals, in broader or narrower forms, is for the sake of common moral practice has a history as long as Western philosophy. From Socrates' insistence that true belief, moral and otherwise, serves action just as well as knowledge, but is not durable without the *logos* (account, explanation) which ties it down, on to Kant's lamentation on the natural dialectic, not only the lure of theory, but the claim of practical (but not interested) service through moral theorization has tempted moral philosophers. Philosophers may like to think of moral theory as a bulwark against laxity; not just the logical foundation of moral judgments but the anchor of robust conviction and the guarantee of unhesitant action.

Who Needs a Scientific Ethics?

Returning once more to Henry Sidgwick, it is interesting to find a less straightforward story on the point of seeking theoretical systematization. At the beginning of *Methods*, Sidgwick seems to distinguish on the one hand the study of Ethics (a philosophical subject) from morality itself, as it is represented in and by common sense, and on the other the study of Ethics as a philosophical tradition from "the plan and purpose of the present treatise" (11–12). That is, Ethics is not morality, but is rather a particular kind of study of morality; and Sidgwick's *Methods* is not Ethics, but rather a particular (and somewhat original) approach to that study. As the work progresses, these distinctions between morality, "Ethics," and what the *Methods* does sometimes blur. At page 77, the "aim of Ethics" is "to systematise and free from error the apparent cognitions that most men have of the rightness or reasonableness of conduct. . . ." A bit later, Sidgwick reminds us "we are accustomed to expect from Morality clear and decisive precepts or counsels . . ." (199) and within pages of this speaks of constructing "a scientific code of morality . . . [whose] very object . . . is to supply a standard for rectifying men's divergent opinions" (210). Is it, then, morality, Ethics, or Sidgwick's treatise that needs the theoretical and juridical form to do what it is supposed to do?

It is in Sidgwick's careful and searching discussions of the intuitional and virtue views comprising "common sense morality," that the slippage becomes most evident. The morality of common sense is just "a collection of such general rules, as to the validity of which there would be apparent agreement at least among persons of our own age and civilisation, and which would cover with approximate completeness the whole of human conduct" (215). Sidgwick thinks that "reflective persons naturally appeal to general rules or formulae" (214), and assumes it "belongs to the ordinary or jural view of Ethics" that "rules of duty ought to admit of precise definition in a universal form" (228). But now it appears that common sense morality is defective by its *own* aims, and must welcome its own systematic reformation by a study of Ethics of just the type Sidgwick's *Methods* affords.

"Most of us feel the need," he says, of general formulas to correct error and uncertainty in concrete judgments, due to complexity of circumstances, personal interests, and habitual sympathies (214), and to supplement our intuitions. Our need is for such formulae as "give clear and unhesitating decisions" (215). It is this practical need, Sidgwick carefully argues, that the collection of commonsense rules of obligation and virtue not only does not, but cannot, meet. These rules are too "deficient in clearness and precision" to "serve as scientific axioms, and to be available in clear and cogent demonstrations" (215). Commonsense moral principles are persuasive only when vague, and become arguable as soon as they are sharpened by careful reflection (342). These vague principles are also apt to come into conflict when applied in some cases, violating the fundamental postulate. They do not, in short, "possess the characteristics by which self-evident truths are distinguished from mere opinions" (338).

By detailed examination Sidgwick demonstrates the resistance of various such principles to exacting statement and systematic convergence in application. Sidgwick finds that the morality of common sense is more a "fluid mass of opinion" than "a deposit of clear and precise principles commanding universal acceptance" (338). This is not for him a reason to question the appropriateness of the systematizing project. While aware of the Aristotelian view that "we can only give a general account of the virtue . . . leave it to trained insight to find in any particular circumstances the act that will best realise it" (228), Sidgwick rejects it for a scientific Ethics that continues "the attempt that Socrates initiated" to define satisfactorily (i.e. to standards of scientific form and precision) the axioms that premise moral derivations. Common sense may be pregnant with durable moral insights, but theoretical midwifery will be required to deliver what common sense itself strains at. Sidgwick not only suggests going in to his review of common sense morality that this is "an effort of reflection which ordinary persons will not make" (215), but observes at the end of it that they need not make it. "In short, the Morality of Common Sense may still be perfectly adequate to give practical guidance to common people in common circumstances" (361) despite its margins of obscurity. But if unsystematic commonsense morality is good enough for common people, whom does scientific systematization in ethics serve?

Initially in reading *Methods* one might have taken it to be a special kind of reflective and analytical ethical treatise for moral philosophers. Later, following the discussion of common sense, one might have begun to think Sidgwick's systematization was directed at the refinement of common moral competence, at "the perfection of practice no less than for theoretical completeness" (263). In the end of the work, however, it is both and neither. The concluding chapters on utilitarianism site scientific moral knowledge in a different place.

Although Sidgwick at the opening of *Methods* demurs from arguing for one method as right, his perusal of methods of moral decision, applying the criteria of scientific form, leads him at the end to present utilitarianism as the "scientifically complete and systematically reflective form" (425) of morality. Sidgwick's utilitarianism is a classical act utilitarianism which holds that objectively right action in any given circumstances is "that which will produce the greatest amount of happiness on the whole . . . taking into account all whose happiness is affected by the conduct" (411). Sidgwick concedes that utilitarianism's theoretical demand of calculative exactness is "grotesquely incongruous" with our commonsense appreciation of the "inevitable inexactness of all such calculations in actual practice" (416). Sidgwick also immediately introduces the now well-worn appeal to the "indirect strategy," the concession that the utilitarian criterion of rightness need not, and generally should not, be that which we consciously strive to fulfill, if the general happiness be otherwise better served. As systematic theory, however, utilitarianism alone "sustains the general validity" of commonsense judgment, while it "supplements the defects" of commonsense moral reasoning and "affords a principle of synthesis" for it. Utilitarianism thus achieves "a complete and harmonious system" (422) which stands to the morality of common sense as a "technical method" embodying scientific conclusions stands to "trained instinct and empirical rules" (425).

If utilitarianism is the technical method embodying conclusions of a scientific ethics, who are the technicians? The final book (IV) of *Methods* contains an answer. Picking up the earlier analogy between ordinary practice and technical method, Sidgwick notes that

> persons of enlightenment and special acquaintance with the effects of the conduct judged, may reasonably inspire us with distrust of Common Sense: just as in the more technical parts of practice we prefer the judgment of a few trained experts to the instincts of the vulgar. . . . Common Sense morality is really only adapted for ordinary men in ordinary circumstances— although it may still be expedient that these ordinary persons should regard it as absolutely and universally prescribed, since any other view of it may dangerously weaken its hold over their minds. So far as this is the case we must use the Utilitarian method to ascertain how far persons in special circumstances require a morality more specially adapted to them than Common Sense is willing to concede. (466)

It is not, then, only that common folk do not usually need a view other than commonsense morality offers, but that it would not be the best (on utilitarian grounds) for them to have just that view which is the "scientifically complete and systematically reflective" one, utilitarianism. Sidgwick thinks that utilitarian exceptions to the vague but commonly serviceable dictates of commonsense morality will be "either for persons generally under exceptional circumstances, or for a class of persons defined by exceptional qualities of intellect, temperament, or character" (489).

While Sidgwick purports to discuss these two kinds of "exceptional" cases, what follows is a carefully reasoned operator's manual for the scientific utilitarian ethic in the hands of an elite, those exceptional in the second way. Sidgwick flatly recognizes the affront to common moral sense itself in the idea of an esoteric morality restricted to an elite. Given it, he concludes that utilitarian decision-making must *on utilitarian grounds* often be covert and/or intentionally misleading, i.e. it should seek for the most part to reinforce for the many and vulgar what is dispensable for the wise and few. Sidgwick judiciously counsels the wise few to take care for such matters as lost power and credibility, negative moral kickbacks of utilitarian attempts at moral reform that are not matched by hoped-for gains, and possible unsavory impacts on the utilitarian operative's own character.

These sections of *Methods*, chapters IV and V of the final book, give new meaning to their common title, "The Method of Utilitarianism," as Sidgwick soberly considers the business of costs and opportunities for the exceptional few. It is hard not to see these as people in positions of political or administrative power, and hard not to view these counsels as tactical and strategic advice for such people. It is they who are at once most in need of a systematic view, because they are responsible for whole systems; and they who are most likely to be able to put such a view into practice discretely and discreetly both, because their power opens workings of that system to them at will, from places of privilege which most others will never enter, or even get a clear view of it. (See Williams 1985, 108–110, on "government house utilitarianism.")

While it is "the Utilitarian's duty to aid in improving" the actual, imperfect moral order (476), Sidgwick advises firmly against wholesale campaigns for change guided by utilitarian insight. He urges a "respectful delicacy" (476) of approach, relating practical interventions to a social order "varying but little from the actual, with its actually established code of moral rules and customary judgments concerning virtue and vice" (474). The net effect of his recommendations would seem to blend a considerable degree of conservatism with a sharp eye for possible surgical interventions supported by utilitarian calculation, especially where these may be shielded from destabilizing publicity (489).

Sidgwick remarks candidly, in concluding the penultimate chapter of

Methods, on the "tendency which Utilitarian ethics has always shown to pass over into politics," and reiterates in the closing sentence that "[a] sincere Utilitarian, therefore, is likely to be an eager politician ..." (495). One might think, historically and practically, that the tendency was likely to be the other way around.

Questions of Authority in/for Ethics

I have dwelt on Sidgwick's construction of moral philosophy because I take him to be, more than an exemplifying figure, a founder of one influential kind of ethics. In Sidgwick we can see, mostly in explicit and even self-conscious forms, a set of ground rules and guiding assumptions that are still very much operative in contemporary moral philosophy, although often in inexplicit and unself-conscious forms. These rules and assumptions define code-like theory building, testing, and fine-tuning, with standard appeal to "intuitions" and vulnerability to intuition-based counterexamples, as the premier genre of, and perhaps simply as "what to do," in ethics. They also pull the field of discussion into a particular shape around an interrelated cluster of other issues, such as moral realism and noncognitivism, moral justification and skepticism, the reality and import of moral dilemmas. The shape of these ongoing contemporary debates reflects not only philosophers' epistemological preoccupations with morality, but their preoccupations with the epistemological status of moral *theories* of the code-like sort, with what sorts of evidence count for and against them, with what type of consistency they require, and with what they might be thought to be "about."

Sidgwick noted that the "plan and purpose" of his treatise parted ways with other historical and contemporary approaches to the study of morality. I think it significant that of the triad of late Victorian moral philosophers within which Schneewind locates him, only Sidgwick, and not F. H. Bradley or Herbert Spencer, is still commonly read and recognized today, (much as we know Mill, but not Whewell; and Bentham, but not, for their ethics at least, Paley or Reid). Bentham, Mill, and Sidgwick are part of a history of the present in which the "scientific" path of theory still beckons, and utilitarianism still out-systematizes everything else around, even as its "grotesque incongruity" with common sense, admitted by Sidgwick, continues to provoke refutations. The refutations in turn evoke either variations on the indirect strategy Sidgwick (and Mill) already conceded was inevitable for utilitarianism, or nonutilitarian theories that try to meet the terms of compactness and systematicity and completeness and determinacy which always so flatter utilitarianism in the end.

Even while Sidgwick's name and utilitarian lineage remain in view, Sidgwick's role as a framer of the TJM and a father of meta-ethics (which submits what we think and say morally to logical analysis and clarification, while abstaining from broaching "substantive" moral matters) has slipped out of view. This is both expressed and reinforced by the contemporary historiography of philosophy, forming in new generations of students of philosophy a sense of "what ethics does." A standard way to periodize ethics (embodied in the organization of many courses, for example) is to begin "twentieth-century" or "contemporary" moral philosophy with G. E. Moore's *Principia Ethica*, published in 1903, three years after Sidgwick's death. It is admittedly a caricature, but not I think a totally unfair one, to say that many students learn that twentieth-century ethics flows from Moore's curious blend of meta-ethical reflection and ideal utilitarianism, and runs off in two directions: One is a trail of meta-ethical skirmishes between various realisms and noncognitivisms, the other a continuing counterpoint of substantive consequentialisms and deontologies, all haunted by egoism and its taunting question, "Why should I be moral?" All of this, the neutral scrutiny of the logic of the methods, the square-off between the "intuitional" and the "teleological" views, the underlying "dualism of practical reason" that cannot reconcile the compelling force of self-interest and universal benevolence, is there already between two covers in Sidgwick's *Methods*, which saw its last edition in 1907.[5] The influence of this particular work on the substance and style of how moral philosophy is done now is very great, but the work and its formative influence remain largely out of sight below the accepted historiographical horizon.[6] My point in hauling it up for view is to make it, and its historical and conceptual specificity, available for examination; and to invite moral philosophers to be at least as self-conscious about choosing the path of code-like theory as Sidgwick was.

I might be suspected of relishing the details of Sidgwick's disturbingly cool discussion of utilitarian cloak-and-dagger. Of course, this alarmingly dispassionate justification of manipulative tactics and covert strategies will jar many readers today. My point in highlighting it has not been to render Sidgwick a sinister figure, nor to imply that the project of moral systematization necessarily implies an authoritarian politics. My point is to underscore Sidgwick's candor and attentiveness in dealing with a question no longer often raised: For whom are the labors of moral philosophers and the accounts that these labors produce? What are moral philosophers imagining as the social realization of the views they propose and defend? If moral philosophy answers a need or has a use, whose need is this and where is moral philosophy used? If moral philosophers aim to represent a capacity, whose capacity is it, or whose could it be? To what and to whose ends and interests is this moral capacity to be exercised? I admire Sidgwick's accountability in these matters, his assumption of the responsibility to speak to such questions, even as his answers to them repel.

Moral philosophy needs to remember these questions, and become again candid about them. When we encounter representations of morality, including philosophers' representations of morality in moral philosophy, we could ask: Who is speaking, and from what positions and interests? Who is the intended audience of these representations? How do these representations embody or reinforce or propose to transfigure social relations, and especially relations of power and authority? This is just to suggest that moral philosophy might give some moral account of itself.[7]

part two

Clearer Views

An Expressive-Collaborative Model

three

Authority and Transparency

The Example of Feminist Skepticism

[I]f I don't speak for those less privileged than myself, am I abandoning my political responsibility to speak out against oppression, a responsibility incurred by the very fact of my privilege? If I should not speak for others, should I restrict myself to following others' lead uncritically? Is my greatest contribution to *move over and get out of the way*? And if so, what is the best way to do this—to keep silent or to deconstruct my discourse?

—Linda Alcoff, "The Problem of Speaking for Others"

Not all the selves we are make you important.

—Maria Lugones, "On the Logic of Pluralist Feminism"

This is a century of moral philosophy in which epistemological anxieties and skeptical threats drive discussion in ethics relentlessly to issues of justification. Yet moral philosophers are typically casual about their own *positions to know* what they claim to represent and theorize. Poses of reflective transcendence and unproblematic authority to define "our" intuitions (or interests, or sense of justice, or concept of responsibility) are part of the manner of moral philosophy as an intellectual practice and a genre of writing. Theories of moral life and moral knowledge, however, are particularly sensitive to questions about the basis of *representative* claims and the *authority* of claimants to enter them. For these claims are not only "about" moral life, but are part of it, and authority is open to moral questions of its rightfulness, as well as epistemic ones about its reliability. Answers to the questions "Who knows?" and "Who gets to say?" are not straightforward in a moral-social world such as ours is.

Ours is a society pervasively segmented and stratified by gender, class, race, age, education, professionalization, sexual practice, and other hierarchies of power and status. Divisions of labor, opportunity, responsibility, and recognition both constitute and follow these hierarchies. These divisions matter significantly, even profoundly, for how people live; they make people live different lives. In a society structured in these ways, there are likely to be differences in views about the nature, structure, gravity, and rational resolution of moral problems among people who live different lives. Differently situated people may face different moral problems or experience similar ones differently. They will have reasonably different understandings of costs, risks, and relevance. They will see different responses realistically open to them in responding to these problems, and find different ways of resolving them to be successful or sane. They may well grasp their responsibilities as different in scope, content, kind, or stringency from those of others differently placed and experienced.

If differentiated social orders demand varied, even competing, styles of moral understanding or different conceptions of agency and responsibility, there are going to be challenging and interesting problems about representing "moral life." Are some, all, or none of these understandings and conceptions the ones that set the standard or provide the stuff for a normative moral theory or moral psychology to represent? Whose understandings of morality are parts of the evidence for determining what morality is? Whose styles of moral thinking define what kind of thinking is moral thinking? Whose senses of self and responsibility show us what selves are like and where responsibility makes sense? And, what is the vantage point from which one is likely to be a good judge of these matters? For ethics, these are problems about defining the field of inquiry itself, and about rights to be heard speaking in it, and to it. These are also problems for the credibility of moral claims within a given society: Who sets the terms for moral judgment, and can all positions in a moral-social order find coherent expression in the moral terms that order provides?

Feminist philosophers cannot be casual about the effects of claims to represent and the assumption of authority to make these claims. Feminist readings and critiques of the tradition and discipline of ethics nurture skepticism about the authoritative and representative poses of men who speak about, in place of, or in the absence of women. But feminists have also had to recognize and resist the lure of unearned authority in their own attempts at constructing accounts for and about "women." For "... systematic, sustained reflection on being a woman—the kind of contemplation that 'doing theory' requires—is most likely to be done by women who vis-à-vis other women enjoy a certain amount of political, social, and economic privilege because of their skin color, class member-ship, ethnic identity" (Lugones and Spelman 1983, 574). The epistemic, moral, and political risks of representing moral life are well illustrated by feminist ethics. At the same time feminist epistemology provides a view of knowledge that helps to identify and explain those risks. Its con-ception of objectivity suggests ways to meet them. I use these materials to defend a model for the close description and critical examination of moral judgment in its social context. I call this model an *expressive-col-laborative conception* of morality. I believe this conception of morality and its epistemology supports a descriptively rich and politically critical approach to ethics and the justification of moral judgments that is not only for feminists.

Feminist Skepticism

Feminist critique of ethics argues that authoritative representations of morality in canonical and contemporary works of the Western tradition of philosophy are marked by *gender and other bias*. Feminist ethics par-ticularly targets for criticism modern moral theories, those neo-Kantian, utilitarian, rights, and contract theories that dominate discussion in pub-lic arenas and in the journals, textbooks, classrooms, and conferences of contemporary Anglo-American academic ethics. While proponents of these views see them as sharply divided over fundamental moral issues, feminist critics see them differently. They see similar preoccupations, images, and assumptions among these modern theories of morality, and a suspicious convergence of these with activities, roles, social contexts, opportunities, and character ideals associated with (at least privileged) men in our society, or with norms of masculinity that apply to them.

A great deal of feminist criticism alleges gender-bias in the *content* of such theories. Preoccupation with equality and autonomy, uniformity and impartiality, rules and reciprocity fits voluntary bargaining relations of nonintimate equals, or contractual and institutional relations among peers in contexts of impersonal or public interaction. It ignores the often unchosen, discretionary responsibilities of those who care for particular others, often dependent and vulnerable, in intimate, domestic, or famil-ial—"private"—contexts. It slights relations of interdependence centered on bonds of affection and loyalty whose specific histories set varying terms of obligation and responsibility. It obscures the particularity of moral actors and relations by emphasizing universality, sameness, and repeatability, excluding or regimenting emotional experience. Ignoring or slighting continuing relationships of intimacy and care, these views feature abstract problem solving to the neglect of responsive attention to actual others. Yet women's traditionally assigned (or permitted) responsibilities—paid and unpaid—center on forms of caring labor in both private and public spheres. These works sustain intimate, domestic, and other personal relations, and tend to the comfort and nurturance, bodily safety, nourishment, and cleanliness of others (Baier 1987; Benhabib 1987; Bowden 1997; Code 1991; Dillon 1992; Gilligan 1982; Meyers 1989; Ruddick 1984; Tronto 1993).

Worse than being incomplete or lopsided, however, these moral theories mystify social reality. For the community of freely contracting peers or mutually respecting reciprocators could not exist without the extensive and required labors of the caregivers, whose physical and emotional work cannot be recognized or valued in the moral terms these theories set (Baier 1987). As Kathryn Morgan puts it, these theories effect the "invisibility of women's moral domains" (Morgan 1987, 220). But it is not only women who thus disappear. Joan Tronto correctly broadens the point: Socially vital caring, maintenance, and support activities are not only gendered, but "raced" and "classed," as "questions that have traditionally informed the lives of women, and servants, slaves, and workers, have not informed the philosophical tradition or political theory" (Tronto 1993, 3). Not all concerns are equally authoritative in society or philosophy.

While most feminist criticism has gone to the content of dominant moral theories, these theories also share a quite specific *form*. This form represents abstraction, generalization, and uniformity as the normal form of moral consideration. I call the underlying conception of morality a *theoretical-juridical model*, and the theories this model requires *code-like* theories.

The regnant type of moral theory in contemporary ethics is a *codifiable* (and usually *compact*) set of moral *formulas* (or procedures for selecting formulas) that can be applied by *any* agent to a situation to yield a justified and determinate *action-guiding* judgment. The formulas or procedures (if there is more than one) are typically seen as rules or principles at a high level of generality. Application of these formulas is typically seen as something like deduction or instantiation. The formulas and their applications yield the same for all agents indifferently. These formulas model what the morally competent agent or ideal moral judge does or should know, however implicitly (Walker 1992; also Baier 1985 and Manning 1992).

The picture of morality as a *compact, impersonally action-guiding code within (or for) an agent* results from a powerfully restrictive set of assumptions about what morality is. It is assumed that morality is essentially *knowledge*, or that philosophers can reflectively extract a core of knowledge specific and essential to morality; that the core of moral knowledge is essentially *theoretical*, of an explicitly statable, highly general, and systematically unified type; and that this pure theoretical core of moral knowledge is essentially *action-guiding*, so that when brought to bear on incidental "nonmoral" information about a situation at hand, it tells "the" agent what to do. Theoretical-juridical moral philosophy sets itself the task of (largely reflective) construction, testing, and refinement of code-like theories that exhibit the core of properly moral knowledge.

The picture of general formulas applied to particular cases projects a stylized and reductive logic of moral judgment, pressing moral consideration toward abstraction. Superfluous detail must be cleared away so that cases can be sorted into broad types that figure in the formulas that unify the moral field. This guarantees uniformity in judgment and action both across cases and across agents, and gives priority to sameness and repeatability by regimenting moral consideration into fixed paths. This moral logic is aptly called an "administrative" or "procedural" one. It envisions impartial application of set policies to all, and best describes participants in a structured game or institution, or administrators and judges disposing of cases in accord with existing rules or laws.

When applied by individuals in interpersonal situations, this form of moral consideration looks evasive; in social or institutional ones it is bureaucratic or authoritarian. Unilateral decision, formulaic responses, and repeatable categorial uniformities displace flexible appreciation and communicative interaction. This kind of moral thought is vaunted in influential literatures of moral psychology and philosophy as maturely objective or impartial. It actually embodies a highly selective view appropriate to certain kinds of relationships and interactions in certain public, competitive, or institutional venues. These are traditionally contexts of male participation and authority, symbolically associated with the masculinity of men privileged by class and race as well as gender (see Frye 1992 on "whiteliness").

Code-like theory has provoked criticism from Aristotelians, Humeans, communitarians, contemporary casuists, pragmatists, historicists, Wittgensteinians, and others in the last several decades. So clear is this schism in late-twentieth-century moral philosophy that talk of "anti-theory" in ethics is now familiar. Feminist criticisms sometimes overlap with these others, but there is a difference.

Feminist ethics pursues questions about *authority, credibility,* and *representation* in moral life and in the practice of moral theorizing itself. When it looks at contemporary moral theory (and the social norms and ideals it reflects), it does not conclude simply that modern (or other) moral philosophy rests on mistakes. It sees instead that philosophical and cultural figurations of moral agency, knowledge, and judgment portray the actual social positions and relations, or views from specific social locations, of some of us, but in abstract and idealized form. When these representations of moral life are put forward authoritatively as truths about "human" interest, "our" intuitions, "rational" behavior, or "the" moral agent, they do not just say what is false. Rather, they uncritically reproduce the represented positions and locations as *normative,* i.e. as the central or standard (if not the only) case.

When this happens, the specific, partial, and situated character of these views and positions disappears. But the experiences of those in other situations and positions appear as "different" or problematic; often, perspectives from other social locations don't appear at all. Not everyone, however, gets authoritatively to define moral life. To have the social, intellectual, or moral authority to perform this feat, one must already be on the advantaged side of practices that distribute power, privilege, and responsibilities in the community in which one does it. Reproducing uncritically one's specific position as the norm is an *exercise* of one's privilege that at the same time *reinforces* it.

This self-reinforcing exercise of authority in moral theorizing can't be dislodged simply by counterexamples, refutations, and counterarguments that stay within the same practices. What is required is critical examination *of* the practices, of the positions to know and means of knowing moral life that these practices assume and construct, and of the conditions that make these positions and means possible. In a social world with specialized institutions of knowledge production and a high valuation of expertise, theory-makers wear the mantle of epistemic authority, of those most entitled to speak because they are in the best position to know. Critical examination of positions to know and means of knowing may support, but can also defeat or circumscribe, the credibility of claims and claimants, including institutionally authorized ones.

Moral theorizing itself is a practice of intellectual authority. Kathryn Addelson reminds philosophers that theirs is a professional status, politically won and politically maintained. Like social workers and religious leaders, teachers and scholars of ethics have powers to legitimize and even to enforce certain understandings of moral life. Presenting these understandings as "discoveries" conceals ways they are sustained in social interactions, including the socially authorized interactions of teaching, lecturing, and theory-making. Unless moral philosophers become politically self-conscious and more inclined toward the empirical study of morality as a tissue of interactions, Addelson warns, they may simply uncritically enshrine existing "gender, age, class, and race divisions" (Addelson 1991, 104–5) in their analyses. Cheshire Calhoun argues this can happen simply by the repetition of patterns of emphasis or exclusion within authoritative discourses on ethics. These produce "ideologies of the moral life"—standard assumptions about moral agency, motivation, or knowledge—that are not logically presupposed or implied by particular theories, but are presupposed to making sense of what is talked about and what is passed over (Calhoun 1988).

Discursive conventions of moral philosophy—its canonical styles of presentation, standard tropes, methods of argument, framing of problems—favor certain understandings over others as well. We usually ignore "you" and "we" in favor of first and third person perspectives in picturing deliberation (while often invoking an untroubled "we" in entering moral intuitions), neglect collaboration and communication in identifying moral problems and resolving them, and regiment moral reasoning into deductive arguments. We rely on schematic examples in which a few "morally relevant" factors have already been selected and from which social and political context have disappeared. We omit stories that explore prior histories and sequels to moral "solutions." We learn these conventions in learning what moral philosophy is from other moral philosophers, and we repeat and enforce them in instructing our students in what moral thinking "is."

All of us depend on languages and patterns of evaluation within which we make moral judgments and explain moral life to ourselves—what I call below the "moral medium." But distributions of social power and authority make some people's uses and interpretations of these resources more effective than those of others. When considering what representations this medium allows, we should ask: What actual community of moral responsibility do these representations claim to represent, and whom do they actually represent? What communicative strategies do they support, and who is in a position (concretely, socially) to use them? In what forms of activity will they have (or fail to have) applications, and who is permitted or assigned these activities? Who is in a position to enforce the rules which constrain them?

These questions are foreign to most contemporary moral philosophy, even to most of it critical of the project of code-like theory. In philosophy, these questions violate a disciplinary self-image formed around the picture of a disinterested search for core moral truth by a process of reflection subject to timeless criteria of precision, clarity, and consistency. Few philosophers today will defend a vision of the Good, supersensible intuition of moral properties or truths, or pure practical reason. Yet the notion of a pure core of moral knowledge, available to individual reflection, lives on.

The idea of a pure and compact core of moral knowledge available to reflection permits moral philosophers to bypass the interlacing of moral vocabularies and practices with other historically and culturally embedded beliefs and social practices. It also shields from view the historical, cultural, and social location of the moral philosopher, and of moral philosophy itself as a practice of authority sustained by particular institutions and arrangements. The purity of properly moral knowledge, the reflective purity of moral philosophy, and the moral philosopher's pose of objective (even "scientific") disinterest are mutually supporting constructs. Feminist ethics challenges a reflective method that is all too apt to reflect the moral experience of someone in particular.

Feminist criticism of ethics, then, gets at questions about the *authority to represent* moral life. It targets the ways gender bias makes moral theories miss or distort much of the matter of social life. It finds that the canonical form of moral theory assumes the viewpoint, and models the prerogatives, of those relatively privileged by power and status. Most distinctively, feminist criticism puts moral theorizing itself in its place—"situates" it—as a specific practice of intellectual authority. This practice assumes powers to define for all of us what may seem obvious, acceptable, or comprehensible only to some of us.

Different Voices, Critical Epistemology

The idea that there is a "woman's voice" or a fund of "women's experience" that is ignored or distorted in mainstream theorizing, and that can serve as a touchstone of corrective or reconstructive feminist theorizing, has had very great appeal. Tapping moral knowledge resident in some women's gendered experience and roles has resulted in a rich lode of creative work on ethics of care, maternal and friendship paradigms of moral relations, and moral responsibilities in situations of interdependence and vulnerability.[1] Yet claims to theorize "women's" experiences, or to represent what "women's" voices say have foundered on the same epistemological challenge feminists direct at nonfeminist views. Not all women recognize the voice or experience theorized as theirs. This ought not to be surprising in a society where gender always interacts with other powerful social divisions of labor, opportunity, and recognition that make women's experiences differ in systematic ways.

Feminists have had to struggle and negotiate over who is representing whom, why, and with what authority. Feminists continue to learn in hard ways that claims to represent are weighty and dangerous, often not only epistemically dubious but morally indefensible (Lugones and Spelman 1983; Moraga and Anzaldúa 1983; hooks 1984; Spelman 1988; Anzaldúa 1990; Collins 1990). At the same time, contests over credibility and authority within feminist theorizing, and between feminist and nonfeminist theorizing, provide ripe examples for a critical epistemology. They reveal how knowledge of "our" lives may be the object of struggle within communities, and they show why communities need to examine the links between their practices of crediting and disqualifying knowledge claims and their configurations of social authority and privilege. Feminist epistemology sheds light on what is happening here and why it is important.

The feminist idea is that knowledge is "an intersubjective product constructed within communal practices of acknowledgment, correction, and critique" of claims to know (Code 1991, 224). As Lynn Nelson puts it, ". . . none of us knows (or could) what no one else could. However singular experience may be, what we know on the basis of that experience has been made possible and is compatible with the standards and knowledge of one or more communities of which we are members . . ." (Nelson 1993, 150). All would-be knowers are *situated* in (typically multiple, overlapping) epistemic *communities*. It is communities, not individuals, that maintain the resources for the acquiring and certifying knowledge. The resources include languages and other symbolisms, methods, procedures, instruments, and technologies (sometimes specialized and technical), but also social interactions in which evidence and reasoning are interpreted, qualified, and disqualified. Resources are used and interactions take place in the context of specific relations and practices of cognitive authority. Some people, more than others, are assumed to know, or know how.

Feminist epistemologists are concerned about background assumptions working alongside or loaded into the cognitive instruments and practices of communities of inquiry. These assumptions may be cultural commonplaces (including stereotypical ones about gender or race), theoretical or disciplinary assumptions that supply the frame within which creditable work is done (established paradigms, well-confirmed theories), or beliefs that seem obvious to, and interests that make sense for, people with certain similar kinds of experiences. These are the things that will typically not need stating or proving within a community of inquiry; indeed, "unreflective acceptance of such assumptions can come to define what it is to be a member of such a community" (Longino 1993a, 112).

Traditional norms of objectivity fit a conception of knowledge as something individuals have or do; these norms aim to eliminate bias due to individual values and interests that differ within a community. But requirements designed to weed out idiosyncratic ("subjective") bias need not touch the problem of concerns, values, interests, or assumptions shared by all members, or by the members with most authority, in a particular community. Certain assumptions may be invisible or seem inviolable to investigators with similar cultural outlook and social experience, or the same education and training. As Louise Antony puts it: "The more homogeneous an epistemic community, the more objective it is likely to regard itself, and if its inquiries are relatively self-contained, the more likely it is to be viewed as objective by those outside the community" (Antony 1993, 212).

Because of this "objectivity effect," the membership of epistemic communities and the relations among their members become crucial. A sound epistemic practice has to look critically at the practices, relations, and background assumptions within its own community. Sandra Harding call this demand on knowledge claims *strong objectivity* (Harding 1993). Strong objectivity requires an epistemic community to examine itself, noticing the discourses, instruments, processes, and relations of authority by which it produces what it claims to be knowledge. Strong objectivity requires forums and institutions that invite and reward evaluation and criticism of knowledge claims that is based on public standards. It requires examination of cognitive authority to make sure it does not cloak cultural, political, or economic dominance or suppress relevant criticism from diverse viewpoints. It requires critical techniques to reveal the specific powers and limits of the discourses and instruments that enable us to know. It needs research on biases and saliencies and the specific ways they make possible what we know and what we can't or don't. "Power-sensitive conversation," in Donna Haraway's words, is the practice of objectivity that "allows us to become answerable for what we learn how to see" (Haraway 1991, 190).[2]

This feminist epistemology is a "naturalized" one, in this sense: It takes actual processes and determinants of human cognition and inquiry as its subject. It sees theories of knowledge as interdependent with, and subject to the same sorts of confirmation or reconsideration as, whatever else we (think we) know (Nelson 1993; Antony 1993). Something this epistemology supposes we do know is that prevalent or authoritative assumptions will shape the direction, practice, interpretation, and results of inquiry, and that social powers can render some people's assumptions arbitrarily prevalent or undeservedly authoritative in inquiry as elsewhere. So this epistemology needs both an understanding of the actual production of knowledges that communities credit and normative standards (at least, necessary conditions) for good epistemic practice.

Normative standards of good epistemic practice endorse social and institutional relations that support effective criticism; effective critical strategies are self-reflexive, historically informed, and politically sensitive. We already know a great deal, and need to know more, about the history and politics of unreliable theorizing and the kinds of epistemic community that shelter it. It is what we already know about this that suggests the normative standards we need. Individuals' epistemic responsibility in the context of their social communities needs to be accounted for, but it is *communal* practices of inquiry that deem knowers responsible and claims credible. These practices must be made explicit, and their reliability assessed. So this naturalized and critical epistemology is a *normative epistemology of knowledge produced by communities*, whose epistemic practices will be intertwined with—formed or deformed by—their other ones.

Now, what might a moral epistemology that reaps results of feminist ethical critique and critical epistemology look like?

An Expressive-Collaborative Model and Its Epistemology

The moral epistemology I defend is a naturalized and critical study of the moral knowledge produced and sustained within communities. This moral epistemology has two tasks. It must identify what kinds of things people need to know to live according to moral understandings that prevail in (any of) their (possibly multiple) communities or societies. And it must supply critical strategies and standards for testing whether understandings about how to live that are most credited in a community or society deserve their authority.

The first task, identifying what people need to know, can mean identifying what they need to know *about,* or it can mean explaining *how* they need to know about that. In the next chapter, I deal with what morality is "about," examining what it is useful to look for and look at in identifying a society's prevailing moral understandings. There I argue that tracing distributions of responsibility yields the clearest picture of the structure of a form of moral life. In the present chapter, my focus is the structure of moral justification: "how" we show our moral competence in entering and defending claims, how the terms and standards for claiming and justifying are kept in place or altered, and what reasonably confirms or undermines their authority. In keeping with the self-reflexive ideal of strong objectivity, a naturalized and critical moral epistemology will steer attention toward the discourses, procedures, and relations of authority that make it possible for some understandings to prevail. It must examine the powers by which and the limits within which we learn how to live, and the fit between the ways certain moral understandings are in fact maintained as credible and their worthiness to govern common life. In my discussion of responsibility in the following chapter and my account of justification in this one I sketch out a view of moral knowledge as communal product and process that makes possible forms of self-expression and mutual acknowledgment, but also constrains them. In doing so I think of morality itself in a different way from the one assumed in the theoretical-juridical model. I call this different, interpersonal and constructive, way an *expressive-collaborative model* of morality.

An expressive-collaborative model looks at moral life as a continuing negotiation *among* people, a practice of mutually allotting, assuming, or deflecting responsibilities of important kinds, and understanding the implications of doing so. As a philosophical model, this representation of morality functions both descriptively and normatively. Descriptively, it aims to reveal what morality "is"—what kinds of interactions go on that can be recognized as moral ones. Normatively, it aims to suggest some important things morality is "for"—what in human lives depends on there being such practices, and how these practices can go better or worse.

Like all such interpretive devices, this model is a creature of its specific historical time and social place, and of my interests in advancing it. The theoretical-juridical conception seems to reflect, for example, interests and problems of an emerging (later maturing) class of male citizen-peers assuming authority in the context of political and economic moderniza-tion, and defining terms of their mutual recognition. I believe that its "monologic" picture of internal reflection to guide action is a prescrip-tion for that special kind of autonomous agency this particular kind of social order requires of those upon whom it confers new privileges. The descriptive and critical tasks of my alternative conception are shaped by interests in the social recognition and participation that individuals have claimed as members of excluded or subordinated groups in many pro-gressive movements of the twentieth century. These claims arise from changes in relations of authority and put further pressure on them in a postcolonial and postmodern world. I like Naomi Scheman's description of this world as one in which "people are empowered to speak in their own voices, out of their own bodies, lives, and communities, not as impersonators of the privileged" (Scheman 1993, 225). The expressive-collaborative view is designed to capture interpersonal and social fea-tures of morality that the theoretical-juridical model hides.

The theoretical-juridical model pictured morality as an individually action-guiding system within or for a person. The expressive-collabora-tive conception pictures morality as a socially embodied medium of understanding and adjustment in which people account to each other for the identities, relationships, and values that define their responsibilities. This medium provides varied resources for moral understanding. There are shared vocabularies and grammars of moral discourse that give us things we can say, and an understanding of when to say them ("kind," "ungrateful," "fair," "wrong," "irresponsible," "promise," "honor," "lie," etc.). There are commonly recognized moral exemplars and para-digmatic moral judgments that show and teach the accepted sayings of such things; we learn the kinds of things "any of us" will recognize as a lie or a kindness, assessments "any of us" would make, like the wrong-ness of inflicting unnecessary or undeserved suffering. There are formats of moral deliberation and argument that give recognized ways to enter reasons and to weigh, elaborate, or disqualify them, such as generaliza-tion arguments, reversibility tests, appeals to empathy, consequences, consistency, self-respect, and more. There are standard forms of imputa-tion ("You knew the consequences," or "That was deliberately cruel"), and excuse ("I couldn't have known," or "I thought she was danger-ous") along with their occasions, limits, and implications ("He's only a child," "You should have thought it over," "Now you'll have to set things right").

These resources give people a common starting place for mutual accounting, but the resources can be renegotiated and their acceptability disputed within the very practices they make possible. We can make moral judgments, assigning responsibility; and we can also raise moral questions about the ways we make them. Morality on this view is constructive: The materials for assigning responsibilities are given, but exactly how to go on with them, how to make them work in particular cases, and where and how to extend or modify them, may not be.

The theoretical-juridical model is powerfully shaped by the assumption that the point of morality is action-guidance; moral judgments are to tell us what to do. The expressive-collaborative view reminds us that guiding decisions on action is but one way morality serves us, and that other things it allows us to do are integral to the distinctive ways it guides us in action. Seeing what to do is one exercise of moral understanding, and action-guiding judgments (in the usual sense) one kind of application of the language of morals. Morality provides as well for knowing and explaining who we and others are as expressed in our values, commitments, and responses. It permits us to know for what and to whom we will have to account when we have done or failed to do something, and what makes sense as a moral reason or excuse. It equips us to reckon failures and derelictions, to understand what can be repaired and what compensated, to assess the costs of choices in morality's own currencies of integrity and appropriate trust. It gives specific form to reactive attitudes of blame, indignation, shame, forgiveness, remorse, gratitude, contempt, and others. It tests the fittingness of what we feel and the tractability of mutual misunderstandings.

Morality's grip on us informs our choices, and so can guide our actions. But so could any sufficiently determinate code of rules or set of commands. What distinguishes morality is not only the many things in which it guides us, but the way it does so. It does so by enlisting us in an ongoing process of self-expression and mutual influence, through an appeal to mutually recognized values. It teaches us to see ourselves as beings capable of considered choices and responsive to mutually recognizable goods, and teaches us that others so see us. In doing so it makes us responsible for ourselves and to others for the moral sense our lives make. It creates common expectations around shared terms of appraisal, creating mutual intelligibility.

In fact, of course, "morality" does not teach us these things; other people do. Any particular system of mutual moral accounting is a cultural practice already there that we learn from others. We arrive at any situation of moral assessment with moral concepts, maxims, deliberative strategies, and intuitive convictions shared, even if incompletely, with some others. So too we come with sensibilities, emotional responses, and senses of relevance and seriousness shaped by a history of interactions in some personal and political environment, and by our places in that. By accounting to each other through this moral medium, we acknowledge each other as responsible. At the same time we renew and refine the moral medium itself, keeping it alive as we keep our identities as moral persons afloat within it.

Mutual moral understanding both presupposes and seeks a continuing common life. It requires a presumption in favor of accounting to others and trying to go on in shared terms. "Sharing" terms, however, means only that their force in defining responsibilities and prerogatives is recognized in common; this much defines a moral community or culture. Just to the extent that terms are shared there is such a community, whether relatively seamless, or nested within others, or obtaining more or less stably at the overlap of two or more distinct others. To share terms in this sense need not mean that the terms in force are endorsed by all, much less that they exist by the consent of all who are required to recognize and respond to them. Nor need it mean that all understand the same things about how the going terms are maintained, and who bears their costs or reaps their benefits. I return to this important fact about moral orders below in this chapter. It is at the heart of the studies of differing moral identities and epistemic positions in part three.

In order to say something about the epistemology of this view of morality, I make the simplifying assumption for now that a moral community is identified by its members' familiarity with some media of moral understanding and their shared and reciprocal recognition that it is these terms and understandings that are in force. What is it, now, that these members know?

On theoretical-juridical approaches, moral agents must master the logic of generalization and abstraction that guarantees uniform judgment on relevantly similar cases by subsuming them under covering principles. The problem of justification on this approach goes to the principles or procedures the moral theory comprises. Claims that such principles are self-evident, or can be compellingly supported by broader background theories of human nature or practical reasoning seem increasingly implausible, for good reasons, to many contemporary philosophers. A "reflective equilibrium" approach, which seeks the best fit between some set of moral principles and our best considered or most firmly entrenched judgments, is widely perceived as more promising.

Reflective equilibrium offers not demonstrable or incorrigible foundations but "reasonably reliable agreement"—coherence—between "our" intuitive judgments about particular cases and those principles we can recognize as "the premises of their derivation" (Rawls 1971, 20).[3] This incorporates the theoretical-juridical understanding of the relation of judgment to theory, without promising unimpeachable foundations for either: Theory and intuitive judgments are to be mutually supporting in the completed view. But precisely for this reason there is a curiosity in the role of (what are now commonly called) "intuitions"—those moral judgments or generalizations that seem obviously or compellingly right to us—on this view. They are seen at once as the *data* for the construction of moral theory (on analogy with scientific theory selection), and as assumptions that are negotiable (revisable, or dispensable) in the course of working out what "we" think morally. "We" (theorizers of ethics?) get to prune and adjust the data going in, selecting the "best considered" ones to set the balance for reflective equilibrium. Further, we may decide to disqualify some of these data if they impede a particular state of epistemic equilibrium that we prefer (out of the many possible ones that will always be available).

But there are no principled procedures for disqualifying moral data short of the moral theories that the data are supposed to constrain. The curiosity lies in the kind and degree of discretion "we" are seen as exercising, not only in fitting theory to data, but in *fitting data to theory*. If moral intuitions are really "datal" they can't be negotiable in this way; if intuitive judgments that are to anchor principles are negotiable, morality isn't science and "we" aren't constructing "theory." But then what are "we" doing here, and why? And who are "we" who enter into the quest for reflective equilibrium, with the discretionary power to decide which of our judgments are well considered, and which will stay and which go?

An expressive-collaborative view makes different sense of this. It drops the dubious image of moral science seeking the covering laws that explain the outputs of an idealized internalized system. It supplies instead the picture of morality as social negotiation in real time, where members of a community of roughly or largely shared moral belief try to refine understanding, extend consensus, and eliminate conflict among themselves. "We" are the members of some actual moral community, motivated by the aim of going on together, preserving or building self-

and mutual understanding in moral terms. We will try not only to harmonize our individual practices of moral judgment with the standing moral beliefs we each avow but to harmonize judgment and actions among us. We need *equilibrium between people* as well as within them.

Moral *equilibrium* is created through shared moral understandings, and creates mutual intelligibility. In it, we know what to expect and what is expected of us morally; how to understand and express ourselves morally in ways that others will, or at least can, understand; not just what to do but what it means, and hence what others will think we mean by it. Moral equilibrium is *reflective* to the extent that we are capable of making it and its conditions and consequences the subject of explicit attention and consideration between us. Mutual equilibria (just as individual ones) may become unstable under reflection, or may be unmasked as merely apparent. A system of complementary breadwinner/housekeeper gender roles, for example, may support a shared understanding between spouses of their different responsibilities in family life, under a presumption of reciprocity and respect. But learning about correlations among power, exit options, and earned income in marriage might reveal to one or both that this arrangement is something other than it seems. A dominantly heterosexual community may move from a punitive or denying attitude to greater acceptance of and tolerance toward same-sex erotic relations. Those who enjoy same-sex relations may be relieved to suffer less or to live less guardedly, but may find "tolerance" infuriatingly inferior to respect. Moral equilibria coordinate beliefs, perceptions, expressions, judgments, actions, and responses. Where present, they may not fully shared; and they may not be present where they are perceived to be. Some may be sustained or sustainable only under exclusion, concealment, or coercion.

Because the maintenance of equilibrium is so central to morality on an expressive-collaborative view, moral agents must learn a logic of interpersonal acknowledgment in moral terms (Cavell 1979). Because people and their relationships are not uniform and situations are not necessarily repeatable, moral consideration on this view presses toward enrichment of detail and amplification of context. Because negotiation of our lives in moral terms is a continuing process, new situations must be mapped onto past understandings and projected into future possibilities. The greater part of moral reasoning will thus be *analogical* and *narrative*.

Analogies test how like or unlike new cases are to familiar or decided ones. Narratives are stories that show how a situation comes to be the particular problem it is, and that explore imaginatively the continuations that might resolve the problem and what they mean for the parties involved. Analogical and narrative reasoning is inductive, and so indefinitely open to the impact of fresh information. These patterns of moral thinking provide for flexibility, rather than uniformity, in adapting existing values to, and honoring standing commitments in, cases at hand. What is at stake in moral understandings is the preservation of integrity, sustainable responsibilities, valued relationships, and certain moral values themselves.

The skills on which these understandings rely are many and varied, and not necessarily specific to morality. Skills of perception are shaped by learning what to notice and how to attend to it; discursive skills by learning how to describe things and what it makes sense to say; skills of responding appropriately in feeling and behavior by learning where feelings fit and what counts as expressing them. The moral epistemology of this view includes close description of and critical reflection on all such skills as belong to a particular form of moral life, the trainings that teach them, the kinds of human relations that make them possible, and the kinds of values and relationships they support in turn. Since many of these perceptive, discursive, and responsive skills are not unique to moral competence, the field for moral epistemology potentially includes every kind of cognition, sensitivity, and aptitude we need to get around competently in any social-moral surround. There's *no pure core of moral knowledge*, much less one to which access might be gained by pure reflection.

Having emphasized the variety and complexity of moral knowledge, I focus now on two features of moral thinking that bear directly on moral justification: *intuitions* —the basic stuff of it, and *narrative*—the characteristic form.

Contemporary moral philosophy is rife with appeal to "intuitions," usually in the role of data for moral theory. Here intuitions are seen as presumptive outputs of an idealized capacity or endpoints of reconstructed moral derivations, and so are served up either as confirming instances of theories that yield them, or counter-examples to theories that fail to yield them or that yield their contraries or contradictories. Most attention is paid to *what* intuitions "we" are claimed to have. Little is paid to the representative status of the claims made in invoking them—that intuitions are characteristically spoken of as "ours" or as something "we" think. Yet the latter is important for the authority these ready responses carry, and rightly so.

It is tempting to defend the authority intuitions are presumed to carry for us by appeal to their "compelling" character; the view that intuitions are "self-evident," at least upon proper reflective survey, mounts this defense. The expressive-collaborative view turns this around: the authority of these moral claims rests on the reason they strike *us* as compelling. What philosophers sometimes describe as our apparently immediate (noninferential) awareness of their truth is, more simply, *our* unhesitating inclination to believe and say these things, either ongoing or in certain circumstances.

This is in turn explained by the fact that such moral claims are ones we have learned from, and been taught by, others to say; or ones that we have learned are unlikely (or significantly less likely than some others) to be contested by those to whom we presume ourselves accountable. Those moral claims will be "intuitive" that we have learned to make in common with others who have received a like moral training or inhabit "our" moral world. Indeed, the ability to enter just these (sorts of) claims appropriately is a condition of being morally competent in the eyes of the training community and one's moral cohorts. One's own moral authority derives from the authority of these judgments as the bases or starting points of a particular form of shared moral life. Anyone who doesn't share enough of, or important enough ones of, these starting points is either a morally incompetent one of us, or just not one of us at all; not, that is, our cohort in the specific practices of mutual intelligibility that morality provides.

Intuitive judgments are relatively fixed starting points and continuing reference points of understanding, reasoning, and discussion. They are simply the judgments most commonly, and so usually initially, taken for correct. From these socially shared bases for moral thinking, deliberation and debate often go forward, occasionally by simple deduction from general intuitive judgments, but often by analogical and narrative elaboration on specific cases or kinds of case. Some intuitive judgments are generalizations which define standard connections between some moral concepts and other moral and nonmoral concepts. ("Breaking promises is wrong," "True friends are there when you need them," "All human beings have dignity and moral worth.") Some intuitive judgments are particular, and function as if perceptual. These we learn to make in learning moral vocabularies through which to report states of affairs directly in (thick) moral terms; absent special circumstances "this" is a lie, "this" cruelty, "this" arrogance.

Many moral judgments are simply intuitive in these ways, and others are mediated by intuitive judgments. The intuitive ones serve as markers of the moral relevance of certain features and guides to the typical moral weight of certain acts or outcomes. But intuitive judgments need to be linked to particular situations by analogy and narrative. In some cases moral judgments result from generalizations standardly understood, applied to cases uncontroversially perceived. In these cases we get instances that conform to the deductivist ideal of the theoretical-juridical view. ("Breaking promises is wrong; this would be promise-breaking; so, this would be wrong.") But these are not the only cases, and perhaps not the most common ones.

Moral judgments often embody complex interactions of moral perceptions and generalizations mediated by analogies and narratives. Sometimes the mediating links are arguable because they are not a matter of course; analogies may be inventive or dubious, cases borderline, perceptions unfamiliar. Sometimes different mediating links are possible; analogies or perceptions may compete, or narratives diverge. Then moral perplexity and disagreement emerges from shared and relatively clear starting points.

Still, intuitive starting points themselves may be called into question; they may be modified, relinquished, or replaced, for they are not better than relatively fixed and common assumptions, not better than where, in fact, we tend to begin. Intuitive starting points may come into question when they lead in application to intractable conflicts or untenable or unintelligible moral positions of a community, or within one. The continuing authority of intuitions depends not on higher-order beliefs from which they may be derived, but on the *character of the common life* they lead us to. The question is whether existing intuitions continue to furnish the standing terms for a negotiation of that life that supports reflective equilibrium among us. This is the form of justification appropriate to them.

The view of morality as progressive mutual acknowledgment and adjustment uses the notion of a *narrative* structure of moral understanding twice over. To say moral thinking is narrative in pattern is, first, a way of seeing how morally relevant information is selected and organized *within* particular episodes of deliberation. The idea is that a story is the basic form of representation for moral problems. We need to know who the parties are, how they understand themselves and each other, what terms of relationship obtain, and perhaps what social or institutional frames shape their options. We need to know how they have gotten to the situation that requires moral attention, for this tells us something about the kinds of attention and responses that are within moral consideration here.

Lovers and strangers, kin and citizens, coworkers and spouses are not bound by all (even if they are by some) of the same commitments and responsibilities. Nor do similar commitments always imply the same demands; actual histories of marriages, friendships, or family or citizen relations may create specific (reasonable) expectations and so set distinct terms of responsibility. Values—fairness, loyalty, kindness, respect—are expressible in various ways; expressions which are appropriate to certain relations, settings, and histories make little sense (or the wrong kind) for others. Ensuring the mutual fairness of a couple's shared childcare arrangements is apt to require measures different from those ensuring the fairness of a medical school's admission policies, the division of a parent's estate among children, or a national system of health care delivery.

Resolution of a moral problem itself takes a narrative form, the form of a transition which links past moral lives (individual, interpersonal, and collective) to future ones in a way not completely determined by where things started, and open to different continuations that may yet affect what the resolution means. Even matter-of-course moral decisions acknowledge an existing history of moral understandings and express a presumption that the same understandings continue to hold. In hard moral cases, the resolution of a quandary or conflict constructs an understanding not available before or modifies an existing one. Either way, what certain values mean or what certain commitments or relationships demand is newly configured with implications for future moral thought and choice. In this way there form continuing stories of individual and shared moral lives.

The theoretical-juridical picture of applying principles to cases is modeled on the deductive relation of validity that holds between some premises and a conclusion, when that conclusion is true if the premises are. This relation either holds or it doesn't; when it holds, it holds under the impact of all further additions of information. In narratives, however, what comes later takes on particular meaning in part because of what preceded it, while what came earlier may finally look very different depending on what happens later. Determining responsibilities in the concrete usually involves grasping histories of trust, expectation, and agreement that make particular relationships morally demanding in particular ways. To know what general norms or values mean in situations now requires appreciating how these have been applied and interpreted before, within individual and social histories. Narrative constructions allow us to take thought backward in these ways, and then forward to explore the costs and consequences of moral choices for individuals and between them.[4]

Resolutions of moral problems—whether in action or understanding—are more or less acceptable depending on how they sustain or alter the integrity of the parties, the terms of their relationships, and in some cases the meaning of moral (and other) values that are at stake. Moral resolutions are more or less acceptable to the parties and the communities they rely on for the conservation of the means of mutual moral understanding. This is why the resolution of a moral problem may be less like the solution to a puzzle or the answer to a question than like the outcome of a negotiation. This does not mean that anything settled on is right, nor that a resolution is right only if everyone can settle on it. A narrative view can be as committed as another to holding that certain things are really better or worse for people, certain responsibilities inescapable, or certain requirements obligating. It is a particular view about the form that demonstrations and justifications take.

Analogies and narratives, more often than deductions, are the patterns through which intuitions and perceptions are invoked to justify judgments, as well as to dispute or repudiate them. These intuitions and perceptions are entrenched by their embodiment and preservation in the moral trainings, discourses, institutions, judgments, and practices of the community which claims to honor them. What that community can in turn claim as justification for these intuitions and perceptions is the habitability and acceptability of the common life to which they lead.

Authority and Transparency

Moral understandings and their enabling stories have to make sense to some moral community. Ideally, moral accounts must make sense to those *by* whom, *to* whom, and (except in special cases of immature or incapacitated agency) *about* whom they are given. This requires that we share with others a moral medium and familiarity with the social terrain of interactions, roles, and relationships to which it belongs. Practices of responsibility mesh and blend with other practices characteristic of a social life.

Earlier I simplified the discussion of intuitions and narratives by assuming that members of a moral community share a similar grasp of roughly the same media of moral understanding. Even in very homogeneous communities, however, this will be an idealization, as variations in moral instruction, familiarity of applications, and individual sensibilities and experiences create differences in understanding. In social or political communities that inherit diverse religious and moral traditions, moral understandings, intuitive and constructive, are likely at best to overlap. In societies divided or stratified by social differences, much of social life will not be unproblematically common, and the parts that are shared may be imbued with different meanings.

From the perspective of an expressive-collaborative view, the deductivist picture of moral reasoning at the heart of a theoretical-juridical approach idealizes a closed moral community: Similar moral judgments are made by everybody, because equivalent moral generalizations are applied alike by everybody to cases which are perceived alike by everybody. In such a community the moral terms are given and their applications are set. This kind of closure on moral understanding could be approximated in an actual community only to the degree that moral authority in that community is locked up, unanimous, and perfectly consistent, and social life so homogeneous that divergent personal and social experiences do not challenge standing terms or their applications. I doubt this is a possible social world, even a "hypertraditional" or authoritarian one. It is, in any case, not our social or moral world, in which we go on under conditions of imperfect understanding, conflict among and within ourselves, and diverse perceptions from different social positions that include dramatic inequities in material and discursive resources.

Imperfect understandings, conflicting judgments, or incomprehension are obviously problems for moral equilibrium. They can be occasions for personal breaches, social fractures, and individual or group violence. But they are also opportunities to rethink understandings or search for mediating ideas or reconciling procedures within or between communities. They can disturb the superficiality, complacency, or parochialism of moral views. Whether they go one way or another depends on the moral and nonmoral interests of contending parties, as well as circumstances (for example, political and economic ones) that individuals may neither recognize nor control.

Consider now the case of a society with diverse nonmoral interests and many distinct or overlapping moral understandings. Such a community has motive and opportunity to continue its moral form of life, but also to experience conflicts within it and challenges to it. This kind of familiar setting—for example, ours—houses moral traditions, terms, and trainings that overlap and diverge at various points. Yet because this society is segmented and stratified by many forms of privilege and disadvantage, not everyone is comparably situated in the continuing negotiation of moral life. Not all intuitions, interpretations, and narrative constructions carry the same authority, or carry authority in the same places. Divisions, instabilities, conflicts of authority, and diverse experiences of social reality provide occasions and materials for critical, and possibly transformative, moral thinking.

Moral terms and assumptions already in place and carrying authority for "our" moral life may be found to render some of us mute or invisible, our moral positions incoherent or inexpressible, our standing as moral agents compromised or unacknowledged, in "shared" life. Sometimes some of us can challenge these terms by appealing to other moral terms or by inventing new ones. Applications of moral concepts to familiar practices may be shifted ("domestic violence," "date rape," "sexual harrassment"), and applications to new or newly visible social practices may change understandings of what those concepts mean (equality as "comparable worth"). There are, however, social conditions for this kind of criticism to emerge. Some coming apart of authority or authorities, or of the fit between ways of judging and practices, opens critical space: Moral understandings may then be questioned that could otherwise go on as before. When members of groups historically or systematically disqualified from epistemic or moral authority begin to occupy positions that carry it, for example, new judgments and new means of judging are likely to result. This kind of change depends in turn on many other changes, especially changes in material circumstances, distributions of power, and access to institutions and arenas that shape public discourses or disseminate them.[5]

The feminist criticism of ethics I have sampled above is in one way unabashedly partisan: It aims to enter claims of and on behalf of women as full moral agents, for this is what women in the Western tradition have rarely been acknowledged to be. In doing so, however, it poses a *completely general question* about the moral terms set for our common life: Where do these come from, and what (or whose) authority and experiences do they represent? Feminist ethics vividly illustrates a kind of critical strategy rooted in what Bernard Williams calls the aspiration toward "transparency" in moral life.

Williams describes this as a "hope for truthfulness" in the ethical thought and practice of society, specifically, that "the working of its ethical institutions should not depend on members of the community misunderstanding how they work" (Williams 1985, 101). Sabina Lovibond similarly invokes the ideal of "a community whose members understood their own form of life and yet were not embarrassed by it" (Lovibond 1981, 158). Or again, in Annette Baier's formulation, "a decent morality will *not* depend for its stability on forces to which it gives no moral recognition. Its account books should be open to scrutiny, and there should be no unpaid debts" (Baier 1995, 8).

The ideal of transparency is at once a moral and epistemic one; it can take thinner or thicker interpretations, but any interpretation will embody some moral perspective or tradition. The demands for transparency embodied in feminist ethics, for example, are, like Western feminism, of specifically democratic, participatory, and egalitarian kinds, squarely founded on moral and political ideals of modern Western social thought. Feminist ethics pursues transparency by making visible gendered arrangements which underlie existing moral understandings, and the gendered structures of authority that produce and circulate these understandings. In doing so it magnifies embarrassing double-binds of modern morality. One is that its "official" conceptions of moral agency, judgment, and responsibility devalue or disqualify other forms of agency, judgment, and responsibility that make the official ones possible in actual social life (Baier 1995). Another is that purportedly universal norms defining moral personhood, rationality, autonomy, and objectivity are constructed in ways that depend on these not being universally accessible positions or statuses under actual conditions (Scheman 1993). The feminist exercise is embarrassing precisely because it exploits a tradition—its own—in which values of representation, self-determination, respect, and equality are common currency. The authority of these values can be used to put in question the credibility of authorities and their claims.

Within a democratic and participatory ethos authorities may be subject to particularly broad-based and egalitarian demands for accountability. But transparency may also be a potent demand in other kinds of social orders. They too may harbor incoherences and contradictions in their own terms or may relieve some parties of the demand to pay moral debts to others in the currency of full or appropriate recognition. They may rely on coercion, manipulation, or deception to sustain arrangements that some of the parties nonetheless presume to justify as interpersonal understandings. A demand for transparency wherever it is put presses on the parts of common life that, depending on trust, are underwritten by credibility. And these, in fact, are many parts of any common life.

Possibilities of critical and speculative thought inhere in real social spaces in real time. How much space there is for criticism or imagination, as well as who can enter it, is determined by social, economic, technological, and discursive conditions that make available real or imagined alternatives to what we think now. These possibilities are not made available *simply* by thinking, as philosophers are prone to wish, nor should anyone assume that the nature and availability of criticism is obvious from just any arbitrary "reflective" vantage point. The demand for transparency is a powerful wedge in this regard, for it can be used to invite report and reflection on moral life from many points of view within it, and even outside it. Reports from some views can open critical sightlines blocked from some others, and can help to reveal how some views hide others.

The Example of Feminist Skepticism

Discussions of moral justification in philosophy are often structured by a standard philosophical "problem of skepticism."[6] This is the threat that there may be no knowledge, because propositional justifications of knowledge-claims will either terminate arbitrarily, curve back into a circle, or infinitely regress. The naturalized, but social and reflexively critical, epistemology I have described locates the problem of moral justification differently. Its problem of justification is a problem about *people's claims* to knowledge and their *credibility* in entering those claims. And if knowledge is embodied in communities of inquiry upon which individual knowers depend, anyone's credibility implicates the credibility of others. The problem of justification becomes: *Who* knows? It is, on one hand, a question about the instruments and practices of inquiry and relations of authority by which communities produce and legitimate their claims to knowledge. On the other, it is about the lives that can be organized around the knowledge claimed. It is about the reliability of the former, and the habitability of the latter.

Moral justification among us appeals to the available languages of morals in their mutually recognized applications. One can push the question of justification farther; one can ask for the provenance of these moral means, and the relative worth of alternatives to them, or to the lives they furnish. Or, at least sometimes, some of us can. The social conditions for the exercise of critical moral imagination must be there; and those who would open these questions and make them stick must have, or must struggle for, a certain degree of credibility. Not all the logical space of moral justification or criticism is already available, because not all possible social spaces are. And neither the space nor the right to enter it is available at will.

When questions of justification do arise, no endless regress threatens, for answers to these questions can only back up so far as there are some standing terms of justification, and practices of appraisal that give those terms sense. Any actual regress that questions the reliability of our authoritative practices and the credibility of our authorities is then quickly pushed forward again to questions about the lives we are willing to live. These matters are hardly arbitrary, as the stakes here include mutual recognition, cooperation, and shared enjoyment of many goods; or else deception, misery, oppression, and violence. In both the backward and forward movement of moral thought there may be contests over who "we" are. Preserving coherence is a powerful constraint in the case of moral understanding, as elsewhere. But what has to cohere in moral life is not just a body of belief, a set of dispositions, different normative standpoints, or particular motives "within" a person.[7] What has to cohere is a set of social arrangements and the ability of a community of people to make a certain kind of stable and shareable sense of themselves within it as they live together.

The questions raised by feminist ethics are only some of those that might be raised about the habitability and worth of our moral forms of life. Moral and epistemic authority matter particularly to feminism because of the historic denial of them to women. But problems about them, about who has them, and why, can be recognized by anyone, and they matter to everyone. It is a central work of moral inquiry to analyze the discursive spaces that different moral views (and theories of them) create, and to explore the positions of agency and distributions of responsibility that these views foreground or eclipse. But these philosophical studies of the logic of moral language, the nature of moral agency, and the conditions of responsibility now have to look at where moral views are socially sited and what relations of authority and power hold them in place. At the same time the inquiry that does this must not forget that it, too, is a practice intertwined with others. As an epistemic practice, it is answerable to strong objectivity, so must render transparent the social locations from which it views moral life and the relations of authority that license it to represent moral knowledge. Feminist skepticism about morality and moral philosophy sets an example for this inquiry. It questions those parts of our knowledge of morality and politics that house the politics and morality of our knowledge.[8]

four

Charting Responsibilities

From Established Coordinates
to *Terra Incognita*

Moral responsibility, I dare say, is a subject about which we are all confused.

—Joel Feinberg, *Doing and Deserving*

But as we all know, it is we collectively who are responsible for allocating and reallocating responsibilities, we who divide the labor and decide if the laborer is or is not worthy of her hire, we who appoint the judges.

—Annette Baier, *Moral Prejudices*

Feminist moral philosophers have found "responsibility" a powerful and sensitive tracking device with rewardingly embarrassing uses in reviewing moral theories and practices. Applied to representations of moral life in philosophical ethics, it has been revealing to see which—or better, whose—responsibilities are spotlighted as representative of "moral obligations," and which (whose) do not show up at all. Applied to common assumptions and arrangements in our (and other) societies, following the trail of responsibilities is a sure way to notice the intimate entwining of moral and social positions that are not all comparably advantaged or esteemed. Some may be intolerable.

One source of enthusiasm for "care ethics" within feminist moral thinking is its power to foreground, dramatically and satisfyingly to many women, the ways responsibilities are gendered, and the arbitrary or exploitative fit between social contributions and recognition. Care ethics provides a conceptual framework that makes vast amounts of caretaking and caregiving activity appear in theory as they are in life— central and indispensable to the continuance, and many goods, of human societies. Caring labors include ministering to the needs of young and old, sick and dying, frail and dependent, as well as securing and reproducing through paid and unpaid labor many basic conditions of life for legions of fully able persons. The lens of "care" magnifies questions about the distribution and recognition of this socially vital labor: Who cares? The distribution of caring labors disproportionately to women in our society, more disproportionately still to women who are relatively poorer and nonwhite, and the low(er) social status of caregiving activities and caregivers, are no longer hidden in plain sight (Tronto 1993). If gender is a feature of status revealed in who gets to do what to whom, it also shows in who is expected or permitted to do what for whom.

Gender partly consists in distinct assignments and assumptions of responsibility, and attracts them. But in this, gender is like other aspects of social identity—age, class, race, and caste, for example—from which gender is never separate, or separately experienced and expressed. And while responsibilities for caretaking or caring labor are indeed fundamental ones, there are numerous things it falls to us to protect or promote, avoid or forgo. There are many whose trust any of us needs to keep and to be worthy of keeping, and many whose well-being is our business or can become our concern. I prefer the more capacious language of responsibility as a conceptual framework for ethics; it invites us to follow the trails of people's diverse responsibilities through different domains. As these trails fork or dead end, they reveal the contours of particular moral landscapes and situate moral actors within them. They trace, as Marion Smiley says, "our configuration of social roles and the boundaries of our community" as well as "the distribution of power between those suffering and those being held responsible" (Smiley 1992, 13). Being held responsible in certain ways, or being exempted or excluded from responsibility of certain types or for certain people, forms individuals' own senses, as well as others' expectations, of to whom and for what they have to account. In such ways we know, or are shown, our places.

An "ethics of responsibility" as a normative moral view would try to put people and responsibilities in the right places with respect to each other. Moral philosophers with diverse concerns—medicine, technology, feminism, partiality—have thought this kind of normative view might have important conceptual resources distinct from those of more familiar deontological, utilitarian, contractarian, or virtue approaches.[1] Robert Goodin's book *Protecting the Vulnerable* (Goodin 1985, hereafter *PV*) is a valuable study in this regard. Goodin presents a developed version of responsibility ethics as one proper part of normative moral theory. His "vulnerability model" is designed to deal especially with the problem of giving a principled moral justification of certain familiar partialities and special obligations, such as those between parents and children or professionals and clients, while avoiding the implausibility of extended egoism or pure voluntarism, and the pitfalls of mere parochialism. At the same time, Goodin wants his account of familiar partialities and special obligations to pay off in a greatly extended vision of responsibilities to, for example, fellow citizens and distant strangers in need, future generations, animals, and the environment.

I wish the route to answers to these vexed questions of our time were so direct, but despite my admiration for Goodin's attempt, I don't think he has found it. For me, it is unsurprising that a relatively quick route through moral theory won't take us there. If moral boundaries are fixed or moved through progressively constructed and socially embodied understandings, these difficult moral problems are for us roads still "under construction." I argue that Goodin's way of developing his central claim about responsibilities fails to support some of his own aims, and neglects to draw out unique features of the responsibilities approach implicit in his own account.

Even so, I think Goodin's analysis locates an important *regulative guideline* implicit in many of our assignments of responsibility. This general guideline of protecting the vulnerable is something less than a theory of responsibility, because it supports specific assignments of responsibility only in the context of local practices, institutions, customary roles, and familiar relationships, on the one hand, and particular conceptions of well-being and human agency, on the other. It is these arrangements and ideas that supply the assumptions and conditions that determine specific assignments of responsibility. Goodin's principle for justifying attributions of responsibility—the principle of protecting the vulnerable—nonetheless serves as a useful guide for analyzing the *organization* of particular forms of moral life: sort through the presuppositions and implications of their distributions of responsibilities. This "geography of responsibility" opens the way for critical assessments of how, and upon whom, responsibilities fall, and how the topography of a particular social life regulates the flow of shared understandings about who is going to be expected to see to and account for situations, outcomes, or tasks. Specific moral understandings in this regard change under pressures of several sorts. One sort of pressure arises from greater transparency of these understandings themselves, and greater clarity about the costs of reproducing them, or the risks and opportunities of holding each other differently to account.

Goodin's Vulnerability Model

Goodin's responsibility ethic is based on the principle that "we are responsible for protecting those vulnerable to our actions and choices." Goodin doesn't claim that the principle of protecting the vulnerable (PPV) orders "the entire moral universe" (*PV*, 117), but he claims it provides the best single account of a very wide range of commonly acknowledged obligations that obtain in "special" relationships, i.e. those which involve some specific history of connection, interaction, or agreement. Philosophers have almost uniformly endorsed the validity of "special moral obligations" (those had by specific people with respect to specific other people (*PV*, 13))—family members and friends to each other, professional to client, recipient to benefactor, promise-maker to promisee. But it is widely felt that no systematic moral justification of these obligations has yet been given that is sufficiently broad, cogent, and systematic. Especially in the matter of "personal" relationships, the "problem of partiality"—the disproportionate or excess benefits we tend to bestow upon ones loved or closely connected—remains a site of contention within moral philosophy.

Goodin believes that his theory will both provide the needed justification and will do more: ". . . the most coherent theory available to explain our special responsibilities to family, friends, and so on also implies that we must give far more consideration than particularists allow to at least certain classes of strangers" (*PV*, 9). That is, the principle that successfully justifies our special obligations will, on Goodin's view, ground "broader notions of interpersonal, international, intergenerational, and environmental responsibilities than are ordinarily acknowledged" (*PV*, xi).

The account that Goodin argues can broadly, systematically, and cogently justify our commonly recognized but diverse special obligations is this:

> [S]pecial responsibilities derive from the fact that other people are dependent upon you and are particularly vulnerable to your actions and choices. What seems true for children in particular also seems to be true for other kin, neighbors, countrymen, and contractors. To

some greater or lesser extent, they are all especially dependent upon you to do something for them; and your varying responsibilities toward each of them seem roughly proportional to the degree to which they are, in fact, dependent upon you (and you alone) to perform certain services. (*PV*, 33–34)

Goodin thus specifies the basic *principle of individual responsibilities* as follows:

If A's interests are vulnerable to B's actions and choices, B has a special responsibility to protect A's interests; the strength of this responsibility depends strictly upon the degree to which B can affect A's interests. (*PV*, 118)[2]

I agree with Goodin that other moral theories prominent in the field do not adequately or plausibly justify the collection of special obligations— and hence the lion's share of ordinary responsibilities—most of us accept and acknowledge. I agree that intuitionism is unsystematic, or, more to the point for me, unanchored and uncritical. I concur that the thesis of voluntary assumption leaves too many core cases (e.g. involving family members) un- (or ill-) explained, and that indirect utilitarian defenses claiming that familiar arrangements "really do" maximize happiness or welfare for everybody are at least unproven and highly dubious.

In an extended examination of the standard collection of special obligations, Goodin makes a generally compelling and resourceful case that the operative principle in each is the same one that directly generates responsibilities out of vulnerabilities, and stringency of responsibility out of degree of vulnerability (*PV*, chapter 4). He persuasively argues, for example, that what binds us to keep promises to the extent that we are so bound is the vulnerability we have occasioned in others by inviting reasonable expectations; that familial and spousal obligations arise from vulnerabilities supported by a particular history of connection as well as the prevalence of certain social customs and legal arrangements; that friends grow progressively more obligated as (and if) deepened involvement and trust cause them reasonably to depend ever more strongly in certain ways on each other. If any such types of relationship obtain without the usual expectations or circumstances and the typically ensuing vulnerabilities, neither do the corresponding obligations apply. Conversely, vulnerabilities which arise entirely out of immediate circumstances of proximity or contact without any history of relationship or understanding may strongly obligate strangers to each other if the stakes are high and the solutions are limited. If a drowning stranger has only me in the vicinity to depend on, this (in most cases) places me under an obligation to attempt or initiate her rescue.

One interesting feature of the vulnerability approach is the way it cuts across one distinction that structures discussions of moral impartiality and vexes moral philosophers. The vulnerability principle does not work by partitioning the beneficiaries of our moral behavior into familiars and strangers. It is just a fact that familiars and intimates will have become more vulnerable to one another through a *history of mutual involvement*. Yet utter strangers may be vulnerable, and so deeply obligated to one another by the purest contingency of unintended *proximity* or *contact*. Still, as will be seen below, the fact of special relationships and their contingencies is a matter of the greatest moral importance on this approach. One virtue of Goodin's account is that it satisfies not only intuitions that special relationships are specially obligating, but companion intuitions that there is something reasonable in their being so, and that the reasons are rooted in the nature of the connections in which these relationships consist, connections that may vary in particular instances with their distinct histories.

Goodin does not only want to convince us of the viability of PPV in dealing with the still-debated problem of special relationships and partialties. He also wants us to acknowledge the systematic power and larger scope of the concept of moral responsibility PPV defines, and to see the principle itself in a particular way. On the first score, Goodin makes aggressive claims about the implications of PPV with respect to individual and collective obligations to unknown and unknowable strangers. On the second score, Goodin claims that his responsibility ethic is a kind of consequentialism. I believe that neither of these claims is right. Seeing where they go wrong opens up a wider view of the social scaffolding of practices and understandings that supports our acknowledgments and ascriptions of responsibility.

Extending Responsibilities

Goodin's central argument is that we almost all accept the standard run of special obligations, but only PPV makes sense of them. Yet PPV has many other applications, particularly to unknown and distant strangers whose miseries we could help to diminish, either individually or (more typically) through collective efforts. So if we have the usual run of obligations we think we do to special others, we have many more demanding obligations than we thought we did to unknown and distant strangers and other sentients (e.g. refugees, starving populations, future generations, and possibly animals or other animate beings).

I sympathize with the spirit of Goodin's conclusions. He attempts to recycle what are no doubt for many of us pretty parochial commitments through a conceptual apparatus that directly generates corresponding responsibilities out of given vulnerabilities. At the same time he hopes to generate a reserve of active concern for a wider array of needy or fragile people and things. The strategy of argument is elegant, but a closer look exposes a serious ambiguity in the key notion of "vulnerability," which gives content to PPV. The ambiguity short-circuits Goodin's argument for the extended applications of PPV.

Goodin defines vulnerability as "susceptibility to injury" or "being under threat of harm" (*PV*, 110) which is avoidable by the omission or intervention of some agent(s). I follow Goodin in treating vulnerability as a triadic relation of the form X is vulnerable to Y (some agent(s)) in respect (or with respect to) N (some important need or interest) (*PV*, 112). Let's suppose we are agreed on which needs or interests have the right sort of importance, or that it is obvious that some needs or interests are of this important type; I return to this below. Of course many people in the world at a given time are exposed to threats to important needs or interests, and some among us could individually or together relieve these threats by some practically imaginable course of action. So if "vulnerable" just means "having one's significant needs/interests open to aid or harm by someone or other," and responsibility is entailed by being "someone who could (possibly) do something to help," then Goodin's argument for the wider gamut of obligations to strangers seems to work (granting relevant empirical assumptions). Call the operative idea of vulnerability here "vulnerability-in- principle." But what was supposed to demonstrate the content and plausibility of PPV in the first place was its efficacy in ordering our more typically recognized special obligations. And in those cases it is not this extremely broad notion of vulnerability-in-principle, but a much more specific one, that is doing the work.

The reason the principle that "we are responsible for protecting those vulnerable to our actions and choices" seems to describe so well the special obligations of promisors, parents, employers, professionals, and friends (as well as passers-by of drowning children) is that these cases involve much more than vulnerability-in-principle, i.e. vulnerability to someone or other. These cases involve what might be better called *dependency-in-fact*, vulnerability to someone in particular, where the one who, as it were, "holds" control of the vulnerability stands in a particular sort of relation to the one who has the vulnerability. The model "derives one party's responsibilities from the other's vulnerabilities" (*PV*, 42) in these cases precisely through dependency-in-fact. Either there are specific expectations induced by a concrete history of relationship (and perhaps a constellation of familiar assumptions and institutions) or there is actual contact, clear opportunity, presumed capability, and limited options. The notion of vulnerability that makes PPV "work" in these cases is something like:

> X is vulnerable to Y in respect to N when X is *actually depending on* or *circumstantially dependent upon* Y to secure or protect N *because* of the nature of their existing relationship, some prior agreement between them or by them, a particular causal history between them, or the fact of Y's unique proximity and capability in light of X's extreme plight.

In other words, someone's having a vulnerability depends on his or her important needs' being potentially answered. But who might be responsible to see to that person's need (and in what fashion and to what degree and why), i.e. to whom, if anyone, that person is vulnerable, is determined by quite specific forms of *connection*. Where a personal relationship exists, the relevant connections are found in the history of relationship and its specific forms of dependence, expectation, and trust, often in the context of culturally common assumptions about relationships of its kind. In role-bound connections, socially shared (even institutionalized) norms of interaction, duty, and desert set the stage. A case like that of the drowning stranger and the passer-by with ability to rescue (made famous by Peter Singer's utilitarian arguments for obligations of the affluent to contribute to feeding the world's starving populations) is different still.

In the last, Singer-type case the "obviousness" of the obligation on Passerby is not supported merely by the stranger's life-threatening plight and Passerby's awareness of it and ability to rescue. It takes the combination of a number of features to confer obviousness on this case. These factors include: clarity of situation (it's clear what's wrong and how to fix it); openness to unilateral action or simply achievable corporate action; limitation of options (Passerby is, or just a few are, in some position to help); obvious and direct relation between actions undertaken and probable effects of so acting; absence of equally exigent (or even competing) demands on behalf of other (perhaps equally deserving) persons; high likelihood of success; low likelihood of undesired consequences; no significant costs, moral, material, or practical, to Passerby or to others dependent on his or her resources. Finally, there is the fact that such opportunities are rare for many people. Or at least they are so for those of us fortunate enough to live most or all of our lives outside states of warfare and conditions of catastrophe. Singer makes the hapless victim a child to boot, foreclosing sticky questions that might arise about drowning murderers, etc.

One may be sure what Passerby is responsible for in this matter, and confident of consensus among those one is likely to query, for all variables here have already been set for the "one thinkable solution" outcome, at least for Singer's presumed audience of culturally similar readers. One may not be so sure, however, whether changes in some variables might diminish the consensus around this example, or whether these variables might bear the same weights within different moral cultures or in dramatically different circumstances. Not all moral traditions take the very young child as the paradigm of "a life worth saving/right to save if any is," at least not in every situation.[3] And does the scenario occur in a situation of famine, plague, or endemic violence, where the floundering child's life is already unsalvageable, and human and other resources are scarce? One may be even less sure whether any of the factors in a Singer-type case has the same moral valence in some other combination, even when moral culture and background conditions are held in place.[4]

The drowning-child-in-the-pond case does function for its intended readers as a moral paradigm of obligatory rescue, but this is because it *is* one: It is a case pared down to "simple saving" with no modifying or countervailing considerations. Far from blazing the trail for complex cases very unlike this one in most of the respects that make it simple, it is a measure of how simple an opportunity to "save on sight" must be for that connection "by itself" to entail the unmitigated responsibility to rescue for the odd passerby. As soon as things become more complicated, the entailment is muddied or the responsibility becomes mitigated. I'm not suggesting there aren't cases like that, nor that what it is right to do isn't obvious; indeed there are, and it is. My point is that there being cases like that provides occasions for our being confident we know what to do and how to judge what is done—*in such cases*. What such cases imply about other instances of contact-and-peril, or in the case that Singer in fact addressed, knowledge-of-peril, is not obvious. There are the relatively fixed points—moral coordinates, one might say—and then come fresh attempts at mappings. As I'll argue further below, making responsiblities fall "directly" out of vulnerabilities requires more than a bit of supporting conceptual and social machinery.

Vulnerability-in-principle defines, as it were, a field of possible responsibility; but only certain sorts of actual connections, dependencies-in-fact, generate moral obligations on specific persons in accord with PPV. Hence, many of the obligations to aid distant or unknown suffering strangers which Goodin defends remain incompletely supported by appeal to PPV alone. Whether a story of connection or contact, and one of the right kind, could be supplied linking specific ones of us to specific vulnerable strangers (e.g. certain starving or refugee populations) remains to be seen. Only that account of connection will show precisely whether these strangers are truly *dependent* or (reasonably?) *depending upon* us in particular ways. Especially in the case of certain collective responsibilities and institutional problems, specific causal histories (of colonialism, exploitation, or discrimination, for instance) or certain forms of immediacy (people sleeping on sidewalks, refugees at our borders or petitioning our courts for asylum) may provide relevant and salient connections. Histories and proximity like these, in some collective as well as individual cases, might pick out particularly obligating circumstances, and might order obligations as more or less significant or exigent. Vulnerability in the relevant dependency-in-fact sense, then, does not just amount to "one person's having the capacity to produce consequences that matter to another" in need (*PV*, 114). But neither can it always be assumed that there "already are" other responsibility-entailing connections simply awaiting discovery, either because of the way the world is or because of the way "our concept of responsibility" works. These connections are (to be) made through forms of practice and the understandings they create or support.

From Vulnerabilities to Responsibilities and Back

A closer look at Goodin's discussion of familiar obligations uncovers not only an ambiguity in "vulnerability," but also reveals how much of the content of the relevant notion of "vulnerability" is in fact supplied by our *understandings* of the relationships, practices, and incidental situations that Goodin takes as his example cases. Common presuppositions and the structures of actual practices in a particular form of social life link vulnerabilities and responsibilities in those cases where Goodin is most successful. Moreover, to a significant extent existing practices and presuppositions define those places where a link needs to be made, and cast the gap in a particular shape that determines which responsibilities will "fit" it. While Goodin does speak to these issues, they have implications beyond those he seems to recognize.

In identifying the ambiguity between vulnerability-in-principle and dependency-in-fact, I assumed in line with Goodin's discussion that there just are vulnerabilities, defined relative to people's (or other beings') needs and interests, and then there just are those individuals or groups who can respond to them. Yet our grasp of vulnerabilities is heavily mediated by background conceptions of well-being and human agency and efficacy, and our understanding of these is shaped as well by familiar practices, institutions, roles, and relations. To see this, consider a prominent weak spot in Goodin's largely persuasive demonstration that vulnerabilities imply responsibilities in the case of special relationships: his discussion of the obligations of parents to their own dependent children.

Goodin assumes parents have duties to provide their own dependent children's food, clothing, and shelter, to protect them from harm, and to educate them suitably for social life. Goodin's main point is that "it was the child's vulnerability, rather than voluntary acts of will of the parents in begetting it, which has been giving rise to the special responsibilities of parenthood" (*PV*, 81). It is indeed more plausible to ground parental obligations in children's vulnerability to parents, rather than in "self-assumed" obligations. A story about parents' being obligated via voluntary commitment is problematic at best, given the practical and technological limitations of contraception at most times for most people, common social limits on women's sexual and reproductive autonomy, and the disproportionate and socially required child-tending responsibility in many societies of female bearers (and other female adults) compared to male begetters. Even when some among us planfully choose to bear a (that is, some) child, only a few of us are beginning to have choices about whether to bear particular children we might, through genetic screening and engineering. And no one yet can choose a particular child *for* conception.

Goodin recognizes, though, that social practices in societies like ours assign parents these special responsibilities of provision for and supervision of children. He sees parental duties as qualified by ability to provide, either on their own or with public assistance; he notes that individuals other than parents can be more capable or better equipped as providers. Yet Goodin attempts largely to naturalize children's vulnerabilities and the link to parental responsibilities. "The special needs of the infant are determined by nature. How they are met is ordinarily determined by society." Parents are "obvious" candidates for "primary" responsibility, "given their crucial causal contribution . . . in the absence of any further social signposts," and "will be regarded" by others as such (*PV*, 82). The idea that needs are determinate quite independently of means and social norms, however, does not stand up, and the obviousness of primary parental responsibility needs another look, too.

General conditions of biological survival for human infants—nourishment, hydration, warmth, tactile stimulation—are naturally given. However, the "bare" biological survival of particular infants can demand, and in our society is frequently secured by means of, technologically advanced, acutely labor intensive, extremely expensive, and socially underwritten means in neonatal units. More generally, societies differ about standards of *adequate* biological survival for those infants allowed to survive (where the latter bound is set in many cases by common practices of infanticide, the "letting die" of severely abnormal neonates, or abortion for preferential, hardship, eugenic, or sex-selective reasons), and set different standards for different infants or for fetuses at different developmental stages.

Furthermore, biological survival is rarely all that is aimed for or thought due by human groups to their infants: What of the child's needs for physical, social, emotional, linguistic, and intellectual development? Socially accepted thresholds of adequate capability may be meager or rather robust. These thresholds are often not uniform even within a society, and may vary with parents' (or others') ability, interest, and resources or with passing social and political agendas, and the limits on variation may not be well or consistently defined. As technologies become available, more sophisticated prenatal interventions may be possible and may be available to prospective parents or others to correct disabilities or enhance capacities. Does a child's vulnerability to parental interventions of these kinds constitute a parental obligation to so intervene if capable?[5] I pose these questions not to imply that needs determination is hopelessly obscure or bottomlessly relative. Rather, needs (and interest) determination on the basis of certain "givens" is made clear always in the context of assumptions about human well-being (or the well-being of different kinds of humans) and the capacities, rights, or duties of human agents, *or particular actors*, to sustain it. The commonly recognized means by which human actors affect each other's well-being, of course, are those social practices that distribute responsibilities (and opportunities and prerogatives) of diverse kinds.

Social practices, like those of certain kinship, family, or other social and institutional structures that sort responsibilities to care for young, for example, not only reflect understandings about well-being and human efficacy (and the propriety of undertakings by any persons or certain persons), but in turn shape these understandings. A society such as ours in the contemporary U.S. has selected a practice of assigning responsibility for basic child maintenance and supervision primarily, and nearly exclusively, to adult members of some (one) nuclear family to which the child "belongs." Public participation and support for these functions in children's early years, essentially ancillary or remedial in this system, are meager, usually punitive, and often stigmatized ("welfare").

These grudging provisions serve not only to express the norms of primary and ideally exclusive parental duties of care, but help to reproduce and propagate them. At the same time, this arrangement institutionalizes levels of response to children's needs that are necessarily variable and often inadequate. In the context of a sharply sex-segmented labor market, lower female earnings, and a presumption that childcare responsibilities fall to mothers, "inadequate" is often the high end. Put very simply, it is acceptable for children in this kind of society to have what their very differently equipped and interested parents (often mothers) give them. Only catastrophic failures that cannot be ignored are addressed, in a regretful or hostile spirit of emergency. Is it really "obvious" who just "is" responsible for a child's well-being? Is the bar of minimal well-being really set independently of practices which determine who will in fact or who must respond? Has the sheer fact of begetting or birthing ever "by itself" uniformly indicated who is the obvious caretaker, in any of several senses ("bastards" smuggled, and wealthy nurslings whisked away, to others' care)?[6]

In fact, Goodin recognizes that "any dependency or vulnerability is arguably created, shaped, or sustained, at least in part, by existing social arrangements. None is wholly natural ... some seem to be almost wholly social in character" (*PV*, 191). This is a premise in Goodin's argument for eliminating unnecessary and undesirable vulnerabilities, and so eliminating the responsibilities that go with them. This view of the social construction of vulnerabilities, however, retains a linear model

of the relationship between vulnerabilities and responsibilities; it is missing one important feedback loop. On it, social arrangements create or
exacerbate vulnerabilities, which vulnerabilities (some of them unnecessary) then entail responsibilities. But as I have argued, delineating and
delegating responsibilities is itself a large and fundamental part of anything we might call a *social* arrangement, practice, or system. The
scheme of distributing responsibilities itself is a determinant, not only of
particular responsibilities, but of particular vulnerabilities as well.
Responsibility assignments render some people vulnerable to particular
others in particular ways for certain things, and thus create specific
dependencies-in-fact. Many of our vulnerabilities take the forms they do
as they are "fitted" to the socially normed responsibilities of others. A
special but important case of this is "needs" being defined in ways that
make them "administrable" in certain kinds of social welfare systems;
one vulnerability that "clients" thereby incur is that they may not be
able to demonstrate that their needs coincide with administrable ones,
or they may have to settle for administrable benefits regardless of actual
needs (see Fraser 1989, chapters 7 and 8).

Another consequence of responsibility assignments, of course, is a distinctive set of vulnerabilities—vulnerabilities to blame and shame, to
loss of others' and one's own respect, if responsibilities that fall to one
cannot be met. Vulnerabilities ground and attract responsibilities (allowing for the loop) and responsibilities ground accountability; when we
duck or muff them, we attract blame. Before returning to this larger system, however, there remains a question about what sorts of things one is
responsible for, when one is responsible for protecting those vulnerable
to one's actions and choices.

Do Outcomes Alone Matter?

Goodin says, "If my analysis of these core notions is correct, then the
principle of protecting the vulnerable must be fundamentally consequen-
tialistic in form. Its central injunction is to frame your actions and
choices in such a way as to produce certain sorts of consequences,
namely, ones that protect the interests of those who are particularly vulnerable to your actions and choices" (*PV*, 114). Indeed, Goodin makes
the stronger claim that "any welfare-consequentialistic theory (of which
utilitarianism is only the most conspicuous example) will necessarily
entail the principle of protecting the vulnerable" (*PV*, 114).

But this seems clearly wrong. Most familiar forms of consequentialism, including standard kinds of utilitarian ethics, require not just attending to consequences, but seeking maximizing (or optimizing, or satisficing) outcomes for all those affected or open to harm or benefit. Certain of one's actions will weigh more heavily on those most vulnerable to one, and PPV confers on us particularly stringent obligations in those cases. But consequentialism may well reach different conclusions; its concern is not simply how strong an impact my actions might have on particular people, but how those impacts affect *aggregate* outcomes for some specified class of persons. Ministering most to those especially vulnerable to me will perhaps make the consequences "best for them," but can hardly guarantee consequences "best for all" without further (and usually dubious) assumptions. One of the most troubling questions about special obligations, after all, is the disproportionate dispensation of resources to the few at what may be, in the aggregate, very great expense to the many. It does not seem that PPV must produce results that cohere with common forms of utilitarian thinking. In fact there is good reason to think the PPV will have to countenance clearly nonconsequentialist elements.

PPV is supposed to have its clearest applications in cases of special relationships. In these cases others are typically dependent on, and even depend*ing* on one for various things. Whether everything for which one is relied upon in such cases is usefully described as a "consequence," however, is debatable. An approach that looks entirely to consequences, in any familiar sense, is likely to miss or misplace the importance of acceptable means and reliable character in stabilizing the relations of trust on which these relationships are founded, and on which much of their value depends.

Goodin emphasizes, for example, that emotional vulnerabilities figure importantly in those special relationships involving intimacy or emphasizing trust or affection (*PV*, 72, 78–79, 83, 89, 98, 105). "Getting money from strangers is not the same as getting it from parents, because in the latter case money betokens something even more valuable—love" (*PV*, 83). "When you are let down by someone who you know does not return your affection, you may feel deeply disappointed. . . . If it is [a friend] who lets you down, you are hurt more deeply; you feel betrayed" (*PV*, 98). One might construe the impact of these vulnerabilities purely quantitatively in consequentialist terms. That is, if one is deprived of help and feels the sting of betrayal, one has suffered more hurt, or more hurts have happened to one; and those in a position to augment hurts additively are those to whom one is more vulnerable. This is certainly one way ("adding insult to injury") that such interests are figured. But if PPV is claimed to make the best sense of our intuitive grasp of responsibilities in these cases, a purely consequentialist interpretation of PPV may do this less well than one which incorporates some qualitative, in fact, roughly deontological features or virtue-based considerations as well.

In filial, friendly, or intimate relationships, what one values is not only the actual outcomes of others' (and one's own) actions, but also the nature and significance of those relationships, and of the specific kinds of trust, appreciation, enjoyment, esteem, and security that those relationships bring to one's life. Suppose a friend might be able to confer very great benefit upon me by acting in a way that is particularly condescending to me, or particularly ruthless or cynical from my point of view. If the beneficial consequences are great enough, I might acknowledge that the benefit achieved, even with the hurt of lost esteem for myself or for the other "subtracted," is in some sense "greater" in magnitude than the total outcome of another course of action in which no such benefit is realized, while esteem is preserved. Cash in a little self-respect for a lot of money? Trade off a bit of mutual trust in a friendship for a substantial career advancement? In these situations, one might rationally prefer, and admirably choose, "less" of some *better* or more *meaningful* kinds of goods; I believe we often do.

Nor need this be because one knows or believes that all things considered one will get "more" benefit in the long run from the relationship's remaining of a certain kind. One might not have any idea as to overall "outcomes" in such cases. One just cares more for certain qualitatively superior states (of relationship, or the expression of character or quality of attitude) in a way consequentialism has never been able to represent or simulate comfortably. "Special" relationships are conspicuous among cases (not all of them moral ones) where certain kinds of things are not weighed in the same scale; so to weigh them is to show you do not know what they are worth, the kind of value they have.

It is even reasonable to think that one can fail to serve another's interest in these special relationships when one acts in ways which do not honor the nature and forms of trust which define them, even when the other party never knows that one's action was unfaithful in that way, and so incurs no feelings of hurt, betrayal, or loss which figure in as actual results. Consider here the harms of undiscovered infidelities, secret betrayals, and unrevealed insults. It is unlikely, of course, that a committed consequentialist will want to acknowledge these forms of harm as morally significant, or will find it easy to represent them calculatively. But if it is part of our commonplace sense of our close relationships that such things may really be harms to us, and not negligible ones, then a consequentialist rendering of PPV diminishes its justificatory value in just some of the areas on which Goodin builds his case. In a recent book, Goodin has simply moved off justifying utilitarianism as a guide to personal conduct, restricting its appropriateness to public roles and public affairs. Goodin lays down the repetitive and tortured remedial quest of utilitarian theories to show us that we are or can be personal consequentialists, saying, "In personal life, most dramatically, there simply has to be more scope for considerations of uncalculating affection, standing rules of conduct and qualities of character" (Goodin 1995, 7). Perhaps there is more scope for such considerations in public life as well.

Here, though, I want to take up a broader view of why purely consequentialist or instrumental accounts of our responsibilities miss something about the nature and point of practices of responsibility. Practices of holding each other responsible *do* have a fundamental and critical role in trying to secure certain states of affairs open to impact by human attention and effort, especially those consisting in or bearing on harms and benefits to other people (or beings). They do have this role, and it is why any socially embodied scheme of responsibilities encodes conceptions of well-being for human beings and others, as well as views about the possible and proper efficacy of human actors in the world. The standing appeal of consequentialism derives from this: We really do, and have to, care how things come out. I have treated Goodin's responsibility ethics at length because I like the way it foregrounds those structures of moral and social life that try to connect people and positions to situations and outcomes that require to be "seen to." This has to be part of the weave of any social fabric. Yet even insofar as practices of responsibility are instrumental or outcome-oriented, they are not only so; they have a number of interrelated functions. And even insofar as they do function instrumentally, they are not organized for mere efficacy (much less maximum efficiency) but serve to achieve their results in a particular way.

Practices of responsibility are as marvelously intricate as philosophical accounts of responsibility have tended to be austere. Practices of responsibility include attributing some states of affairs to human agency; taking ourselves and others to be (variously) answerable for these; setting terms of praise and (more elaborately) blameworthiness, excusability, and exculpation for what is or is not done, and for some of what ensues as a result; and visiting (in judgment, action, speech, and feeling) forms of commendation, or of criticism, reproof, or blame, on those judged in those terms. Sometimes rewards and honors are bestowed, or sanctions, penalties, or punishments applied. These range from smiles to military decorations, and from withdrawn confidences to death by lethal injection.

But practices of responsibility are not only ones of assignment. They also include ones of accepting or refusing, deflecting or negotiating, specific assignments of responsibility. There are given ways of contesting, defending, or excusing oneself; inviting or limiting one's exposure to expectation or damages; showing regret, contrition, or remorse (or contempt, indignation, or derision) over one's (alleged) responsibility; offering apologies, reparations, compensations, restitutions. A more or less rich repertory of feelings, experienced and expressed, accompany these realizations and interactions. The things for which we hold ourselves and each other responsible are various, too. We can be responsible for specific tasks or goals, roles with discretionary powers, acts and failures to act, outcomes and upshots of actions (not always controllable or foreseen), contributions to outcomes that are not ours alone, and attitudes, habits, and traits.[7] Specific distributions of responsibility roughly map this complex terrain of who must account, how far and for what, to whom. Peter French calls this, amusingly but with serious point, The Responsibility Barter Game. "The minimum achievable score is zero, though it is seldom attained if the player is really in the game" (French 1992, 2).

It is indeed an important end of these arrangements that certain things get done, and that people and valued things be kept out of unnecessary harm's way. The way these arrangements do this is to keep afloat a system of mutual expectations and self-expectations. Since arrangements and people are imperfect, however, it is equally important that the system of mutual expectations supply not only norms for performance, but norms for disappointment in performance or the expectations of it. We need to know this setup provides recourse and remedies, known places to go to when damage is done or desired things undone, and assured satisfactions of accountability and blame, material and not, all in a context of shared *recognition*. The system not only aims to secure outcomes (for the most part), but to keep reproducing the specific shared understandings, and the awareness of them as shared, in which the system consists. When in good working order, practices of responsibility not only exert pressure toward production or prevention of outcomes, but in doing so shape, correct, and enliven individuals' senses of responsibility and strengthen the common fabric of trust in people's senses of responsibility. Such efficacy as these arrangements aim at, then, is *efficacy through mutual recognition*.

Yet they also aim at renewing the fund of recognition itself. Practices of responsibility renew the common fund of shared understandings and the fact that they are shared in several ways. They function *manipulatively*, putting pressure on performance (and due preparation, care, informedness, effort, and self-control), aiming to reproduce conforming behavior. They do this by creating awareness of the sticks of blame and reprisal or the carrots of approval and reward. They function *regulatively* in circulating understandings of what is required of us and how we might be asked to account for it. It is here that specific distributions of responsibility to and for persons, by situation, role, and relationship, are made common knowledge within communities or in some parts of them. Our attention is thereby guided toward some people and some features of situations and our own behavior (and not toward others). In holding each other responsible, we also *express* feelings and attitudes that stroke and soothe or burn and sting; the reactive attitudes work at once as pressures on, and as messages about and emblems of, one's connections to others, and what balances of trust are there to be tipped. Our practices cue us about when to feel these things, and about the meaning, as well as the mode, of their display. Finally, these practices *define* and *articulate* a conception of agency (how much of what happens in the world belongs to me or puts claims on me), the natures of particular relationships (what friends, cousins, compatriots, are "for"), and the boundaries of communities (whom it is our business to look out for and account to). (See Smiley 1992, especially chapter 9.)

I don't mean to suggest, of course, that our practices do, or that we learn to do, these things separately. We just pick up things about what people expect, and how people react, which excuses work, what repairs are appropriate, and so on. This is just another case of how startlingly replete even small bits of social knowledge tend to be. A whole system comes with them, but it's rarely very easily surveyable. So much of what we know about this is hidden in plain sight; and there is a lot we do not know, or cannot notice, unless we are looking from certain places.

Geography, Transparency, and "Our" Concept of Responsibility

Philosophers' discussions of responsibility—or moral responsibility—have long been dominated by moral metaphysics and moral psychology, exploring the structure of the physical or the human mental universe in order to discover if, and if ever when, we are responsible. Sometimes philosophers claim that inquiries into responsibility are tests of whether "our concept of moral responsibility" can face the facts, or of what that concept—either "our" concept or "the" concept—"is." It is not clear to me that there is "a" concept of moral responsibility, even one that is "ours," much less that there is one, ours or someone else's, that just gets the facts right. I think talk of "the concept" or "our concept" of moral responsibility is not very helpful, and can be very misleading. Where do we look to find it? Does it show in what people say, or what they do, or what they feel? And which people's judgments, on which occasions, reveal it? Which concept is "ours"?[8]

I think instead that there are many-faceted practices of responsibility, as I have been very roughly describing them, which give what is meant by "being responsible for." I don't see any sharp, principled, or noncircular demarcation of "moral responsibilities" from others, and so I have not tried to observe one throughout this discussion. It seems true that we are most likely to invoke the notion of moral responsibility in cases of where stakes are high, or cases where dependability or dereliction is apt to reflect on character, or cases where we know we are relying entirely on the informal system of pressures of mutual recognition, where there are no official judiciaries or enforcers. None of these marks of moral responsibility makes any clean theoretical cut, however. "High stakes" have to be moral stakes (human welfare, honor, self-respect, not expensive real estate); performance has to reflect on moral character (not energy or extroversion). And we do also speak of moral responsibilities with respect to many of the same actions that institutions and tribunals, police forces and jailers respond to. In some cases responsibilities may have to achieve some institutional reality before moral opprobrium reliably attaches to their desertion.

Even the ubiquitous authority moral judgment seems to enjoy—that it can be invoked, it seems, in any context—may not be a feature of morality but of one particular form of it, one whose teaching instills a sense of demand that philosophers end up calling "overridingness." It is also sometimes said that "anyone" may make moral judgments, without special powers or office. But that's not descriptively accurate, either. Making a moral judgment is assuming a kind of authority, at least the authority of grasping and speaking for a common standard (Smiley 1992, 239). *Not* just anyone has standing to enter any and all judgments, including moral ones, even if an ascendant modern political morality pictures moral equality or a "kingdom of ends" as an ideal. The architect of that ideal did not take all adult human beings to possess that kind of standing in it, and in this was not unusual. In actual moral communities, both ones imbued with egalitarian ideals and ones that are not, whole categories of people are typically disqualified from the standing to make moral judgments, or to make them in certain contexts or upon certain others—e.g. small children, lunatics, outcasts, infidels, women, outsiders. It is a separate question exactly which exclusions or disqualifications are (rationally or morally) justified.

It seems what we have are our practices of responsibility. What we get out of these practices is one set of solutions to a universal human problem: reproducing a form of social life by means of pressures—the manipulative, regulative, expressive, and definitive functions—of mutual accounting in terms of shared understandings of responsibility. I am inclined to call any such system that works in these ways a moral form of life. It is another question what may be said for or against any specific system (see, for example, Baier 1993).

I agree with Bernard Williams's claim that while there are universal "materials" for the construction of conceptions of moral responsibility (for example, human causal power, intention, state of mind, and needs for responses to harm or damage), "There is not, and there never could be, just one appropriate way of adjusting these elements to one another ... [in] one correct conception of responsibility" (Williams 1993, 55). These materials may be interpreted and weighted differently in different times and places, but may also be so at the same time and place when serving different purposes, e.g., in commonplace understandings and in the criminal law. I think, though, that these different "conceptions" really get their content from the practices that embody them. The practices seem to show that "responsibility" consists in *many* facts, in the context of judgments, perceptions, feelings, and reactions shaped in particular (and only roughly coordinate) ways.

Philosophers very often treat the reality and nature of moral responsibility as a question of fact "prior" to the business of normative ethics. Indeed, the "problem of determinism" is supposed to threaten the fact of moral responsibility, and (so) there being a proper point to moral judgments and the justificatory projects of normative ethics at all. Yet, Joel Feinberg noted a long time ago that "moral responsibility" cannot pick out a precise and absolute fact about agents or actions that requires no human beings' practical adjudication (Feinberg 1970). More recently, Marion Smiley has provided a striking analysis of how judgments of causal responsibility and blameworthiness (standard constituents of moral responsibility judgments by many philosophers' lights), always adjudicate relevant facts in light of *normative*, often *moral*, assumptions about such things as social roles, community boundaries, or normal or expected levels of informedness and self-control (Smiley 1992). Smiley demonstrates the operation of substantive norms *within* our practices of judging causal responsibility, but also shows why our practices are dynamic and contestable. They can be changed not only by the intro-duction of new facts, or by changes in social roles and normative expec-tations, but also by successfully shifting burdens of blame and responsibility to new places. This pulls normative assumptions along in train, configuring (or reconfiguring) roles and communities as a conse-quence (see also Calhoun 1989). Moral suasion, power or authority of several types, and simple opportunity can be catalysts for this change.

Smiley understands that causal responsibility assessments are gudied by our looking forward to whom it will make sense to blame. At the same time she sees that actually blaming someone or anyone for certain outcomes feeds back into our understandings of what it makes sense to hold human being responsible for. If our society now ponders, for exam-ple, duties to aid or rescue distant populations in need, no few premises in a philosophical argument can "demonstrate" the fact of our responsi-bility. What is needed is the progressive entrenchment of habits of judg-ment and practices of effective blame-placing (most likely on collective entities such as governments, and then individually on those who sup-port or tolerate their policies) that will shift the standing norms guiding negotiations of responsibility (see Calhoun 1989). This might involve countenancing some new or emerging facts (global interdependencies, new political balances of power) and might involve seeing existing facts anew or with a different emphasis (disproportionate consumption of resources by wealthy nations, citizens' responsibilities in democratic societies for government priorities and policies). It will necessarily involve making these facts appear in stories of dependency and connec-tion, stories of sorts we find compelling. I think it is because these stories are now more often told that these moral questions have begun to take the forms they have. When Philippa Foot once wanted to point out that morally motivating reasons could not be produced automatically by some magical kind of imperative, she spoke of morality as a "volunteer army" of those who care about liberty and justice (Foot 1978, 167). While the image of purely elective affinity seems to me misleading with respect to socially entrenched norms, this image fits well those who have taken up the burden of shifting practices of responsibility (whether to thicken and extend connections or to sever them, to open up communities or to more vigilantly police their boundaries).

I suggest that we have an urgent need for *geographies of responsibility*, mapping the structure of standing assumptions that guides the distribution of responsibilities—how they are assigned, negotiated, deflected—in particular forms of moral life. The brief examination above of links between vulnerabilities and responsibilities suggests that this structure is likely to be complex, and that much of it may hardly be visible to us from within because of its apparent "naturalness." Neither is this structure all there is to practices of responsibility. There is the reproduction of the supporting sensibilities, dispositions, and feelings which make participants responsive to moral pressures from within and without, and the roles of blamings and praisings, and more formal sanctions, that keep shared understandings circulating and authoritative. These ecologies and economies of responsibility need to be looked at too, and we may need to look harder and from different angles, to notice what is too familiar to see.

These studies can show the extent to which patterns of ascribing and deflecting responsibility are socially shaped and differently shapeable. The point of seeing this is not just better descriptions, however; it is to be able to appreciate what is gotten and what is lost, what is secured and what left to chance, when responsibilities are shaped in one way rather than another. For the justification of familiar or redrawn responsibilities lies in the values in and of the lives to which distinct distributions of responsibilities lead. "Special relationships" have been a bugbear of impartialist theories in ethics, and a *cause célèbre* of communitarian ones. Closer looks at how responsibilities are distributed and reproduced show, I think, that moral forms of life are typically organized around highly differentiated social-moral positions, defined by different responsibilities, and different standings to give accounts or demand them. We are all of us "special," in some respects. We are not all responsible for the same things, in the same ways, at the same costs, or with similar exposure to demand or blame by the same judges.

In particular instances this may be a harmless or useful social division of moral labor, or it may be something unsavory. Sometimes it is a privilege or a mercy to be exempted from responsibilities; sometimes it shows you are nobody, or less of a somebody than someone else. Assignments of responsibility are a form of moral address, but some are addressed as peers, others as superiors or subordinates. Much moral epistemology takes as its topic how, or how best, "the" moral agent knows, reasons, or decides what to do. If moral orders are often, in fact, complex networks of different positions, people need to understand who they are, and where they are, in these orders, to see what in particular they are responsible for, and to whom. A basic and urgent work of moral theorizing, then, is seeing more clearly how the mesh between social positions, identities, and responsibilities works, and whether it works for some and against others. This is the subject of part three of this book.[9]

part three

Self- (and Other) Portraits

Who Are We, and How Do We Know?

five

Picking Up Pieces

Lives, Stories, and Integrity

I started out believing that life was made just so the world would have some way to think about itself, but that it had gone awry with humans because flesh, pinioned by misery, hangs on to it with pleasure. Hangs on to wells and a boy's golden hair, would just as soon inhale sweet fire caused by a burning girl as hold a maybe-yes maybe-no hand. I don't believe that anymore. Something is missing there. Something rogue. Something else you have to figure in before you can figure it out.

—Toni Morrison, *Jazz*

... what I want is for you to feel, around the story, a saturation of other stories that I could tell and maybe will tell or who knows may already have told on some other occasion, a space full of stories that perhaps is simply my lifetime, where you can move in all directions, as in space, always finding stories that cannot be told until other stories are told first, and so, setting out from any moment or place, you encounter always the same density of material to be told.

—Italo Calvino, *If on a Winter's Night a Traveller*

In John Barth's novel *The End of the Road*, a man finds himself inert, paralyzed by indecision in a railway station. He is given three rules to follow by a quack doctor. The rules (lexically ordered) are Sinistrality, Antecedence, and Alphabetical Priority: Choose the thing on the left, or the thing that comes first, or, if these don't apply, choose the thing the name of which begins with the earlier letter of the alphabet. The doctor adds that there are other rules too, and although they're all arbitrary they're useful. Obviously they're useful only insofar as you'd rather do anything than nothing at all, and useful or not they bear no resemblance to a moral code, path, or sensibility. They touch on nothing human beings care about. They are unresponsive either to particular circumstances and what is happening in them, or to people and what might happen to them. They are mechanical not only in their rote character, but in their blindness.

They also go nowhere; they have no point or meaning, not even a direction or tendency. A life lived by them would be utterly consistent and consistently meaningless. Barth's man has no character. His patterns express nothing about the value of what is chosen, nor about his valuation of it, and so nothing about the kind of person he is, in the sense in which we in fact care what "kind of person" we and others are. Anyone looking on would be stumped as to what meaning such a life could possibly have, and things are no better for Barth's man himself. He can give no better account of his life to himself than to anyone else.

Now consider former minister and high school teacher the Rev. Robert Shields, profiled by reporter David Isay for a segment on National Public Radio's *Morning Edition* (NPR 1994). As he has for over twenty years, "no less than four hours each day," the Rev. Shields "surrounded by a half dozen IBM Wheelwriters," creates a record of 3,000 to 6,000 words a day of everything that happens to him. Shields says: "I don't leave anything out. I start it in at midnight and go through the next midnight, and every five minutes is accounted for. Twelve-twenty to 12:25 I stripped to my thermals. I always do that. Twelve-twenty-five to 12:30 I discharge urine. Twelve-thirty to 12:50 I eat leftover salmon, the Alaska red salmon by Bumblebee, about 7 ounces. Drank 10 ounces of orange juice while I read the Oxford Dictionary of Quotations." He records the weight of the daily paper, everything he eats and buys, his blood pressure and pulse, all mail he receives; he wakes himself at two-hour intervals to record his dreams. "It's my makeup. It's my nature, I suppose," he says; stopping would be "like stopping—turning off my life."

In a sense, the Rev. Shields is at the opposite end from Barth's man. The Rev. Shields is certainly a "character" in one familiar sense of that word. His life is not only directed, but is singularly consumed, by his relentless verbal reproduction of it, which appears to have intense personal importance to him. He has a constitutive project, he's on a quest, and he's got a life plan, but it's not the kind of thing Bernard Williams, Alasdair MacIntyre, or John Rawls had in mind. Even if Shields is doing nothing wrong, his singleness of purpose and the resulting unity of his life are simply ridiculous. Shields himself cannot explain why this absurd endeavor holds his life in thrall. His life and the character it expresses are no more intelligible than that of Barth's man. We are inclined to think of them under psychiatric categories, for neither exhibits an intelligible *moral* personality.

The rigidity of Barth's mechanical rules and Shields's obsessive project are comically bizarre. Their stories are hyperbolic parables of life-orderings gone haywire. Yet it might seem that a set of ordered rules or an overarching goal with which one identifies could be the right kinds of structure for a well-ordered life, so long as they involved the right kinds of *content*. In fact, accounts of moral integrity as a specially admirable property of whole lives have often appealed to some kind of principled consistency or unconditional commitment with respect to morally important matters. But this invites the question what kinds of things matter morally, and whether things of that kind can be so ordered, both at a time and over time. And what is the relation between the moral ordering of lives and the things that give them individual meaning?

All moral philosophies have views about right or value. Not all respond equally or in the same ways to worries about the overall shape and content of lives, or to hopes that they might be personally worthwhile as well as interpersonally defensible. I think it is reasonable to expect moral philosophy to shed some light on how to steer a morally responsible course throughout our lives among valuable things and important commitments, while giving place to the wish that our lives might express the people we in particular are. I believe the structure of an *ethics of responsibility,* nested within an expressive-collaborative view of morality (chapter 3), is responsive to these demands. It aims to accommodate the richness and diversity of what people have reasons to care about and take responsibility for. It accommodates the varieties and vagaries of very different lives people may want to, or have to, lead.

This kind of view, however, proposes no philosophical metric to help us determine when we have assumed just enough meaningful and sustainable responsibilities in just the right order. Rather than a defect, I find this to be a virtue of the view. I do not think there is a principled way of ordering for everyone in advance the numbers, kinds, combinations, and weightings of things that matter morally, and with respect to which we may well be called to account. I don't think we simply haven't *yet* found an all-purpose solution for all of life, or for all lives, to the question of how far to go with which morally significant commitments, where to stop, or when to compromise or change course. The vicissitudes of projects of high moral theory in this century might well make one skeptical about the likelihood of achieving that. I think the resistance of our lives to this treatment is due, in part, to the nature of things in our lives that morally matter. It is also due to the nature of these lives themselves. Morally significant things, our responses to them and responsibility for them, play very important parts in our lives, but our lives are not only about or propelled by them.

Yet to say there's no principled way is not to say there are no ways at all. People solve these problems in their lives all the time in ways that may be found more or less morally sound for good reasons. One thing I want to show is how a kind of responsibility ethics clarifies the structure of the moral accounts people actually tend to keep and give. It sees these accounts as individual and individuating narratives of lives that are particularly our own. But these narratives, even if individuating, cannot be private or idiosyncratic. They serve purposes of *shared* understanding, not only of self-guidance but of justification and criticism. We are neither unfortunate enough to have to go it all alone in trying to find and keep an acceptable and vital moral order in our lives nor lucky enough to have the last word on whether we have succeeded.

The other thing I want to show is how this kind of ethics does something it may be thought unable to do: to supply an intuitively recognizable understanding of *integrity*, and to defend the central importance of it. It is true this kind of ethics does not support a view of integrity that equates it with maximal evaluative integration, unconditional commitments, or uncorrupted fidelity to a true self. This ethics does not find those conceptions of integrity true to the changing, deeply relational character of human lives and the ways we make sense of them. Those conceptions do not reckon with how much and how inevitably most lives are entangled with and given to others, as well as to chancy circumstance beyond our control. If we consider the several kinds of stories by means of which we keep our moral accounts these features of our lives come to the fore.

I defend a view of integrity as a kind of *reliable accountability*. Its point is not for us to will one thing nor to be it, but to maintain—or reestablish—our reliability in matters involving important commitments and goods. This view exchanges global wholeness for more local dependability, and inexorable consistency for responsiveness to the moral costs of error and change. It trades inward solidity for flexible resiliency at those points where lives, fortune, and several kinds of histories meet. This view of integrity takes utterly seriously to what and to whom a person is true, but looks with suspicion upon true selves. It features the role of stories in making sense of lives, but is skeptical about certain overly ambitious or monopolistic narrative demands on selves. It links our senses of meaning and responsibility to the stories we can tell, but notices that "we" are not all in the same discursive positions any more than we are all in the same social ones, and that these are importantly linked. There are moral problems with the social distribution of narrative resources and the credibility to use them, which this view can help us see.

Strains of Responsibility

I model the structure of responsibility ethics here in my own way, but I hope this way captures something important about a variety of related views, including ethics of care that have been favored by many feminists. The basic claim about the structure of our responsibilities is this: Specific moral claims on us arise from our contact or relationship with others whose interests are vulnerable to our actions and choices. We are *obligated to respond* to particular others when circumstance or ongoing relationship render them especially, conspicuously, or peculiarly dependent on us.[1]

This kind of ethics requires a view of moral judgment with significant expressive, interpretive, and (where possible) collaborative features. If actual dependency or vulnerability (and the circumstances or histories of commitment and expectation that create it) is the basis of many moral claims, the specific nature, as well as the relative priority and stringency, of the claims cannot generally be determined in the abstract. Rather, prior abstract orderings of values ("honesty over convenience"), generic obligations ("treat persons with dignity"), or generalized conceptions of roles or interests ("friends deserve loyalty") are only rough guidelines; they need to be interpreted for the instance at hand. Sometimes prior conceptions or orderings will be altered or set aside when the nature of the particular case shows them to be irrelevant or unresponsive. Where available, a shared search for mutually acceptable resolutions (or for an understanding of what is irreconcilable) is preferable to unilateral decision.

Here's a problem some find with this approach. In a typical human life there will be many relationships that create varying degrees and kinds of dependence, as well as countless episodes in which unfamiliar others may be rendered dependent on us without their or our intent or control. Responsibility ethics draws together cases where developed relationships thick with commitment or expectation put demands on me; cases where incident or emergency put me in a position to provide significant aid to, or deter significant harm from, perfect or virtual strangers; and cases where I may become aware of my ability to help others who do not immediately confront me. Is there any end to the number and types of demands that on this view morally claim my attention? Could a life responsive along these lines exhibit the commitments and concerns distinctive of the one who lives it? How could a person make, or keep, this life her or his "own"? Responsibility ethics might seem to defeat personally meaningful life-ordering by visiting a veritable plague of commitments on each of us. It might even be claimed that such a view ignores, thwarts, or threatens a person's *integrity*.

Indeed, Carol Gilligan, explicating one version of an ethics of responsibility, called this "the conflict between integrity and care" (Gilligan 1982, 157). Any human being, immersed in the complex, varied, and changing relationships and episodic contacts of real life might be scattered, depleted, and "constantly compromised" (ibid.) by an unlimited demand for responsiveness. This integrity problem is analogous to one raised by Bernard Williams with respect to both utilitarian and Kantian moral views.[2] Both impartial maximizing of goods (whatever they might be) and impartial respect for persons (whoever they might be) seem to demand that personally distinctive and meaningful projects, commitments, and relationships be jettisoned, and that agents view them as dispensable, whenever impartialist moral demands conflict with them, as they surely often (if not always) do. Because personally distinctive "constitutive" commitments carry a life forward, giving it meaning and making it one's own, impartialist morality seems to deny us a life truly ours. Is responsibility ethics at least as bad, if not worse?

Some feminist critics think that Gilligan's identification of an ethic of open-ended responsiveness with women is deeply mistaken. They think it valorizes stereotypes of bottomless feminine nurturance and self-sacrifice that continue to haunt women while politically disempowering and personally exhausting them (Grimshaw 1986; Houston 1987; Card 1990; Friedman 1993). A care "ethic" can look like the lamentable internalization of an oppressively servile social role. Some critics of Williams, on the other hand, suggest that his plea for the agent's integrity is a defense of self-indulgence or a cavalier refusal to accept legitimate demands morality makes on us (Conly 1983; Herman 1983; Flanagan 1991). And it is tempting to caricature Gilligan's and Williams's discussions as sentimental rationalizations of feminine ("What's a mother to do?") and masculine ("A man's gotta do what a man's gotta do") stereotypes.

These criticisms have merit, yet I sympathize with something both Gilligan and Williams are trying to do. They are straining against a formulaic view of selves and their others, lives and their commitments, and the role of morality in binding or shaping these. Both try to get the meanings, motives, commitments, and connections that move individuals through their distinctive lives into the right relation with morality's guiding and constraining force within those lives. Gilligan in fact argued that people's real problems of conflicting responsibilities need to be "separated from self-sacrifice" (Gilligan 1982, 134) and reconciled to "the truth of their own agency and needs" (138). The larger truth involves "the fact that in life you never see it all, that things unseen undergo change through time, that there is more than one path to gratification, and that the boundaries between self and other are less clear than they sometimes seem" (172). And Williams, despite deep ambiguity in his notorious discussion of a fictive "Gauguin" whose abandonment of his family may be retrospectively "justified" by artistic success (Williams 1981b), acknowledges elsewhere that commitments constituting personally meaningful lives are normally formed within the bounds of morality (Williams 1981a, 12–13). Both use "integrity" to stand in for a demand, either within or against morality, for some space a self can call its own, although it is likely that they think differently about the self who needs to stake this claim.

It is not always clear in these and other discussions exactly what integrity is supposed to be: Doing what's right? Doing what you, particularly, believe is right? Doing what's particularly and morally acceptably right for you? Doing what it takes to keep yourself or your life all in one piece? Having moral commitments so conflict-free and/or a record of performance (and prediction?) so flawless you never have to say you're sorry? There's no detaching a picture of integrity from some view about the nature of morality. I think an ethic of responsibility within an expressive-collaborative framework can acknowledge a moving horizon of commitments and adjustments, allowing individual distinctiveness of situation and commitment. It preserves livable flexibility in tandem with reasonable reliability.

Three Kinds of Narratives: Identity, Relationship, Value

Narrative understanding of the moral construction (and reconstruction) of lives is central to understanding how responsibilities are kept coherent and sustainable over substantial stretches of lives that, in important—but not imperial—ways, remain people's own. The idea is that a *story* is the basic form of representation for moral problems. Many situations cannot be reckoned with responsibly without seeing how people, relations, and even the values and obligations they recognize have gotten there. Since any morally problematic point might turn out to be part of the history of some later one, many problems are "solved" only to produce a sequel of personal and evaluative implications and remainders. Anything we do now may bear on what we are responsible for later on. These views reflect the idea of moral responsibility (in prospect or retrospect) as attaching to persons, a conception of a person as identified at least in part by a history, a history as constituted by patterns of action and response over significant periods of time, and actions themselves as conceived and reconceived in terms of their relations to what precedes and what follows them.

It is not only for moral purposes but also for purposes of intelligibility over time that we read and reread actions and other events backward and forward, weaving them into lives that are anything more than one damned thing after another. The sense-making connections we exploit in doing so are of several kinds. Some are putative causal ones. We can describe someone's feelings as *scarred* or her replies as *defensive* only by presuming a present that results from something in the past; a decision only *restores* someone's dignity if certain kinds of things are found to issue from it. Other connections are sequential. There can be an opportunity to *regain* trust only where it has already been lost, and a man's *final* break with his youthful political convictions can only be that looking back. Sometimes sense-making connections serve to bundle up varied or repeating actions into legible configurations, such as neglecting a friendship or trying to disown a past. In such ways, features, trajectories, and whole segments of lives are given intelligible roles and even thematic meanings.

In these ways we make sense of what someone has done, what someone does or doesn't care about, or who someone is. Often we make sense of one of these by means of the others. For such things we may be held, or hold ourselves or others, responsible. To know what to hold ourselves or others responsible for requires identifying the separate and mutual histories and understandings we bring to situations requiring response. Three kinds of stories are central to living responsibly a life of one's own. We need to keep on keeping straight who we are, and who we have given others to understand we are, in moral terms. We also need to sustain or refurbish our understanding of moral terms themselves, of what it means to talk about kindness, respect, friendship, or obligation. I call the needed stories ones of *identity, relationship*, and *value*. In taking these up I begin in the middle, as we all in fact do, with relationships.

A *narrative of relationship* is a story of the relationship's acquired content and developed expectations, its basis and type of trust, and its possibilities for continuation. A response may be owed to others because some prior history of actual contact and understanding makes it reasonable for them to depend on me for something and reasonable for me to know of their reasonable expectation. Then it is morally important for us to acknowledge the past character, present state, and future possibilities of that relationship. It shows us what is owed, why it is owed, and what latitude there may be for postponement, substitution, or release. We must also consider what this relationship, imagined in various continuations, revisions, or terminations means for both (all) of us. In cases of purely episodic dependency (an unknown stranger in need of assistance), and where the needs and interest are entirely obvious or where the situation is urgent (a drowning child), there is no antecedent story of relationship to explore, and the imaginable interpersonal sequels are typically limited as well. These are very short stories of our moral lives, but they still may end more or less creditably, and their matter and implications may be significant parts of larger stories that reveal how well or badly we live or how easily we can make moral sense of ourselves.

So, sometimes we must do things for others because they need it and because our ongoing relation to them makes us most likely or apt to supply it. Sometimes we do things for others as a way of creating a relationship that will become committing in that way, or as a way of honoring a history of relationship that has been so. And sometimes we do, and must do, things for people we did not and will not know, simply because their need is so critical or extreme, or because it is so easy for us to respond, or because there is no one else to. Things are more complex when the different demands of different persons or the different demands of the same person pose conflicting options. I must weigh different continuations against each other, deciding how much can be accommodated and what might best be sacrificed.

It is at this point, concentrating on the relationship-centered narrative, that an actor's integrity seems most strained. Integrity seems threatened because it seems that someone is pressed to define how she goes on in terms derived from others' needs and demands, and others' unpredictable situations. But the narrative of relationship is *not* the only relevant one. Two others figure in an adequate moral construction of a situation.

The agent's own *narrative of moral identity* is a persistent history of valuation that can be seen in a good deal of what a person cares for, responds to, and takes care of (Walker 1987; Meyers 1994). There are too many people, values, and possible realizations of those values by and for those people for any of us to respond to all of these. In fact, most of us, whether with thought or by habit, set definite priorities among values, develop highly selective responses, and pay acute attention to particular kinds of things as well as people. Some devote primary energy and attention to friends or family, others to institutional roles, political involvement, or creative pursuits. Some care specially about honesty or loyalty, others about alleviating suffering or political change. And of course we all care specially for some particular others, whether out of our love, gratitude, or pity, or their merit, need, or right. *None* of these habitual or characteristic devotions licenses avoidable cruelty, destructiveness, or indecency to *anyone*. But the limits of minimal respect and minimally decent values are very broad ones. There are indefinitely many ways of going on acceptably within these moral boundary conditions; there are many specific versions of moral excellence as well.

The significance of the ongoing narrative of moral identity is not only that we typically do have some such characteristic patterns of valuation but that we should. It shapes and controls our history of responses to others in ways we can account for. The narratives of relationship I sustain, the ways I combine and order them, the continuations I find more valuable than others, and the losses I am willing to accept or impose are controlling structures of the moral life that is specifically mine, even where its matter includes an unpredictable lot of demands that originate with others with whom I'm connected by history or occasion. This is as true of episodic or distanced relationships to strangers as of intimate, personal, or committed ones; it is as true of choices about problems on the large scale as it is about those of everyday and close-by. There are always too many suffering strangers and worthwhile causes on the large scale. We *will* be selective, whether in individual or collective contributions. These selections reflect and refine a moral identity that gives our deliberations greater focus and refinement. Equally important, they let others know where we stand and what we stand for.

The narratives of relationship and identity inevitably intertwine. Our identities, moral and otherwise, are produced by and in histories of specific relationship, and those connections to others that invite or bind us are themselves the expression of some things we value. Yet there is a third kind of narrative that spans and supports both of these. It is a history of our shared understandings of what kinds of things, relationships, and commitments really are important, and what their relative importance is. This is the *narrative of moral values* progressively better, and sometimes differently, understood.

Throughout a person's life, moral choices confront her not only with problems of applying values and principles she acknowledges and understands to fresh cases but also with many problems of coming to understand how new situations are or aren't instances of certain previously acknowledged values or principles, and exactly what those values or principles really mean. Learning to refrain from dominating a child, condescending to a student, or depending too much on a partner may involve a new or extended understanding of what respect or self-respect can be. Terminating a lengthy friendship may involve insight into what friendship now means, or what loyalty does not.

Many moral choices reaffirm values and principles already understood and applied to new cases in familiar ways. Others bring under renewed scrutiny and reinterpretation those very standards themselves. So the narrative of "who I am" (or "who we are") and the narrative of "how we have gotten here together" is threaded through by another story, one about "what this means." The last involves a history of moral concepts acquired, refined, revised, displaced, and replaced, both by individuals and within some communities of shared moral understanding. Any moral concept has at a given time a familiar set of applications that reflects a history of choices made in light of it; think of the short, dynamic histories of modern concepts of "equality" or "rights." We learn progressively from our moral resolutions and their intelligibility and acceptability to ourselves and others who and how we are and what our moral concepts and standards mean.

This is essential to keeping moral justification coherent within and between us. I have to make sense to myself of what reasons I have for doing things, and this means not only valuing kinds of things but recognizing when it is those kinds of things that are at stake or at issue. One might be able to acquit oneself if one is able to say, "I was fair (kind, faithful, loyal, honest, generous, reasonable, etc.)"; yet it may be hard to decide whether one is entitled to say it. The indispensable test of both is submitting one's justification to others, sometimes (or especially) including others affected by my actions who might have wished for another outcome, always including those whose judgment one has reason to trust, and perhaps some untried bystanders for good measure. You may not get others to agree with what you have done, but you need them to recognize a possible moral justification for it in what you have to say for yourself.

Such tests are entirely fallible, and to make matters worse, the results may be mixed. This is because moral guidelines are not mechanical like Barthian rules, and this is because of the kinds of things they aim at and the purposes with which they aim at them. They aim at things important for us such as are recognizable between us, and which depend on people's care and responsibility for their maintenance. They aim at these things so that we can sustain a framework of mutual accountability that will work to preserve them. In the best case, this framework can preserve our understandings of the importance of these things even where it fails to prevent conflict over them or damage to them. Moral guidelines are not mechanical because things of importance are multiple, often multiply relative (in terms of importance to whom, for what, when, given what else), and (so) not obvious. This complexity is increased by the aim of shared understanding. Moral justification, then, is from the first and at the last interpersonal. It is with and from others we learn to do it, and learn that we must. It is to others we must bring it back to do the work it is intended for: to allow and require people to account to one another for the value and impact of what they do in matters of importance.

Just as—and because—individuals reshape their understandings of the values that ground reasons, so too do communities of people who hold each other morally accountable reconfigure over time the shared understandings that supply mutual justifications. Even the most private parts of our lives require a public justification, where this means shared intelligibility. "Private" justification in this sense is otherwise known as hypocrisy or self-deception. (And these are different again from simply acknowledging that one doesn't pretend to have anything to say on one's behalf, morally speaking. Given the alternatives of hypocrisy and self-deception, there are places where this is not the worst position one can take, even morally speaking.)

It's the coherence of each of the three narratives, and connections among them, that makes a distinctive moral life out of what could otherwise be an odd lot of disparate parts. Fabrics of life so woven may be more smooth or more knotty, some neatly and closely repetitive and some bold or even eccentric; different moral lives will have these forms of richness and regularity in varying degrees. A life's being so organized to some extent enables the person living that life to decide with good reason how and what to select, within the limits of moral acceptability, for most (or some) attention. At the same time, a life legible in these ways gives promise to others of reliable performance and accountability of specific kinds. This *nongeneric accountability* is one way the life we have is truly our own, and not interchangeable with others'.

Stories that support particular self- and mutual understandings and the distinctive responsibilities they entail are stories of distinctive and committing partiality. But they are only ever partial stories, ones limited by or dependent on other stories, and subject to change. A life which fails to support some such narratives seems unowned even if benign. Barth's man has no meaningful stories to tell, while the Rev. Shields's life has imploded into a megastory that is about nothing except its own telling. Just how much coherence and continuity make for integrity? I've already said I believe there is no satisfactory principled (i.e. formulaic) answer to this. But I do have a story about this. My answer comes in two parts. The first is about integrity's being not the coherence and continuity themselves, but something else they make possible in varying degrees, one's *moral reliability*. The second is about why more coherence, consistency, or continuity is not necessarily better, especially over the long haul of a life. We need only so much as will serve.

Integrity

"Integrity" is a term powerfully loaded with aesthetically attractive associations of wholeness and intactness. Magnetic images of unity and unspoiledness have exerted their pull on philosophers' discussions. It is not intuitive meanings by themselves but the sense a concept of integrity makes within a larger picture of moral life that argues for that concept. Even so, I too can invoke a familiar meaning, and images less pretty but sturdier, in supporting a view of integrity that reckons with how much of our lives is given to others, to change, and to things we cannot hope (and sometimes shouldn't wish) to control. Think of "integrity" used to describe the sturdiness of structures people have built, the property of holding up dependably under the weights and stresses these structures are apt to encounter given the purposes to which they are put and the conditions they might encounter.

I suggest integrity as a morally admirable quality is something like that. I think of integrity as a kind of *reliability*: reliability in the accounts we are prepared to give, act by, and stand by, in moral terms, and dependable responsiveness to the ongoing fit among our accounts, the ways we have acted, and the consequences and costs our actions have in fact incurred. This includes keeping reasonably straight what we are doing and whether the accounts we can give of it make sense; following through short and long term on what we have given to be expected; recognizing we can't always choose our tests or control all results for which we may have to account; and being disposed to repair and restore dependability when structures we have built in our lives teeter or fail.

Cheshire Calhoun has recently argued against several kinds of wholeness and purity views of integrity (Calhoun 1995). These views not only equate integrity with other things—volitional unity, psychological identity, the purity of rightness—but render integrity as essentially a self-directed and self-protective virtue rather than one "fitting us for proper social relations" (253). Calhoun proposes instead a relational view of integrity as "the virtue of having a proper regard for one's own judgment as a deliberator among deliberators" (259), of standing up for one's own best judgment under pressures and penalties from other people. A person shows integrity in taking responsibility for her part in the collective work of determining how to live. Hypocrites lack integrity, for example, because they deliberately mislead us about what is worth doing (258).

But hypocrites do not necessarily mislead us about what is worth doing; they do mislead us about what it is *they* may be relied upon by us to do. As codeliberators they may represent worthy and admirable views. Yet even where they do so, they knowingly mislead us into reasonable expectations of performance on which we might, to our grief, rely. If we do so rely, and are deserted, the last thing a committed hypocrite will do is account for herself by acknowledging it was her moral veneer, not the trust it invited, by which she steered her (and so our) course. She will either redirect her moral display to fresh audiences, or try to reengineer its credibility in our eyes. This leaves us in the original lurch; and it lays the welcome mat down for us or others on the edge of the next abyss.

I share Calhoun's view that it is a relational conception of integrity we need, a conception that makes it interpersonally, and not just intrapersonally, indispensable. Responsibly contributing to the common deliberative weal by testament of conviction and action under social pressure is a central aspect of the moral reliability I have in mind. I want to place more emphasis on the fallibility and limitations of both our deliberative efforts and our attempts to live up to their results, and how and whether we face what we are accountable for even (or especially) when things come apart. I want to get at how integrity is reliability not only at the outset, in the having of firm and coherent convictions and publicly expressing them, but also after the fact, in various reparative responses, sometimes including changes of moral course. The point coming and going is our being reliably responsible in matters of our own and others goods, as well as keeping clear and vibrant the shared understanding of them.

Narratives of moral identity, relationship, and value help us determine matters we may be more or less reliable in, and so more or less securely relied upon by ourselves and others. But these are *kinds* of stories; it's a short step to noticing that within any life there may be multiple actual narratives of a given type—more than one story of identity, relationship or value. With respect to relationships this is obvious. I am someone's daughter, sister, lover, friend; a colleague, teacher, and neighbor to more; and a friend of several kinds to many others; and so on. My self-understanding and sense of accountability might vary in these relationships (and I may not equally respect, like, approve of, or understand myself in all of them). If I do endorse some collection of these versions of me, I may not be able to cover them with any single story. My interpretations of values and the application of principles may not be uniform across different domains, relationships, or roles. My moral identities may also be plural. The structure of my commitments in certain official roles may differ from that in private encounters, for example, or my life may show stages or alternating periods during which my orderings and understandings of value may be distinct. I do not mean only that one may be inconsistent or undependable, although this is true. I mean also that one may be *differently reliable*, depending on what is at issue. Most people are.

Sometimes one has to *become* differently reliable than one has been. Circumstance can thrust upon one new responsibilities that require the reordering of others, or situations can reveal that existing responsibilities are no longer jointly sustainable. Sometimes the pressure for change or redistribution or differentiation arises out of moral concern itself. It's importantly misleading, though, to figure all the shifts and changes in the moral structure of people's lives as if morality itself were the engine of these people's lives. It's not. Sometimes people and possibilities just change; lives are regularly reordered by complex synergies of choice and chance. This may mean certain commitments are off, with various consequences, including moral ones. In some cases one may be culpable for injuries or losses to others. Then new reliabilities are at issue. One may be more or less reliable in repairing or compensating for damage; or one may simply be relied upon to own up, whether one can fix anything or there's anything left to fix. Whether or not there is damage to reckon, the reestablishment of reliability after changes in course—not staying in formation as before, but being *again reliably responsible* from here— may be fairly described as integrity. Sometimes, it's a matter of starting over when everything's gone to hell.

In thinking about integrity, I'm trying to curb a temptation to focus exclusively on admirable performance right out of the gate, that is, on cases of sticking by principles or doing as one believes despite temptation or pressure. In fact, people are often said to have integrity when they've already muffed things, miscalled outcomes, left damage, and then take such responsibility as ensues. Again, it's common to attribute integrity to someone who finds a way to honor commitments or act creditably in a situation compromised by someone else's bad behavior, recklessness, or ineptitude. Sometimes the two combine when someone shoulders burdens of setting right what he or she alone has not made to come undone. A central use of "integrity" then is to describe not only people who act well from, as it were, a standing position but also people who own up to and clean up messes, their own and others. People who don't beg off, weasel out, or deflect flack toward others as life lurches on have integrity. That some people never do this, and most people cannot always do this, makes integrity something admirable. We are lucky that many of us do this as often as we do; very much that we value for us and between us would be lost without it.[3]

I take these observations about integrity to be commonplaces. Integrity is commonly associated with forms of responsibility-taking where people might be tempted to do otherwise and things would go noticeably easier for them (and sometimes worse for others) if they did. It is especially linked with specific performances or histories of choice where opportunities to get away with or from something (such as the expectations one has invited or the comeuppance one deserves) are forgone. Often people restrict judgments of integrity to specific performances impressive in these ways ("it took integrity for her to . . . ," "he showed integrity when he . . ."). Integrity doesn't need to have a whole-life referent. In short, integrity involves being reliably accountable in terms of commitments and values, and ready to respond to the results of the accounting. It can be more or less *local*.

None of this requires a moral actor whose life is "of a piece," whose defining commitments are unconditional, or who is being faithful to a true self.[4] Lives are usually of many pieces, not always stably processing in unconflicting parallel lines. If one has more than a single significant responsibility or cherishes more than a single person, thing, or value, it is not possible to guarantee that the demands of some may not condition the fulfillment of others. And if a self is a bearer of values and responsibilities for them, and these are multiple and sometimes competitive, then the self to which one would be true is not just given. That self is constructed and affirmed in intertwined histories of identity, relationship, and value. A good deal that is true *of* it consists in what it finds it can be true *to*.

A view of selves that fits with this ethics is one in which a self itself is understood in terms of a history of relationships among its various temporally distant and concurrent aspects. We are layers of various overlapping histories of traces of many encounters and relationships; these coexist in various states of stratification or alternation as we live our lives. My present self owes debts to my past one, and my future self is deeply dependent on the choices and self-understandings of my present one. I owe things to myself in these and perhaps other ways, just as I owe things to others for which they reasonably or crucially depend on me. This layered, nested, and "ensemble subjectivity" might sound a little exotic; I have tried to show that it and its kind of integrity are familiar.[5] I have suggested we not think of this integrity as something inward and nonrelational, something buried deep inside to which one answers and may answer more or less truthfully. Instead, we should think of it as the actual display of reliable accountability and resilient dependability that we have many occasions to measure in each other and ourselves by the yardstick of shareable justification applied to narratives of varying lengths.

Morally guiding narratives are very coarse grids over the complexity of lives. If they were not coarse grids, we would not be able to use them, any more than we could use a map that replicated a landscape in every detail. Their point is the simplification that allows us to mark out and follow a route. First-person stories rightly enjoy a significant privilege, for although they often collect what has gone before in later edited or revised versions, their use is importantly prospective. We use them to determine how we might or must go on with the life only we, after all, can lead. Their privilege, however, is not that of incorrigibility. Others may call them into question, may impeach our cogency, sincerity, or integrity in trying to account for ourselves by means of them. Others may be in a position, in more ways than one, to press upon us corrections or alternatives. That this is so belongs to moral justification as essentially *between* people. But the pressures exerted on our mutually sense-making stories need themselves to be morally evaluated from more than one point of view.

Stories We Can Tell

People's lives aren't stories, but we do, it seems, tend to understand them in that way. A burgeoning field of narrative psychology studies the conditions of this form of understanding of our lives, while claims on behalf of narrative as a form of moral understanding have taken root in ethics. In one of the best known of these, Alasdair MacIntyre has claimed that people's lives *are* stories because "action itself has a basically historical character" (MacIntyre 1981, 197). MacIntyre further claims that a self is "the subject of a narrative that runs from one's birth to one's death," and identifies the meaningfulness of that narrative/life with "its movement toward a climax or *telos*" (202), a structure that he describes as a quest (203).

The idea that a life is or has or will support a single or master story is vastly stronger than the claim that an action "is a moment in a possible or actual history" (199). The story in which some action is a moment might be a simple, local, or short one, one story among others within a life. And an action's being a moment in a story need not mean more than its being understood as some action or other only in some story or other. Our *re*descriptions of parts of our lives may transplant actions from one story to another, or may individuate actions themselves differently. Telling and retelling parts of our lives, we might avail ourselves of multiple and changing descriptive options. We don't need a view stronger than this: People make sense of, or give significance to, events in their and others' lives, including their own and others' actions, by embedding them in some story or other. Yet such story lines as make sense of different actions might be many, local, fragmentary, or discontinuous. Ones that persist are apt to have earlier and later editions.

There are, further, reasons *not* to assume that such story lines are, can be, or should be global or largely unified or strictly continuous. *Can* one imagine a totally or maximally unified life? Above I suggested this did not fit with the normal complexity of human lives, hopes, and cares. When I try to imagine maximal integration I find myself imagining something either desperately simple or intolerably suffocating. I picture new strands of story with unforeseeable implications being smothered to avoid potential conflict or threat. I picture tired stories being dutifully tended and maintained because they are integral to the existing plot. I picture something especially onerous for those who feel that others have had a disproportionate hand in writing stories for them that are limiting, cruel, oppressive, or alienating to some things they sense but do not (yet) have stories available to express. I picture frustration for ones whose stories have withered or blown up or grown painfully strained, and who need quite new ones. These are at least reasons to be suspicious of maximal integration as a *uniform* ideal. So much of the matter and form of stories we can tell are not things we can unilaterally choose or control, and some of us less so than others.

Yet the idea of maximal, substantial, or overarching unity exerts an attraction on otherwise very different contemporary moral philosophies. MacIntyre likes the image of a quest, and Charles Taylor adopts it as well (Taylor 1989). In John Rawls's influential work "a person may be regarded as a human life lived according to a plan" (Rawls 1971, 408), a more buttoned-down but still fairly robust version of central organization both as a presumption of and prescription for lives. Bernard Williams criticizes Rawls for thinking life plans can nail down rational evaluation (in particular, judgments about the worth of lives and the actions that determine them) *in advance*. When it comes to the retrospective assessments of choices Williams likes to defend, however, his tastes run to cases of "life roulette," in which the tenability of a *whole life* (or the agent's integrity in it) hangs on whether a high-stakes constitutive project pans out (Williams 1981b, 33–36). It's not only philosophers who like the idea of a single dominant story line. Biographers are ever tempted by the master trope which contains and lends color to a telling of someone else's life. But some evidence suggests that real life and real time life-narrations are changeable, flexible, and strategic, even while constrained by significant assumptions.

Some recent studies of specifically autobiographical memory find that memories are found in tellings of who we are and where we've been, and that these tellings retrieve and reconstruct events selectively (Neisser and Fivush 1994; Rubin 1986). The production of our accounts of ourselves follow socially recognized forms and occasions of telling. They are sensitive to how we remember, and for whom, and why. They are controlled by both standing and shifting purposes, and rendered in "culturally

familiar narrative forms" (Bruner 1994, 47). Even where inaccurate, our
rememberings show certain typical forms of error or bias; some of them,
for example, involving general beliefs about the likelihood of consistency in people or situations over time. Studies of jury deliberations
show that third-party reconstructions of events and behavior are also
accomplished by composing continuing stories; credibility of third- as of
first-person narratives follows both general criteria of plausibility (detail,
causal connection) and background assumptions that vary with jurors'
experience (*New York Times* 1992).

Many features of our accounts of ourselves vary with cultural environments and social situations. Conceptions of personality, and narrative templates and practices, are among the things that tell us how to
tell. Anthropologist Clifford Geertz remarks, "The Western conception
of the person as a bounded, unique, more or less integrated motivational
and cognitive universe, a dynamic center of awareness, emotion, judgment, and action organized into a distinctive whole and set contrastively
both against other such wholes and against its social and natural background, is, however incorrigible it may seem to us, a rather peculiar idea
within the context of the world's cultures" (Geertz 1983, 59). Michael
Walzer describes an immediately recognizable late-model version of this
centered self: "It is not every kind of life that is lived according to a
plan. Today we commonly think of our lives as projects, undertakings in
which we ourselves are the undertakers, the entrepreneurs, the managers
and organizers of our own activities, extended over time, planned in
advance, aimed at a goal ... —this is what we mean by a *career*"
(Walzer 1994, 23).

These career selves would seem to be ideal subjects for highly unified
lives. Although the career self enjoys special prominence in some contemporary American moral philosophy, late-twentieth-century Ameri-
cans in Jerome Bruner's studies of spontaneous autobiographical
accounts are fond of decisive "turning points" (Bruner 1994, 41). Even
if these are career selves, they seem to change careers occasionally.
Bruner thinks his narrators trade off global consistency in order to
retrieve a position of decisive agency at times; in our culture, he adds,
turning points often appear as "second chances." Thus are there culturally normed patterns for the stories of our lives and their parts.

But do all people have that first chance to be this or some other culturally dominant and valued sort of self, or to tell any story of their lives
or the parts of them? I think the answer is obviously "no," and this
bears on which lives are judged to have integrity.

Hard(er) Lives

One view is that people who are subordinated or oppressed cannot possess integrity, or are likely to be able to achieve only a hobbled or inferior version of it. This is then one more injustice done to those who are oppressed: A significant moral good, and a source of self-respect and others' admiration, is denied to them. This view may be supported by the thought that subordinated people's lives are evidently not their own, either insufficiently under their own control for them to set their own courses more than marginally, or too ridden by others' control and demands for them to follow through reliably on such courses as they might set.

I reject this view. Although I assume that very many things human beings have to or want to do are made harder, even excruciatingly costly, by deprivation or oppression, I think the belief that integrity is out of reach for people under conditions of social disadvantage represents a confusion, a mistake, or a temptation. The assumptions underlying this belief need to be confronted and resisted. If lives are our own because of the circumstances thrown our ways and because of the distinctive commitments and attachments we make under those circumstances, and if integrity is admirable reliability in response to such demands as we then face, the issue for integrity is how well we respond to our lot and its demands. There is no reason to think that many human beings under circumstances of subordination, oppression, or unfreedom of many types do not exhibit valor, perseverance, lucidity, and ingenuity in staying true to what they value within the confines of their situations. These very confines may set the stage for exemplary achievements in just this regard.

There can be a confusion here between displaying integrity and possessing autonomy, especially in the uncontroversial sense of possessing some minimum of self-determination and socially approved or protected latitude for choice, defined either absolutely or comparatively. There is a difference between being forced to live a life very much not of one's own choosing, or being deprived of means or opportunity to live a life one most or more prefers, on the one hand, and failing to lead whatever life one happens to have with integrity, on the other. Integrity in the reliability sense and autonomy in the social-political sense may co-vary inversely. Terrible social burdens and injustices are born by many with courage, dignity, and fidelity to what and whom they love, whereas the

social privileges of others permit (and perhaps contain or deflect the effects of) irresponsible, craven, or dishonorable commitments and actions.

Neither will it do to identify integrity with something like autonomy in the more elusive and disputed psychological sense of one's being under control of the rational parts of one's self, or the parts of oneself one most identifies with, or the parts of oneself that best stand up to critical review, or the skills for the relevant kinds of review itself. Let's suppose one could connect integrity with these modes of psychological function and show that these modes are morally valuable, or superior to some others. Then the view that socially subordinated people lack integrity would be the claim that they (invariably? typically?) are psychologically (if not morally) stunted or damaged, that they are incapable of optimal forms of adult self-awareness and self-control. Of course, some people might be so incapable, but does one want to suggest that this incapacity or childishness inveterately or especially tracks social disadvantage; and if so, which ones? Which oppressions, marginalizations, or subordinations would be parts of the etiology of this particular incapacity? For they are not all the same. Oppressed or subordinated people do not form a natural kind, nor are conditions of subordination uniform.

Leaving autonomy aside, might there be reason to think that subordinated people are less true, within whatever limits apply, to what they care about because they are more corruptible or less resolute? I don't think we need to assume that people under varied conditions of disadvantage are typically more likely than more privileged others to be swayed or bribed or timorous or cravenly ingratiating or self-abasing or opportunistic or duplicitous. And it would be distorting to equate conscious strategies of evasion and survival to which people must resort under direct threat, supervision, or control with general depravity. These strategies may be the very things that allow those in subordinate positions to make and be true to commitments of their own. No one should assume that lives lacking certain or many privileges are characteristically or uniformly reduced to the compliance, complicity, even slavishness, that their oppressors demand or their betters fantasize. As Maria Lugones reminds those with white-skin privilege, "not all the selves we are make you important" (Lugones 1991, 42). These hypotheses sound more like familiar rationales for subordination or disadvantage than like critical responses to it.[6]

bell hooks confronts directly the association of moral inferiority with

poverty: "I went to college believing there was no connection between poverty and personal integrity. . . . I was shocked by representations of the poor learned in classrooms. . . . I had been taught in a culture of poverty to be intelligent, honest, to work hard, and always to be a person of my word. I had been taught to stand up for what I believed was right, to be brave and courageous. . . . These lessons . . . were taught to me by the poor, the disenfranchised, the underclass" (hooks 1994, 167). In classrooms where the topic is ethics, I too have heard unself-conscious comment on the lesser capacity or rectitude of those who are less advantaged by those more so.

Cruelties and burdens imposed by oppressive conditions inflict miserable costs and terrible losses on people, including psychic ones. Being rendered unable to undertake certain commitments or being thwarted in one's best attempts to fulfill them, and the frustration, rage, and shame this can provoke, may be among the costs and losses. I don't deny this, and I don't suppose hooks would either. But the nature of the costs and their toll on individuals are apt to vary with individual situations, temperaments, and resources of several kinds. There are differences in the supports supplied by oppressed communities to their members, and differences in the degrees of control and forms of enforcement that different hierarchies demand. It is the blanket assumption of diminished integrity I reject as unnecessary and implausible.

This assumption is also perilously mystifying. It deflects scrutiny of the kinds of responsibility and tests of commitment that privileged positions may allow some to duck or hand off to others (Tronto 1993). It also diverts attention from the ways individuals' lives and the stories they could tell of them may be *disqualified* for some audiences as expressions of moral achievement no matter what those individuals do.

Not everyone is allowed or enabled to tell just any life (or other) story. The stuff of lives to be told, the discursive means available for telling them, and the credibility of storytellers are apt to differ along familiar lines of class, gender, and race, and perhaps along other lines, even rather local ones, as well.[7] Life stories, including moral histories, will take shape in response to specific constraints, and for some people may be shaped as much for them as by them. Kathryn Addelson reminds us that "some people have the authority or power to define the terms in which their own and other people's stories are to be officially narrated" (Addelson 1991, 120). And some people's standards of intelligibility may rule "informally," protected from challenge by the challengers' lack of socially recognized credibility.

This suggests another view about a special problem of integrity under conditions of subordination or oppression. The recognition of integrity (as of other esteemed qualities or achievements) may be denied to those subordinated, and the life-interpretations that support the ascription of integrity to them may be replaced or erased, by others. The others who can do this are those with the power to confer this recognition authoritatively in the eyes of others like them. Some people's disqualification from giving certain accounts of themselves and being understood in the ways they intend to be can be part of the apparatus of "culturally normative prejudice" (Meyers 1994, 51–56). One obvious way to disqualify people is to restrict recognition to certain roles or pursuits, and to preclude certain people's occupation of those roles or engagement in those pursuits. This strategy will fail, though, whenever it is noticed that integrity and other morally valuable qualities are not in fact coincident with or utterly dependent on the occupation of specific social roles; possession and exhibition of courage, for example, are not restricted to battlefield behavior.

What works more effectively in moral disqualification is rigging not only some aspects of lives but dominant interpretations of them, thereby biasing the understandings of ourselves and others that the interpretations serve. To the extent that lives themselves can't be cut to fit the approved stories of them, the socially sustained authority of some people and some stories will make offending or anomalous matter of some others' lives disappear or appear distortedly—and this despite whatever self-descriptions offenders might prefer or invent (Addelson 1994). If for the official record, formal or informal, some people's self-respect is insubordination, their courage impulsiveness, their loyalty stealth, their magnanimity stupidity, their rational restraint servility, then their integrity cannot be coherently claimed, or if claimed, the claim cannot be credited.

Vivid first-order depictions of a savagely oppressive social order and the actual workings of rigged intelligibility are found in American slave narratives. These stories detail the unrelenting cruelty, the commonplace violence, the continuous humiliation of being held as property, and the denial of humanity visited on black slaves, as well as the bizarre strategies of tailored intelligibility needed by white Christian masters. They also present stunning counterexamples to the blanket thesis that oppression precludes integrity. Indeed, one of the strongest impressions made by stories like Harriet Jacobs's *Incidents In the Life of a Slave Girl* (Gates 1987) is of the extraordinary moral integrity shown repeatedly by their protagonists, often under conditions that seem unendurable.

At the same time, stories like Jacobs's exhibit strategic finesse in addressing their intended audiences. Sometimes their authors invoke conventional norms (e.g., sexual purity, scrupulous honesty) to give plausible, if contextually oversimple, justifications of what they do. At others, they admit to defying these norms with forms of stealth, deception, violence, or "improper" sexual behavior, but appeal to readers' sympathy, or more riskily to their identification and empathy, in defense. They must convincingly demonstrate their capacities for moral judgment and responsibility, even while being careful never simply to presume their entitlement to the rank of moral subjects. Narrative devices and conventions are used to subvert or outflank resistance to the credibility of these accounts and the moral urgency of what they tell. These are artful "counterstories" (Nelson 1995), which are as interesting conceptually as they are emotionally moving and historically important.

Of course, these stories are political documents and rhetorical feats; I am not suggesting they are the everyday stories that most of us use to make sense of our lives, or that Harriet Jacobs herself so used hers. What these narratives exemplify are the possibilities for cogent and powerful stories of moral achievement and integrity under unendurable conditions. Their rhetorical art shows acute awareness of how difficult it might be for these stories to be received as credible accounts at once of outrageous injustice and exemplary moral achievement under its yoke. Their ingenuity shows something about obstacles to ordinary sense-making narratives and about possibilities of overcoming them. They illuminate the complexities of unrigging and reweaving eccentric and deadly webs of interpersonal intelligibility constructed so that some people are "inexpressible" to some others as persons at all.

At times, some people are expressible to others only as a certain kind of person. Women vastly more privileged than slaves have contested their canonical, gendered scripts of motherhood, daughterhood, sexuality, or housewifery. The reason is not simply that these gender scripts are normative or relational, for men's are too. These are normative stories of relational and *subsumed* identities, ones which are seen in our society as functions of, or in terms of functions for, someone else (whether or not women themselves always so see them).[8] The women to whom they apply are pressed toward self-descriptions that serve plot functions in someone else's tale within societies in which having one's own story, quest, or career is emblematic of full moral agency (see chapter 6). Subsumed self-descriptions buttress claims on women's dependability that are at once disadvantaging and not individually negotiable. Normative stories may be so culturally legislative for some women's lives that alternative stories are not found intelligible, or are translated into failed (or crazy) versions of the normatively preferred ones. One might still exhibit integrity within these constraints. But the costs of achieving it may be unnecessarily steep and ill-distributed, on the one hand, whereas its achievement may yet be ignored, denied, or deflatingly misdescribed, on the other.

When feminists discuss integrity, and they have done so conspicuously, their concerns look different from those of nonfeminist accounts that focus on wholeness or purity (Calhoun 1995; Davion 1991; Lugones 1990; Card 1989; Hoagland 1988; Rich 1979). The feminist discussions are concerned with impediments and resistances to women's understanding what they themselves are doing. They address irresolvable conflicts between self-interpretations available to women (and others) in found and chosen communities, endorse radical, life-disrupting changes feminist consciousness may induce, and challenge women to resist pressures and bribes to turn against themselves or other women. I think many feminists are concerned with the fit or the misfit between women's self-understandings and women's social lives.

Women and men in many situations of subordination, oppression, or marginality may find themselves targeted for normative narratives that are already given, coercive, not negotiable, and disadvantaging. Maintaining integrity is hardly the only challenge in such straits, but it is important to understand the kind of challenge it is. My account of the supporting narratives of identity, relationship, and value, under demands of interpersonal intelligibility, offers a framework for looking at ways we keep clear what we are to ourselves and others and what our moral values actually mean. Some challenges to doing this fall differently, or more heavily, on some people than on others. I've urged critical examination of the social definition and distribution of discursive resources, credibility, and dominant conventions of intelligibility. These determine whether and how lives can be told, to whom they can be told, and what effects their telling has. Available ways of telling lives in stories, and their social intelligibility and prestige for certain audiences, raise questions. Who's kept quiet? What's left out?

Coda: A Cautionary Tail

Narrative constructions of lives rest on particular assumptions about those lives and place particular demonds on them (see, for example,

Smith and Watson 1996). Moral philosophy needs to examine the usefulness, "naturalness," and effects of narrative construction in moral philosophy and elsewhere. Narratives impose structure and make an important kind of sense, but so do motifs, tropes, emblematic patterns archetypes, styles, rhythms, or themes. The vogue for narrative stylization breeds more-is-better temptations toward narratives of ambitious kinds—global ones with robust emplotment and a climactic momentum, for example. Perhaps narrative ethics and psychology are too comfortably fitted to disciplines that produce those enterprising career selves, who'd better always make sure they know where they're going and who'd better always be going somewhere. These are the selves who are "made" for those saving second chances. Why so few chances? Did everyone have a first chance? And, who's keeping score?[9]

six

Career Selves

Plans, Projects, and Plots
in "Whole" Life Ethics

Far safer to practise being articulate about the external and ideological bases
of selfhood, because this leads to straight talk about the kind of community
and the kind of culture we want to protect.

—Mary Douglas, *Risk and Blame*

There has been a metaphysical prejudice always that if a thing is really real,
it has to last either forever or for a fairly decent length of time. That is to my
mind an entire mistake. The things that are really real last a very short time.

—Bertrand Russell, *The Philosophy of Logical Atomism*

"Autonomous man," that centerpiece of modern Western culture and
protagonist of modern moral philosophy, has come in for quite a drub-
bing in ethics recently. That this man is disembodied, disembedded,
unencumbered, affectless, isolated, detached, unpleasantly self-interested, defensively self-protective, abnormally self-reliant, and narcissisti-
cally self-reflective was a drumbeat of the past decade or two in certain
quarters. Communitarians have tended to argue this could be *no* actual
man at all, while feminists have tended to argue that this could only
actually be some *man* (a male individual quite particularly placed) in the
social life of a society like ours. These objections pull in different directions: One has autonomous man as a kind of myth or fiction, while the
other has it as a projection of the real social position and prerogatives of
some of us, albeit in a highly idealized rendering. Somewhere between
false consciousness and real privilege falls the shadow. But the stake for
critics in exposing autonomous man as either illusory or unrepresenta-
tive is similar. If there is something wrong with this picture of a (or

"the") moral actor, there is something wrong with the moral philosophies that presuppose or elaborate it, as important forms of modern and
contemporary moral theory do.

In this chapter, I come neither to bury autonomous man nor to praise
him, but to ask what he is, really. I examine the guises in which he
appears in three influential depictions of "the moral agent" and "the
moral life" in twentieth-century ethics—those of John Rawls, Bernard
Williams, and Charles Taylor. There is something wrong in these
philosophers' depictions of moral agents and their lives. They treat an
aspirational ideal for a moral agent as if it were a constitutive requirement of being one, and they treat as a uniform measure an ideal to
which not everyone has been encouraged or allowed to aspire even in
those places where the ideal has obtained. My interest in these mistakes,
however, is to show how they are rooted in something not uncommon
that these philosophers are doing. They are presenting a culturally
embedded and socially situated ideal of character, a richly normative
self-conception that certain selves in particular places at specific times
find intimately familiar and personally compelling. But they are presenting it as if it were a kind of culturally transcendent constitutive fact
about being a "person" or "agent" or "moral subject" at all; as if it
were just "our nature," instead of something some people had learned,
perhaps by an arduous and restricted apprenticeship, to try to be.

If I am correct about these mistakes—this "misplacing" of autonomous man—this still says nothing about the moral worth of the ideal
or the particular forms of life which support or demand it. It will only
clarify what it is we are appraising if we go on to a moral evaluation of
this moral ideal. The difference between *situating* a moral ideal and
morally evaluating it is important, because to spotlight connections
between philosophical conceptions and culturally specific practices,
ways of life, and positions in them, is often taken, and often intended, as
a deflationary strategy, as a kind of unmasking, debunking, or discredit-
ing of the philosophical conceptions. But my own conception of morality is that of culturally embedded practices of responsibility. So I cannot
look upon the intricate meshing of moral with other social practices in
specific lifeways as second best to some other kind morality, much less as
a kind of scam. A socially critical moral epistemology needs to look at
that mesh closely, however, so that it can begin to understand what
moral understandings it makes available (and to whom), enforceable
(and by whom), and both of these at what costs (and for whom).

The moral philosophers I discuss below are doing what moral

philosophers do. They are reflecting, refining, and elaborating certain images of moral personality and relations, certain exemplary moral identities and allied lives, certain distributions of responsibility of particular kinds. Moral philosophers do this from within their situations in the midst of social identities, institutions, and practices, some of which are more familiar or salient to them than others are. Yet consistent with the genre of moral philosophy as we have it, the accounts they produce of certain positions, postures, and lives often are given and taken as disinterested, indeed rationally critical, examinations of what moral agency, autonomy, or responsibility simply "are," and what people and lives look like when they exhibit these. These accounts, however, are not just descriptions. They are idealizations and defenses (one might say, idealized defenses) of certain conceptions: They affirm these as terms which should govern our moral assessments of ourselves and others.

While depictions like the ones examined below are not just reports, they are hardly mere fancies and speculations, either. These accounts defend ideas and ideals that are familiar to people who share in a particular form of social life to which these ideas and ideals belong, and for which they make a kind of sense they might not make elsewhere. The philosophers' defenses participate in maintaining or transforming moral understandings fitted to the form of social life the philosophers share with others to whom these conceptions make sense. These forms of life depend on many things, including things repeatedly and characteristically said about them from authoritative positions, including the positions of moral philosophers, and accepted or repeated in many other places. But a lot of other things must obtain for the things that are said to make sense. These include many specific features of ways we live now; or, to put the right emphasis on it, ways *we* live *now*. My aim, then, is to situate a certain normative conception of a moral agent in the places in which it makes sense and in the viewpoints from which it seems obvious or compelling. But this involves noticing other views from other places.[1]

Life Planning

Kathryn Addelson has recently offered a troubling slant on depictions of persons and their lives in contemporary philosophical discourses featuring autonomy and rational choice. Addelson calls the universalist ethics of autonomous actors an "individualist planning ethics." It enshrines as a moral ideal the proper and successful form of life of middle-class people in a particular kind of liberal-democratic and capitalist society pervaded and directed by experts and their special knowledges. A "planning motif" is "*basic* to the individualist ethics of democratic state and market" (Addelson 1994, 45), Addelson says, but is reproduced by some contemporary moral philosophers—some among those experts with special authority to describe and define things—"as if it captured the truth and reality of human nature and social and natural environments" (116). Rationality and autonomy (characteristics with premier value in certain kinds of modern ethics, sometimes treated as necessary or constitutive conditions of moral agency, even personhood) are strongly identified with being able to adopt a plan of life and carry it out.

Unsurprisingly to readers of contemporary moral philosophy, Addelson quotes a famous passage from John Rawls's *A Theory of Justice* as the star example of life-planning rampant on a field of middle-class expectations of control, stability, and (socially mediated) reward. The passage quoted includes the statement that

> a person's good is determined by what is for him the most rational long-term plan of life given reasonably favorable circumstances. . . . We are to suppose, then, that each individual has a rational plan of life drawn up subject to the conditions that confront him. It schedules activities so that various desires can be fulfilled without interference. It is arrived at by rejecting other plans that are either less likely to succeed or do not provide for such an inclusive attainment of aims. (Rawls 1971, 92–93, quoted in Addelson 1994, 108)[2]

Addelson unsettlingly juxtaposes this familiar passage from Rawls with one from Lee Rainwater's 1960 book *And the Poor Get Children* based on a study for Planned Parenthood of how to overcome obstacles to "family planning" in the attitudes of working-class people. This passage is not likely to be familiar, so I quote most of what Addelson quotes:

> The ideas of family planning and planned parenthood embody a particular world view, a particular way of looking at the world and oneself. . . .
>
> Planning means that one looks ahead, orients himself toward the future, and commits himself and others to some courses of action. Middle class people are used to doing this, and the ramified consequences of looking ahead and making commitments characterize the middle class way of life in connection not only with the family but

also with the worlds of work, education, voluntary association, and the like. Middle class people live in a matrix of commitments toward the future, in terms of personal goals, and to other people in terms of reasonably clear-cut obligations. Planning thus involves a picture of the way things will be in the future and of the way one will be and act then (Rainwater, quoted in Addleson 1994, 107).

I can't do justice to the way Addelson uses this comparison in her book about cognitive authority, the social contests that make moral problems public, and the moral responsibilities of professionals, including philosophers, as participants in this process (see Addelson 1993 for a briefer account). What Addelson emphasizes just here is the contrast between Rainwater's clear recognition of the "class basis" (and we might say, more broadly, the cultural specificity) of the ideal and expectation of "planned lives," even as he endorses the "maturity" of the outlook, and the absence of this kind of awareness or admission in Rawls, even as "a persons's good" is defined through the notion of a life plan.

One might complain that it is unfair to Rawls both to exhibit this view out of context of the whole of his book, and to fail to note that Rawls has now, long since, situated his views about justice. They are ones meant only to exhibit the structure of a conception of justice rooted in a particular kind of modern, liberal-democratic society (Rawls 1980 and 1993). But many other parts of the original book support the construction of the principles embodying justice as fairness, and it is not clear how local those supporting ideas are acknowledged by Rawls to be. When Rawls introduces life plans in the passage just cited, he identifies the theory of the good that implicates them as a "familiar" one going back to Aristotle, and present in Kant and Sidgwick (Rawls 1971, 92). The Aristotelian principle of enjoying the perfection of our capacities, which is intimately connected in Rawls's account with the planning structure of a good life, is "accepted" as "a natural fact" (428). In later work Rawls does see his conception of justice not as the true one, but as "now the most reasonable for us" as members of a certain cultural tradition at a particular historical point. The social role of this conception of justice is to justify certain arrangements to all citizens "whatever their social position or more particular interests" (Rawls 1980, 517). Yet this conception of justice is rooted in "our" conception of ourselves as persons and is addressed to those "who regard their person and their relation to society in a certain way" (ibid).

When the quoted passage is placed in fuller context (407ff.) it intensifies the sense that Rawls is indeed talking not only about a particular kind of life but speaking from assumptions available from a particular kind of place within it. It is in these pages that Rawls affirms the rationality of "postponement" (410), the importance of "scheduling" (ibid.), the virtues of "inclusiveness" (412) (arranging to satisfy more aims rather than fewer), the demanding architecture of "subplans suitably arranged in a hierarchy" (411) that reflects a hierarchy of desires. The main thing is to know where one is going over the long haul in order to get as much as possible of what one wants; one's wants in turn had better be known very much in advance, too. Fortunately, local "revisions" "do not usually" threaten the overall structure (ibid.).

These and other considerations lead to the remarkable and oft-remarked "guiding principle that a rational individual is always to act so that he need never blame himself no matter how his plans finally work out" (422). The right kind of planfulness puts one "above reproach" (422). At the same time, though, it makes one liable to moral shame. One is morally shamed by those failures of planning and action that lead to busted plans and the loss of others' esteem that this invites (444). When the form of planned living is joined to the Aristotelian principle—that we especially enjoy the exercise of our realized capacities, and the more realized and complex the capacity the more we enjoy it—there's a bit of "a race" between increasing satisfaction and the "strenuous and difficult" learning that supports it (428). The planning itself sounds strenuous and difficult, but Rawls emphasizes that the characterization of the planned life is "hypothetical" and does not imply that one should be "continually planning and calculating" (423); planning activities, too, are to be fitted into a rational plan of life in ways that make sense (424).

In a variety of respects this is a perfectly recognizable kind of life—to me, and I suppose to many of Rawls's readers. Many of the kinds of things many of us have wanted and were proud to have gotten were available only at significant prices of planning, postponement, preparation, prevision. On the other hand, there is something puzzling and alien to me in this brief characterization, even adjusting for the obvious simplication and idealization. I am puzzled that someone would think the degree of clairvoyant control involved in Rawlsian life-planning could possibly be part of a normal form description of the way "people" do and can go about their lives, regardless of the social environments in which they go about them. At the same time, I recognize with resentment how many things that *are* parts of a normal form of life for very many people in a particular social environment count (and are felt) as failures and occasions for shame, when they appear under the aspect of lack or loss of control. They appear under that aspect in the very form of social life that makes the successfully planned life both a (restricted) possibility and a powerful ideal. The entropy of pregnancies and illnesses, the unpredictable care of vulnerable and dependent persons, and the shabbinesses of poverty and its lack of insulation from the catastrophic effects of "changes at the lower levels" of plans (411) are among these.

I think Addelson's main point here cannot be rejected out of hand. There is a recognizable norm at work here, recognizable to people in a certain kind of society where its fulfillment both requires certain specific kinds of resources and powers, and in turn tends to confer more of these. But the question to be posed is, would this conception of our persons make sense to just any one of "us," much less to anyone anywhere? Could it? I believe the answer to the latter is pretty obviously "no." Individually and robustly planned lives could not, for example, have made sense to very many people in Western societies several hundred years ago. It is important to pause over this question on the way to the one that is central to moral theorizing: Should this form of life make sense to us, indeed, command our allegiance to the many practices and institutions that make it, more than available, to various extents *required*? We need to assay its actual conditions, costs, and alternatives.

Rawls says, to sum up his explanation of the planning structure for whole lives, "If this conception of plans is sound, we should expect that the good things in life are, roughly speaking, those activities and relationships which have a major place in rational plans" (411). This can be read in two ways. Rawls presents it as the outcome of a correct analysis of the structure necessary for human lives to achieve goods of the sorts that human lives offer. Alternatively, it can be read as a reminder not to expect such goods as are on offer in a society that elevates and exacts life-planning to be awarded to one without having done it. It could remind us not to expect some kinds of goods to be easily available in such a social world at all if those goods are not compatible with, or the result of, hierarchically planned, prudently inclusive, and patiently scheduled lives. Rawls is concerned, of course, with the way available goods are to be handed around, and has produced one of the outstanding recent theories, in and for our culture, of their fair distribution. But we need also to keep space open to query (in and for our culture, but not only by attention to it) the costs of the practices of living that produce such goods, and the distributions of satisfactions, shame, and reproach that not only follow from, but drive, this form of life.

Constitutive Projects

No Rawlsian life-planning for Bernard Williams. Williams has trenchantly criticized Rawls's picture of life plans as a theory of practical rationality. Williams believes in an "ongoing disposition to practical deliberation," (Williams 1981b, 33) but nothing at once so ambitious and wrong-headed as a plan for a whole life. The false model entertained by Rawls, Williams thinks, is "one's life as a rectangle ... presented all at once ... to be optimally filled in" (ibid). The model ignores that the size and continuation of the rectangle are up to me; I might choose at some point not to go on at all (Williams 1981a, 13). Yet supposing that I do go on, what I do at any time will condition what I later think and desire. Either I evaluate my life from the particular set of preferences I have come to have at that time, so that my standpoint of evaluation isn't fixed; or, I evaluate all the times of my life from some fixed standpoint constituted by preferences I happen to have at a specific time in my life, but then my standpoint of evaluation may not be relevant. So we cannot gain that fixed and relevant standpoint of evaluation, as it were, "external" to the whole rectangle from which alternative ways of filling it might be objectively compared. Hence, "the perspective of deliberative choice on one's life is constitutively *from here*" (Williams 1981b, 35). One of the most interesting, though controversial, consequences of this view of rational, including moral, assessments, is that it works in both directions: I can only deliberate and choose from here, but I may only be able to adequate assess some choices *from there*, that is, later when the results of certain choices and ways of living are known. Here I want to look not at Williams's disputed defenses of moral luck and retrospective assessment, but at a favorite idea of Williams's that is central not only to those points, but to his defenses of partiality against both utilitarian and Kantian demands.

Williams's attempts to make sense of "our experience of our own agency and the sense of our regrets" (Williams 1981b, 22) feature the notion of a *constitutive project*. Constitutive projects answer "the question of why we go on at all" (Williams 1981a, 10); they are those commitments and undertakings (including important or treasured relationships) which propel us into our futures by giving us a reason for living (Williams 1981a, 13). These projects are "constitutive" because they are the condition of my existence. Without the desires they ground, "it is unclear why I should go on at all" (Williams 1981a, 12), while the presence of such desires either prevents our raising the question of whether to go on, or provides its affirmative answer. These desires Williams calls "categorical" (Williams 1981b, 11).

It is worth pausing over the assumption that there is or ought to be an answer to "the question" of why we go on at all, or that one ought to expect an answer, or a generic sort of answer-type, to that question from "us." Perhaps the question about going on only comes up in some particular kinds of situations, perhaps different ones for different people, and perhaps for some not at all. Reasons are supplied to meet certain and various demands; we might ask whether one typically has, or ought (is rightly expected, and by whom) to have a reason for going on another day, or some number of them. Let us give Williams the question for now, in order to notice some ambiguities surrounding his suggestions that constitutive projects supply its answer.[3]

Williams allows that some project's being constitutive for someone does not imply that its loss or frustration compels the person to quit on life. He says, "Other things, or the mere hope of other things, may keep him going. But he may feel in those circumstances that he might as well have died" (Williams 1981a, 13). Nor does Williams in fact claim that some single, central project is characteristically the polestar of each life: "Of course, in general a man does not have one separable project which plays this ground role; rather, there is a nexus of projects, related to his conditions of life, and it would be the loss of all or most of them that would remove meaning" (Williams 1981a, 13). A ground project is said to give meaning to someone's life "to a significant degree" (Williams 1981a, 12). Is it to a significant degree, then, or at all? Still other remarks suggest it might be not some degree of meaning, or not that alone, but some *kind* of meaning that ground projects supply, not simply something to do next, but a bona fide "reason" for living.

The stronger claim was that "one's pattern of interests, desires and projects . . . constitute the conditions of there being . . . a future at all" for one, not merely what one is likely to do with it, or to what extent what one did was likely to seem worthwhile. Not just any desires are apt to fulfill this role; the desire to avoid pain (in fact often an intense and driving desire) is Williams's example of one that does not. It is "more distinctive and structured patterns of desire and project" which do this, for they alone are "adequate to constitute a character" (Williams 1981a, 8). In fact, it seems a person's having a character *is* "having projects and categorical desires with which that person is identified" (Williams 1981a, 14).

If having a character is identical to, or requires, having constitutive projects, then if, or at the point where, I ceased to have such desires and projects, I would cease to have any character at all. This cannot be right in any familiar sense of "character." But if having categorical desires and constitutive projects is merely sufficient for having a character, then it is the desires and projects (and so a particular kind of character, the kind propelled by and identified with just such desires and projects) that keeps one going; simply having just any old character need not play that role. But then, why bring character in at all here? Well, "character" might be functioning here as term of appraisal: It's only people with constitutive projects who "really" have a reason to go on at all, who have "character" in this special sense. Then perhaps others go on with no particular reasons, nothing, as it were, to say for themselves. On this view, constitutive projects (or a nexus of them) provide, not simply whatever it takes to go on, but a "significant" way of going on, a way with—or as a person of—"character." This makes sense as a normative discussion of character, one which plumps for a superior type, but it is pretty clearly not what Williams intends his discussion to do.

The discussion of character and projects from which I have drawn here, in "Persons, Character and Morality," is to serve the argument that impartial morality, whether utilitarian or Kantian, makes unreasonable demands on people: "it is quite unreasonable for a man to give up, in the name of the impartial good ordering of the world of moral agents something which is a condition of his having any interest in being around in that world at all" (Williams 1981a, 14). The unreasonable demand is that we surrender not only our constitutive projects, but "what is involved in having a character" (ibid.). The discussion starts off with the claim that projects help to constitute a character, and aims to discuss "the connection between that fact and the man's having a reason for living at all" (Williams 1981a, 5). It concludes with the claim that such projects are a "necessity" for "unless such things exist there will not be enough substance or conviction in a man's life to compel his allegiance to life itself" (Williams 1981a, 18). The argument is: If everybody must have categorical desires to have reasons to live, and everybody must have constitutive projects to have categorical desires, but impartial morality thwarts constitutive projects, then impartial morality makes it impossible to have reasons to live. But, now, what was the connection between this and having a character?

Everybody who has a functionally integrated personality (and that is perhaps only to say, a personality) at all has some kind of character in the familiar sense. And some people no doubt have life-driving loves, works, or devotions—"projects"—to which they are so committed that the loss of these projects might be experienced as the collapse of a whole life, leading, if unrelieved, to emptiness, despair, and perhaps to suicide. Williams seems fascinated by lives organized in the latter way, and the sorts of intense, or intensely focused, meaning they support. Yet it is just this sort of life-structure that creates the high-stakes situation that flirts with total wipeout, ever verging on the possibility that, having gone for broke, one may just have to quit the game. Williams's other famous discussion of constitutive projects—those of Gauguin and Anna Karenina in his defense of moral luck—features just such games of "life roulette," where all the chips are put on one color (Gauguin: paterfamilias or painter), or even one number (Anna: Vronsky). Of course, Williams designs these cases expressly "under the simplifying assumption that other adequate projects are not generated in the process" (Williams 1981b, 36) of gambling on the unique and so fateful (and in Anna's case fatal) one. But then they are very special cases. Even if these cases illuminate the way categorical desires and their grounding projects structure assessments, regrets, and reasons for living *in lives where they do so*, it is unclear what these lives have to do with other lives, much less how having projects that work like this is tantamount to having any character at all.

Here's an interpretation of the conflicting pressures in putting "character," and life-driving "meaning," together via the notion of a "constitutive project." It explains the usefulness of the equivocation on "character" in Williams's discussion. "Having a character" stands in for a common sense fact—everybody has some character or other—so the appeal to character against impartial morality has the widest scope; it's at stake in everyone's life. Yet it requires to be stretched to cover a questionable claim, that having character at all requires having literally life-driving, make-or-break commitments, so as to result in a conflict between impartialist morality's guidance for living and what actually keeps "us" alive—a kind of reductio. A conflict with less than life-sustaining commitments would just pit these moralities against some desires or certain kinds of happiness, and maybe just some people's desires and happinesses, an old story which is coherent in many versions. And then the battle would have to be joined on the ground of which kinds of persons and desires and lives are better.

My interest here is not after all in the success of Williams's arguments, but in tracking the picture of selves and their lives that emerges in them. Allowing for a skew toward romantic or existential scenarios, the underlying vision is of a kind of life that a person experiences as handed over to him or her, with a sort of internal imperative to *make* it meaningful. This kind of life is "up to" people themselves; their own commitments and "projects" bear the burden of "giving" it meaning. In this life people would tend to face direct and indirect demands, from themselves and presumably from others, to rate that life for its worthwhileness, and so to be responsive to the question, "Why do I go on at all?" That question might be understood not only as the ultimate one on the razor's edge, but as a standard maintenance routine. These individuals must be *able* to rate their lives for meaning, and if it is theirs to make the life meaningful—they must make it so and its meaning must be meaning for them—the ratings will have to reflect their success at something *they* care about. Thus, "projects." And thus "character" less as a description than as a dimension of appraisal of how well people succeed at this kind of life. It is hard to see yourself as (much of) a character in this scheme unless you can give this kind of account of yourself.

Williams's characters charge themselves with taking hold of their lives in a particular way: They demand of themselves a sort of meaningful career, whose meaning is subject to their own reflective assessment of it. And this meaning seems for Williams a test of whether that life itself, its very existence, can earn its right to go on at all, in *their* eyes. Williams has written vividly of ways some dominant pictures of morality, reflection, and choice are impossible, or where possible, frightening, to map onto our understandings of our selves and lives. And those of us who read Williams are apt to recognize, and many of us probably share, these understandings. But might just anyone understand these understandings of self-possession, its prerogatives and responsibilities, much less wish to honor them? Michael Walzer remarks that there are alternatives to lives "undertaken" as careers: inherited lives, socially regulated lives, spontaneous lives, or divinely ordained ones (Walzer 1994, 23–24 and Walzer 1993, 169). And a life fully shared with others will often be taken up, or taken along, by those others as much as undertaken by the one whose life it is. Very often in his writing, Williams emphasizes the cultural location of our moral beliefs and the particular concepts that make them possible. But some of his views about selves and what organizes their lives flirt with categorical imperatives, though not of the Kantian kind.

Quests

Williams's selves are certainly possessed of—in fact possess themselves in the mode of—a kind of "inwardness" that Charles Taylor takes as one hallmark of a distinctively modern self. A central theme of Taylor's work is that this self's social and moral "sources" lie at various distances back in, and beyond, the modern era. Taylor's approach is determinedly historical and historicist in ways neither Rawls's nor Williams's is. Taylor, however, is not attempting a causal explanation of the rise of modern identity. His question about modern identity and its moral aspects is not about how it happened but "why people found (or find) it convincing/inspiring/moving" (203). Taylor calls this question an "interpretive" one. He seeks elucidations of the complex relations between ideals and "a wide range of practices—religious, political, economic, familial, intellectual, artistic . . ." (Taylor 1989, 206).

Interpretations start with something given to be understood, and Taylor starts with "a historically limited mode of self- interpretation . . . which has become dominant in the modern West" (Taylor 1989, 111). I want to look at a particular spot in Taylor's discussion where his self-consciousness about historical limits seems to waiver or drop away as certain "inescapable structural requirements of human agency" (52) make their appearance.

Taylor's signature theme is *strong evaluation*, that human beings cannot make sense of themselves outside some evaluative framework that contrasts actions or lives as qualitatively higher or lower in kind, and not merely by degree or within some procedural formalism. Taylor says it is "inescapable, i.e. that it belongs to human agency to exist in a space of questions about strongly valued goods, prior to all choice or adventitious cultural change" (31). Exactly which differences Taylor seeks to mark by talk of "strong evaluation" is not entirely clear to me (although it's something utilitarians, Kantians, and "naturalists," on his account, try to circumvent), but it's clear enough the role he gives it. Strong evaluation of human lives and their features is fact, not artifact; it is prior, not posterior, to the many kinds of practices mentioned above. Taylor believes human beings have an "ineradicable" craving to be "rightly placed in relation to the good" (44), and only frameworks of strong evaluation give them a relevant measure of this.

It is not Taylor's view about good that I want to look at, but a view about selves that Taylor annexes to it. What human beings crave and must have in some form, according to Taylor, are answers to the question: Who am I? These answers articulate human beings' identities, which are defined by "commitments and identifications" that express some strong evaluations or others (27). To know who I am, in this sense, I must know the kinds of things that are worth doing or out of the question. But people do not face disconnected (Taylor might say, completely "punctual") doings: What's up for consideration depends upon where I have got to, and where I find myself later may depend on what I do (or not) now. This introduces, as we might put it, a longitudinal dimension of what Taylor calls "the self in moral space." Taylor says it is, like the higher or lower moral latitudes mapped by strong evaluation, "another inescapable feature of human life," "that we grasp our lives in a *narrative*" (47).

Now I agree that our understandings of ourselves (and others) as actors "has temporal depth" (50). This comes with the causal structure of actions, and of the sense we make of them under intentional descriptions. Placing certain events as actions, and as particular ones, involves certain assumptions about where they come from and what they effect. More richly, from the standpoint of practical deliberation, we necessarily undertake to set, switch, or continue our courses, in Williams's nice phrase, "from here," where "here" is some position we have gotten to, and from which we will have moved on in some more or less consequential direction.

This point about the intelligibility of those events which are actions, however, is compatible with the stories' that reveal events as actions being very short ones. Someone ahead of me brushes by a display in the market, knocking a box off the shelf; I notice, pause to stoop, pick it up, and restore it to its place. It's obvious that I have done something and what I have done, both to me and to anyone else looking on, it's a perfectly intelligible intentional action. If I stoop to straighten my cuff, continue the exercise routine, show obeisance to my master or my husband, miss a snowball, or check my backache, these actions, too, are intelligible as such within their stories, where some of these are normative, even moral, ones. Some of these stories are simply local and fragmentary (although of course they take place within my continuous spatio-temporal trajectory as a physical being), while others may entail more elaborate or extended sagas. An action's requiring a narrative context means only that it can be understood as some action or other in *some* story or other.

Taylor recognizes this point about "the structure of any situated action . . . however trivial" (47), but insists that the inescapable feature includes more than this, in fact much more than this, both in quality and quantity. "[A]s a being who grows and becomes I can only know myself through the history of my maturations and regressions, overcomings and defeats" (50). Not only do "[w]e want our lives to have meaning, weight, or substance, or to grow towards some fulness. . . . But this means our *whole* lives" (50). Endorsing Alasdair MacIntyre's description of a human life as a "quest," Taylor holds that when I choose to go on with my life in an existing or a new direction, "I project a future story, not just a state of the momentary future but a bent for my whole life to come" (48). And he goes as far as to say human persons are "counted" as such—as one self and only one self—by their existing in a space of questions about the good in "the shape of my life *as a whole*" (50). This, Taylor admonishes the reader, "is not something up for arbitrary determination" (50).

Something's certainly up here, and it's a lot more than the temporal structure of an intelligible, even an intelligible moral, action. In these pages equating selfhood itself with having and sustaining a whole-life narrative, there's a repeated back and forth. Acts and valuations are either trivial or fateful, momentary ("punctual") or life-spanning, arbitrary or constitutive; there seem not to be any possibilities in the middle range. Taylor says he is not interested in making sense of our present actions in "such trivial questions as where I shall go in the next five minutes but with the issue of my place relative to the good" (48). Put like this, the claim threatens to become a tautology, if by supposition all decisions are trivial that are not issues of my place relative to the good, and only those decisions that are fateful for my whole life are issues of my place relative to the good. But Taylor is supposed to be arguing *to* the necessity of actions being invested with a meaning connected with one's whole life.

In fact, sometimes where I shall go in the next five minutes is of life-altering importance, whereas it might turn out that whether I married Jack, abandoned art for agriculture, or made a risky choice to cross the border without papers didn't make a whole lot of difference in the long run. Any of these might make a greater or lesser difference to the way I live my life and my evaluative perspective on it through stretches of varying lengths, but not even choices that seem fateful at the time necessarily reverberate through one's life as a whole. I don't always know which it's going to be at those times, even at times when I ponder just that. As Williams correctly says, I can't guarantee from what later standpoint "my major and most fundamental regrets will be" (Williams 1981, 35), nor, for that matter, my deepest relief or most profound satisfaction.

Whole lives and parts of them may make more or less "sense," and different kinds of it, from different points within them, and in various perspectives at those points, including moral perspectives invoking substantive qualitative discriminations. On the other hand, someone's life between the ages of 38 and 42 might simply have been lived contemptibly, and there's an end to it. Moral assessability and long-term intelligibility co-vary in different ways.

What if one's whole life does (or is believed to?—an interesting question I pass over here) make sense in terms of a certain kinds of pattern, but it is not the pattern of quest or striving, development or aspiration? What if one's life repeats a motif—generosity of spirit, championing underdogs, tilting at windmills, shedding one's skin—for example, like playing a theme with variations? Or what if one faithfully (or relentlessly) plays out in one's life a persona, or (arche)type—earth mother, tortured genius, aesthete? Taylor is quite aware that stories of linear development, progress, continuous gain and growth are distinctively modern "forms of narrativity" (105). But he doesn't tell us how premodern (or non-(Western)-modern) motifs for organizing whole lives are to be rendered with the kind of emplotment that reveals their narrativity.

But what if one's life simply fails to be tell-able in a single, "coherent" life-spanning narrative? Anyone's life might be chronicled, recorded as a temporally ordered sequence of doings and happenings, but "narrative" here seems to demand some significant degree of emplotment, where what goes before can (at least later) be seen to have laid a kind of groundwork for what ensues, or where what comes later confers significance on what led up to it. Taylor gives the example of the tea-and-madeleines passage in Proust where the narrator "recovers" the apparently "wasted" time of his life up to then as really a "preparation" for his work as a writer.[4] But: What if he did not?

Taylor's comment on this is brief and revealing. If my past is "unredeemable" I "accept a kind of mutilation as a person; it is to fail to meet the full challenge involved in making sense of my life" (51). If I can "fail," though, what I can't escape is not the whole life that makes some kind of strongly evaluated sense, but a negative judgment, at least from Taylor's perspective, on the life that does not. If one can fail, it is *one* who fails, a person who has failed to do enough, or the right kind of thing, with *her* life. And if the result is "mutilation" this seems not to mean that one ended up *not* a person, or (literally) some fraction of one, but that one is the wrong kind of person, a marred person, a person who lived badly—apparently very badly, for "mutilation" is a very strong evaluation in anybody's view. If the whole-life meaning-test is for individuals who are unquestionably persons (to what else might it apply?) whose lives are to be measured by it (and so there is something given for the measuring), then Taylor is defending a view about the *best* kind of life, not about what is involved in merely being a person or having a self or a life "at all."[5]

Taylor's self-conscious historicism, his usual firm sense of the way ideas and ideals are "embedded in practices" (204), seems to drop away when it comes to the requirement on lives to be "whole" in a way that makes a proper story. This seems to be an instance of a "strong evaluation"—whole lives that can be figured as quests are "incomparably higher" than others—that wants not to be historically limited or culturally placed, but transcendental.[6] My guess is that by its lights most people, here, now, and elsewhere are incomparably lower; yet even if we are fallen selves, we are selves just the same.

Taylor's strongly evaluative partition of moral characters seems vastly more demanding than Williams's. Williams requires only a project or few to serve as the reason to go on for a while at a time; Taylor seems to require a whole life's falling into place along some dominant story line. But maybe Taylor's requirement is not so strong, because the stress on narration seems to place peculiar emphasis on retrospective tellings that put the past in the right, i.e. leading, light. This could turn out to be easier than it sounds unless there are some nontrivial constraints on one's narrative options and editorial prerogatives. Narratives of conversion, for example, can accommodate any old mess of a life up to the point of being found, saved, enlightened, or recovering; this may be one reason these stories have such power for so many people, at least in our society. But are those lives then incomparably higher than others that went through phases and stages with discontinuities and shifting evaluative perspectives? Can picaresque lives that are robust and satisfying be narratively joined enough to qualify? And what of lives for which a yarn can be spun like Wittgenstein's thread, twisting fibre on fibre so that no one fibre runs the whole length, but the strength is in the overlapping of many fibres? (Wittgenstein 1958, #67). Do they qualify? I should think it depends on what's *in* them. I do not think Taylor has made the "necessary" connection between some kinds of content and the globally narrative form.

The whole-life story motif is not simply historically locatable. It's as old as Last Judgment stories, including pre-Christian ones, and as recent as psychoanalysis and many self-help and recovery movements. But its progressivist forms may have a connection with a particularly modern story form. I do not mean the modern genre of the novel. I mean another kind of writing in which lives are *recorded* to an unprecedented degree in many daily practices and central institutions of a certain kind of society, and progressive or "developmental" histories of individuals are routinely kept. Many procedures and institutions require individuals to have and to be able to recount "normally" continuous histories—of residence, education, or employment, for example. In fact, many systems, practices, and institutions construct these histories for us, whether or not we are aware of it (Foucault 1979, 191–92). We should want to know what kinds of value reside in these forms of life in which records of one's life are expected to be kept, by one's self and others. We need to notice what rankings and valuations are made possible or inevitable in this way, for what kinds of social recognition or qualification adequate narratives make their authors eligible. Who is the intended audience and presumptive judge of the continuities of our many institutionalized, normal form narratives? What kinds of person, and what sorts of worth, are they designed to reveal?

Dominant Identities

I myself defend a certain kind of narrative ethics of responsibility as an alternative to the systematizing search for high theory, but I am very hesitant about how ambitious the required narratives should be. This is in part because I think the narrative intelligibility of actions is often local. There's just no plausible move in general from making sense of an action in some narrative context to needing to see it against the backcloth of an entire life. It is also because I find the more ambitious claims about the inclusiveness and centrality of plans, projects, and plots questionable as descriptions of actual people's actual lives, where these lives nonetheless seem decent, good, or admirable. At the same time I think influential conceptions of persons and their lives found in moral philosophy do represent something real.

Instead of saying that they represent some people's real lives in highly idealized form (a useful but potentially misleading shorthand), I'd rather say that they reflect the reality of certain specific social norms that confer special value and visibility on those lives which can claim to embody them. I call these socially normative ideals of personhood *dominant identities*. In many cases of these, no lives embody them stably and for the most part over the long haul, while most lives cannot hope to look much like what these normative ideals require at all. The reality of these social norms consists in the pressures they exert on people's attempts at self-understanding and their possible representations of themselves to others, and in many things required of many people to keep the pressure up.

Kathryn Addelson has done a great deal to find out how this works. Addelson might say that what I am calling dominant identities are part of a social world's "official story" the regeneration of which requires keeping quite a lot *out* of view. Lives that show how restricted the scope of the dominant identities really is may get in the way of official stories, and so may realities within the very lives that are assumed to embody the dominant identities. The point about these dominant common understandings—e.g. of what "people" are like—is not that they are true, but that they are dominant. They are a "public" face of a social world that its members recognize as theirs. This means that dominant identities are not well understood as something "had" or "done" by the (often) select group of people to whom they are standardly attributed. They are a "collective" (though not democratic or egalitarian) product of people in social worlds where many must do, attend to, and ignore certain things in order for that identity to be performed and claimed by some. And this may include the performance and ascription of *other* (nondominant: subordinate, marginal, deviant, or diminished) identities to some other people. (See Addelson 1994, especially chapters 5 and 6.)

It is easy for philosophers to reproduce or echo aspects of these visible and valued social identities in idealized forms when trying to elucidate what "agency" or "personhood" means. It is to a significant extent unavoidable, as moral philosophers speak from a particular cultural place, and mean to speak comprehensibly to others in it, about it. Moral theorizing, like other actions and practices, is "from here," a cultural place we have got to, and from which we head off in some direction or other. And from a particular "here," and certain places in it, some lives stand out for notice as obvious or best cases of persons, while others fail to stand out clearly, or in their own terms, or at all. The point for moral philosophy is not that the dominant identities of certain social orders are wrong—inauthentic, corrupt, mystifying, oppressive, or oppressing, though they might turn out to be upon examination. It is that this is something for moral philosophy to examine about actual social lives and their alternatives. It cannot be examined if it is not noticed that normative ideals of personhood that make their ways into moral philosophy *are* culturally and socially shaped, *and* that such ideals do make their ways into moral philosophy. With that fact kept in focus, links between available goods and actual positions are clearer. Clearer, too, are the roles philosophical depictions, along with other representations and practices, play in shaping how we see those goods and positions, and the value we place on them.

Whole-Life Ethics in the Modern Style

Rawls, Williams, and Taylor represent a fairly broad spectrum of Anglo-American ethics. While Rawls is squarely within the analytic tradition of systematic moral theorizing, Williams is arguably its most successful gadfly. Taylor (and MacIntyre, see chapter 5 in this book) is part of a more programmatic opposition to the tradition Rawls and many others continue. This opposition sometimes makes odd bedfellows, occasionally linking communitarians, Aristotelians, pragmatists, Marxists, Christian ethicists, and feminists, although different ones of these at different points on different occasions.

Along another axis, Rawls, Williams, and Taylor have in common a profound antagonism toward utilitarian moral ideas that threaten the separateness of selves and their rights to hold themselves, or the plans, projects, and strong evaluations with which they identify themselves, dear. If they are standing philosophically in the path of the utilitarian juggernaut—the system to beat all systems—of fully administered lives to which are distributed (only?) fully administrable goods, what are they standing for? I find in their otherwise diverse views in (and on) moral philosophy a kind of convergence, an insistence on the theme of a person's mastering the structure of his or her "whole life." Now, one's whole life as the subject of moral concern is no modern novelty, but an ancient idea. I think it is the kind of mastery insisted upon that is revealing. I believe what it reveals is a dominant identity that is quite familiar.

What seems distinctive about the kind of concern with one's whole life found in Rawls, Williams, and Taylor is its manner and its object. It is not only that people are seen as being open over the course of their whole lives to appraisal of their actions or characters. Nor is it that a conclusive appraisal cannot be made until the results of a whole life are in. Of course these selves will have to account for what they do and have done. But Rawls, Williams, and Taylor seem particularly insistent on having them account for their life's work of *reflective self-monitoring itself*, for that seems to be really what their required plans, projects, and plots show about them. These selves are threatened with fundamental forms of reproach, bordering on disqualification *as* selves, if they cannot demonstrate their continual watchfulness over their running of their lives, to prove this kind of self-conscious stewardship by showing how deliberately, mindfully, or artfully the lives are planned, projected, or plotted. They do this by having a plan to point to, a project to declare, or a story to tell that is "their own"; their readiness to produce it upon request shows it has been rehearsed and refined by them to themselves all along the way.

The supposed imperative of individuality in modern life always sits uncomfortably alongside the grinding and levelling forces of mass culture, bureaucracy, and normalization. Perhaps the individualization of the modern individual that reconciles these is not individuating creativity, spontaneity, originality, or uniqueness, but the individualized division of moral-social labor that makes each superintendent of itself. I think Rawls, Williams, and Taylor each impose a test on persons—indeed of human beings' being persons—of a whole life under *conscientiously conscious self-superintendence* of a verifiable kind.

This returns us to autonomous man, seen as a dominant identity. The "career self" that appears in Rawls, Williams, and Taylor is both equipped and required to account for itself through particular arts of accounting that give evidence of continuing conscious and designed self-superintendence. Its ability to do this entitles it to extremely valuable recognitions and rewards, preeminently respect and rights that it can claim on the basis of its good standing as a self-superintendent; its good standing, that is, among other self-superintendents in good standing, to whom it is required to account. Autonomous man's eery independence is often remarked; he is supposedly "disembedded" and "unencumbered," insulated and isolated. This seems to me to miss something essential about this modern individual. In being prepared for self-command through his entitlements, he is prepared for a superintendence of his life that will be juried by his peers. These peers will decide who among them has risen to that task, and they will express that judgment by requiring and receiving the appropriate accounts from those who have. There are no autonomous men alone.

Each, then, is superintendent of him- or herself; but only ideally, for the autonomous person is clearly a dominant identity, an idealized picture of an exemplary person in a certain kind of society, a norm that no one fulfills all along for the long haul, and many never come close to fulfilling at all. A certain kind of society holds out to us, and gives some of us, to varying degrees and at different costs, the gift of (roughly) autonomous lives. It unquestionably is a gift, a special kind of good available in this kind of society (but not, of course, compatible with all other possible goods, including many that can be seen clearly, and even enjoyed, within this kind of society). It is a gift that keeps on giving, but only with some steep investments of time and effort, and the continuing recognition of autonomous peers.

Time and effort alone do not guarantee that recognition. For many are neither prepared nor permitted to display self-possession through the kind of self-superintendence imaged by Rawls, who is identified with the Kantian tradition involving rational autonomy, as well as by Williams and Taylor, who are not.[7] Some selves are neither required nor permitted to account for their superintendence of themselves, because they are overseen, and in certain ways accounted for, by others. These selves have lives, but they either do not get (or are not expected) to lead them, or do not get to claim that they do. There are in our social world, as elsewhere, dominant identities and other identities.

I have not here argued for or against the collectively imagined and enacted late modern version of autonomous man, the career self, as a moral paradigm of a "person." I have argued against a few prominent attempts at presenting this richly specific ideal as a thin but necessary idea of what persons, selves, or human agents "are," rather than as a component or product of some forms of social life whose admirability remains to be examined. That examination demands a look at identities other than dominant ones, in our own social world and perhaps in others.

seven

Made a Slave, Born a Woman

Knowing Others' Places

From this trivial and anatomical observation is deriv'd that vast difference betwixt the education and duties of the two sexes.

—David Hume, *A Treatise on Human Understanding*

Ain't I a Woman?"

—Sojourner Truth

It is that act of speech, of "talking back," that is no mere gesture of empty words, that is the expression of our movement from object to subject—the liberated voice.

—bell hooks, *Talking Back*

Bernard Williams's *Shame and Necessity* is an inquiry into the ethical ideas of the ancient Greeks, in order not only to understand them, but to "free us of misunderstandings of ourselves" (Williams 1993, 11). Williams believes the Greeks were different from us, but the differences are not those that have often and influentially been claimed. Specifically, Williams rebuts the "progressivist" idea that we moderns have developed significantly beyond the Greeks in the maturity and refinement of our moral conceptions. He argues that insofar as we differ from the Greeks in basic ethical conceptions, theirs were in better shape. He also claims that we in fact rely on "much the same conceptions" (4) of agency, responsibility, shame, and freedom as the Greeks did, without acknowledging that we do so. We have changed ethically, then, neither as much nor as creditably as we like to think, nor in some of the ways we are used to assuming. To comprehend this is "to recognize some of our illusions about the modern world" (7).

In a vivid chapter Williams considers the common and (on his account) erroneous wisdom on the distance between the Greeks and us with regard to *slavery*. Moderns congratulate themselves by crediting distinctly modern moral views with revealing why slavery cannot be morally justified. In particular, modern morality rejects *necessary social identities*. A necessary identity is a social role or status that is inevitably or comfortably well fitted to the people whose social position it is, because of some naturally occurring feature of those people. The idea that there are necessary identities is the view that some are born for (rather than born to) and naturally suited (rather than more or less forcibly fitted) to certain social roles or stations. Modern people are often said to have achieved moral and other insights that discredit this view, insights that the ancient Greeks, for example, are thought to lack.

Williams persuasively argues that there are two things wrong with this view of what makes us different from the Greeks on slavery. One is that Greeks did *not* generally think their institution of chattel slavery was just to its victims, and did not generally morally defend it. Another is that Greeks did *not* generally see those impressed into slavery as "made" or naturally ordained for it. On the contrary, the prevailing view was that impressment into slavery was "a contingent and uniquely brutal disaster for its victims" (117). Coercion, not nature, made slaves, and Greeks were not pretending otherwise. Aristotle's well-known but hopeless attempt to show that some are slaves by nature is exhibited by Williams as an aberration, an attempt to "square the ethical circle" (110) by showing that something which obviously requires force happens "by nature."

Greeks did not morally justify slavery by claiming that slaves were by nature such, but on Williams's account they didn't see slavery as unjust, either. Williams explains that "considerations of justice and injustice were immobilized by the demands of what was seen as social and economic necessity. That phenomenon has not so much been eliminated from modern life as shifted to different places" (125). The Greeks did not think "slave" designated a necessary (that is, naturally inevitable or fitting) identity. Instead they thought the role of slave was necessary *to* a kind of social order, and to that extent someone (although no one in particular by nature) "had" to be a slave. Here is a very uncomfortable sameness between us and the Greeks. We, too, largely acquiesce in the existence of miserable or demeaning lots, which are culturally and economically "necessary" parts of our given form of life, and to which people are consigned largely or completely (it is often said, and perhaps believed) by individual bad luck. A modern liberal ethos, according to

Williams, differs from some ancient and other ones in recognizing that questions of justice should not be simply silenced by necessities, and that measures of justice should be applied to institutions and practices that contribute to determining whose lots the undesirable ones are to be. The aspiration in modern liberal views is thus that no one's "bad luck" in this regard should be abetted by social arrangements. This difference is something, but not so large as a commitment to preventing anyone's luck from being that bad.

I find Williams's rough account of the Greeks' "extra-moral" acceptance of their form of chattel slavery convincing, although oversimple. Aristotle's view may not have been representative, but it surely wasn't idiosyncratic, either. Williams cites, for example, a bit of "archaic aristocratic material" from Theognis that finds the slave's physical person slavish: "A slave's head is never upright, but always bent, and he has a slanting neck" (114). The idea of natural fittedness—physical, intellectual, temperamental—to social role was old then, and continues to get older. And the quoted remark is characteristic, then and now, of one way the idea is sustained: by inducing in or requiring of people certain physical or behavioral traits as marks of a social role, and then using those marks in turn to justify those people's assignment to it. In this, as well as in the acceptance of unluckily bad lots, "we" are not so different from the Greeks.

It is rewarding nonetheless to see Aristotle's naturalized account of slavery revealed as Aristotle's, not "the Greek," one. It illustrates something we need to learn to notice routinely: that there is not simply "the Greek" or "the modern" view of morals, or religion, or society. Some views are at a time more authoritative, entrenched, institutionalized, or visible than others. Some views resident in a given place and time are more widely circulated, more energetically vended in conspicuous places, or better preserved for posterity than are some others. If we were inclined unwisely to take Aristotle to speak for the "ancient Greeks," the lesson is not only one of historical near- sightedness or canonical smoke. There are gaps now as long ago between what is seen or thought and what can be said, and between what is said and where it can be heard. What interests me in Williams's discussion is related to this. I want to explore in more detail what goes into making some social identities "necessary," and how this involves, among other things, the ways certain things about people can be noticed and known, or not.

I'll start by looking more closely at Williams's useful but lightly limned notion of a "necessary identity," probing the contrast Williams

uses to bring out its meaning, a comparison between the Greek's attitudes toward slaves and to women. "Being a woman," Williams holds,
"really was a necessary identity" (122) in the ancient Greek society.
Here Aristotle, construing "a genuinely necessary sexual identity as a
naturally given social identity" (123), represents the rule rather than an
exception. Williams's point is not that women's social role in Ancient
Athens is better justified morally than that of slaves. It is that there were
different understandings within ancient Greek society of the apparently
contingent (or only conditionally necessary) lot of a slave and the apparently (simply) necessary lot of a woman.

The central contrast Williams draws is that the Greeks had ways to
know, and knew very well, that it was bad to be a slave and chance that
anyone in particular became one. But if the Greeks could or did know it
was bad to be a woman, there was at any rate no "real possibility" (120)
they could see, and so no matter of chance, of becoming one (or not).
Anybody in particular at birth simply *is* a woman or not. Williams
thinks the Greeks here failed to see something *we* see. We, he thinks, see
the "necessity" of a "sexual" or "biological" identity, but do not equate
that with a social one, whereas the Greeks are said not to see, or to be
able to see, that. I'm going to argue that neither of these claims is right.
The Greeks might well have seen something Williams seems to think
they could not have, whereas Williams fails to see something he might
have. To show this I'll follow out what Williams sees the Greeks seeing
or not, noticing what Williams himself sees.

At least one Greek (Plato, handed off rather gingerly in this discussion
as a "utopian") did see something clearly that Williams doesn't see.
Human beings are inevitably (although not always unambiguously—as
surely some of the Greeks knew) sexed. But Plato knew that being sexed
isn't, in the sense relevant to this discussion, an identity, whereas being a
woman, in the relevant sense, *always* is. Williams thinks the Greeks had
one thought too few, but I fear he has one thought too many here.
Williams supplies the thought that there is some "identity" already there
in the fact of being sexed. He forgets that not all females in a society
have the same social identity. Williams's account of what the Greeks
knew about slaves and women, and how they knew it, also neglects to
distinguish between there being evidence of coercion into and within a
social role, and the coercers having to acknowledge that evidence and
admit what it is evidence for. Yet Williams's discussion provides significant clues to the maintenance, if not the construction, of "necessary

identities," both in where it goes for an explanation and in where it goes wrong.

There are necessary identities, but they are not all or nothing. They do not consist in (real or alleged) facts that people so identified have certain properties, but in relations among these people and others that involve both facts of coercion and power and norms of credibility. The necessity of necessary identities has not to do with their content, but with how firmly but invisibly they are held in place. Necessary identities are an epistemic and social accomplishment, and a precarious one requiring steady maintenance. These identities, finally, are not necessary for the ones who bear them, but for others who need to legitimate the ways they treat the bearers or to foreclose examination of those ways. It is very important to understand these matters, for necessary identities are no antique fact; they are alive among us today.

How Did the Greeks Know People Weren't Born to Be Slaves?

Ancient Greek society, Williams says, had an institution of chattel slavery, and important features of the social and economic lives of free people were dependent upon this arrangement. To the extent that the Greeks accepted that way of life in the polis, it was necessary that some people occupy the role of slave. Most people, however, did not believe that there were some particular people, or particular kinds of people, such that it was necessary that those people be slaves (or, be slaves if anyone was). So "slave" is not a necessary identity of anyone who is one.

Williams does not explain much about which of the Greeks accepted the way of life that was the polis (and why), and to what extent they envisioned alternatives to this way of life or thought them realistically possible. H. D. F. Kitto (Kitto 1957, 132) cites an estimate that there were perhaps 125,000 slaves in Attica (65,000 in domestic employment, 50,000 in industry, 10,000 in the brutal environment of the mines) just before the Peloponnesian War, and a total Athenian population of something over 100,000. If slaves, at least, are assumed not to have "accepted" the mode of life requiring their status, then perhaps a majority of participants in this mode of life did not find it acceptable. But then, slaves are not "Greeks," in the sense in which this is never simply a fact of birth, but a social identity predicated upon certain facts, which include those of birth.

Williams focuses on the other point, how the Greeks knew no one in particular "had" by nature to be a slave (and thus, that it was not a necessary identity for anyone), and how the Greeks knew it was very bad indeed to end up being one (and thus that there was no morally justifying it). The two bits of knowledge are related. It's a bad lot to be a slave because one is forced into it and subjected to force within it. But what needs to be forced into a place (and kept in it, and shaped to it by force) is something not inevitably, on its own account, (necessarily) in it and fitted to it. Slavery was a status with clearly coercive modes of entrance which could be visited on one arbitrarily (being captured, taken in war, or forced by indebtedness), and with official possibility of exit through manumission. One could come to be a slave and cease to be one. While it might seem no one could fail to appreciate the badness of arbitrary subjection of individuals by and to violence, Williams appeals to an additional source of evidence. He emphasizes theoretical condemnations of slavery that survive, as well as the "complaints of slaves themselves, frequent in drama and certainly, in everyday life" (112). Given all this, people in the ancient Greek world could not but recognize the "arbitrariness and violence" (123) of their kind of slavery. The system was taken for granted, but so were the grounds for its victims' complaints (112). Slavery was undeniably brutal and bad not only because of the kind of system it was, but because those to whom it was brutal and for whom it was bad *said* so.

How Did the Greeks *Not* Know Women Weren't Born to Be What They Were?

The Greeks knew coercion, not nature, made slaves; but they believed that nature, not coercion, made women. This is Williams's contrast. The Greeks did not see that women weren't born for their role; or, whether or not they saw this, that women's role was something women might have reason to hate, resent, or complain of. What is it that women were born to be in the ancient Greek society, and what about this did the Greeks not notice?

In the case of women, Williams says, the conventional view was: "There was by nature a position to be filled, and there were people who by nature occupied it" (118). The mistake of the Greeks, Williams says, was "to construe a genuinely necessary sexual identity as a naturally given social identity" (123). What is the "genuinely necessary sexual identity" that the Greeks confused with something else? It is obviously the fact of individuals' *being sexed*, and the necessity is that individuals be sexed to fulfill one of two biological roles in sexual reproduction.

There must be biological males and females to reproduce sexually, the former necessarily to beget, the latter necessarily to bear, children. This is the sense in which there are "by nature" positions to be filled, and people who "by nature" fill them. The Greeks are supposed to have confused this sexual role with "a naturally given social identity." Which one? Following the parallel Williams draws with slaves, and noticing the social position Williams treats as a possible target of complaint, the social identity in question is (actual or possible) "wife" in the Greek household.

The Greek society had an institution of chattel slavery, and it also had an institution of private familial households in which "free" women and children, and (collectively) many slaves, were contained. Clearly, fundamental features of the social and economic lives of people were dependent on this arrangement. To the extent that the Greeks (including women?) accepted the way of life of which this kind of household was a central part, it was necessary that someone occupy the role of wife, a woman belonging to a free man as a source of private and sanctioned sexual, childbearing, child-rearing, and household services. So far this is like the case of slaves, but here's the difference as Williams identifies it. Most people believed that there were some particular people, that is, a particular kind of people, such that it was necessary that *those* people be actual or potential wives (or, be wives if anyone was). These people are women. So actual or potential "wife" is a necessary identity for women.

Williams says the Greeks erred in seeing the fact of being sexed female as naturally giving someone the social identity, wife. But this cannot be right. For the Greeks it was *not females* who were necessarily the ones who were wives if anyone was. Many (perhaps most?) females were by no means necessarily destined to be the wives of free men. Indeed, many females were necessarily not the ones who were or were to be those wives, because many females were *slaves*. The social identity "wife" was hardly naturally given to female slaves. So if "genuinely necessary sexual identity" refers to the fact of being sexed female, and so for bearing rather than begetting in the matter for which being sexed is "genuinely necessary," sexual reproduction, the biological fact of being female does not necessarily confer the identity of wife. In fact, it does not necessarily confer the identity "woman." Not all females are women, in precisely the sense in which it is, necessarily, women who are wives.

Not all females are women. If you've not heard this before, it will sound bizarre. Yet it is common in social systems where gender is one hierarchical order among others. Consider the example of the nineteenth-century antebellum United States. The nineteenth-century cult of true womanhood characterizes chastity, modesty, delicacy, frailty, and spirituality as "women's" true or proper nature. But an equally common understanding among whites about the nature of black women (especially but not only slaves) characterizes them as licentious, sexy, brazen, sturdy, and earthy. There is no contradiction here; black females aren't women in the relevant sense. A dominant story about "women" is meant to apply to females of a particular social standing, those of the dominant class. Poor white women are something else again. In short, as soon as "woman" so much as begins to involve an *identity*—a socially recognized status determining relative standing, duties, prerogatives, and possible functions or stations—then there are either several kinds of "women" or just one (reserved to females of the ruling or dominant class). In either case the identity "woman" is *never* constituted simply by being sexed female. You may be born a woman, but being born female (as it is biologically necessary that some members of a sexually reproducing species be) doesn't get you there (see Spelman 1988).

For the Greeks as for everyone else, in the sense in which there is a natural position to be filled and it is the nature of women to fill it, "women" means "females." The relevant position is bearing rather than begetting, and females by nature do that. But females as such are not ordained for the wifely roles made necessary by the Greek institution of the household; only some females are born to that, for the Greeks. So it is false that the Greeks construed females as naturally given to wifehood in the household. The Greeks did not confuse being female-sexed as such with being wife-material. In the sense in which it is true for Greeks that women were naturally given to that role, "women" means (roughly) "female-sexed members of particular social class (or classes)." The females who were born to be wives already bore an identity that is not naturally given. This class-bound identity "woman" is a "sexual identity" in that sex is a necessary condition for assignment to it, but it is a (contingently) necessary identity only in a particular hierarchical social order. This class status and wifehood are necessary only in that relative sense that "slave" is, too: They are roles necessitated by institutions taken as given, but these institutions are constituents of one among possible ways of life.

Were the Greeks unable to notice what Williams himself overlooks, that even having been born female, one might not have been a "woman," where this refers to an institution-dependent social identity of some females and not others? No. Plato's discussion of male and female guardians in the *Republic* shows clearly that Plato saw the fact of being sexed to involve a specific biological function—childbearing (not including child-rearing) in the case of women and child-begetting in the case of men—that was not necessarily a socially articulated role, an "identity" in the sense relevant in this discussion. Female guardians in Plato's imaginary state are those females sufficiently gifted so that they no longer have to be women in most of the senses of that social role belonging to the wives and daughters of free men in the actual Athenian state.

Plato easily explicates a distinction between the fact of being sexed, which is necessarily true of members of a sexually reproducing biological species, and any socially organized role, by picturing the male and female guardians as dogs, and picturing the issue of sex as bearing entirely on how they are matched for (eugenically) desirable breeding. The successful issue of engineered matings is whisked away to nurseries, the unsuccessful to someplace else, unauthorized stock is destroyed. Socially, male and female guardians do not become mothers and fathers in our or the Athenians' conventional sense (i.e. where this involves socially articulated forms of relationship with specific children whose care or supervision one undertakes, whether birth-children or not). Child-tending is not a part of the social role of guardians (although the education of guardian children for guardian life is part of the role of male and female guardians equally). The guardians' role is to rule or fight. The senses in which male and female guardians are mothers and fathers biologically, are strictly complementary: One begets and one bears. The sense in which they are mothers and fathers socially is identical, each being a member of the same "parent" class of the whole generation of children born after a single round of begetting.

While Plato introduces this discussion with assurances that this will seem "incredible," it's all explained straightforwardly in a few pages (*Republic* 449–467). The colorful device of picturing guardians as dogs provides a simple way to focus on sex as a fact "necessarily" pertinent to breeding, and otherwise variably combinable with social roles of different design. The latter is true, Plato readily sees, even within a single society, including the ideal one of the *Republic*, where of course very few males and females are guardians. Being born male or female is never by itself determinant of social role. And why should Plato not have seen this, or have been "utopian" to have seen this, when it was simply a fact about his own, *actual* Athenian way of life? Sexes aren't social identities, and social identities are never constituted by sex alone; they weren't in Athens then, and they are not now. Or, to put the point another way, sex is a significant biological fact about someone, but the kind of social fact it may be—how it constitutes or even partly determines an *identity*, and which one—varies.

Williams does not fail to point to Plato as the "famous exception" to the supposed conflation of biological sex and social status, noting Plato's consequent proposal to abolish families among the guardians. He contrasts this with Aristotle's view that abolishing families is inconceivable, because the family is a "natural institution" to which the "role of women" is essential (123).

Yet the "inconceivability" of abolishing the particular arrangement of private familial households is not different from the "inconceivability" of abolishing chattel slavery as the Greeks had it. A certain way of life would survive neither abolition. The fact that females bear and males beget young, however, would survive both, for that is no social fact. Plato and Aristotle both understand this. Plato justified abolishing families (only) for men and women of a certain social class, to the ends of a particular social order imagined in the *Republic*. Aristotle's justification of the necessity of families is, too, for men and women of a certain social class to the ends of a particular (existing) social order; the mini-aristocracy that is a family cannot be realized among male and female slaves themselves for Aristotle—there's no one to be ruler. Plato and Aristotle both saw the kind of family with which they were familiar as a particular institution fitted to possible social orders which might be defended. Neither saw this family as a necessity for organizing reproductive relations between males and females just as such. In fact, in ancient Greece there were different systems of reckoning status and lineage for those born of free and those born of mixed (i.e. slave and free) parentage, regardless of sex, and such rules organizing familial ties could and sometimes did change (Patterson 1982, 140). Of neither does it seem right to say, as Williams does of Aristotle, that he construed biological sex itself as a necessary social identity.

I am not then convinced that the Greeks could not know that even having been born female, one might not have been a "woman," where "woman" refers to a social identity (or some number of class or status bound identities). They certainly were aware at least that there were very different social roles for free and slave females, as for free and slave males. Nor does it matter if the social difference between free and slave males was (even on average) much greater than between free and slave females. There is no surprise in its being the case in a patriarchal, class-hierarchical, slaveholding society that there is—literally—nothing like being a well-born, free, adult male. No one ever seems to confuse the social identity of well-born free male with the "genuinely necessary sexual identity" of being sexed male; everyone knows there's more to it than that. What requires explaining, then, is not why no one conflates being a biological begetter with a quite particular political-social-moral identity, but why it is so easy to equate being a biological bearer with one. It is not after all some unnoticeable elision of sex to gender that we know enough not to do, and the Greeks did not know enough not to do. The Greeks *were* able to know that it isn't so simple, while sometimes "we" (including Williams, apparently) can *forget* that it isn't. I think the real difference between the situations of women and of slaves lies elsewhere. It lies in the *recognition of coercion* in the case of slaves, but not in the case of women.

Williams says, "The role of women could be taken for granted by most Greeks as natural. . . ." I do not doubt this, but I want to examine *why*. I have argued that since there are different roles for females of different class or status, taking for granted the naturalness of any women's roles cannot simply be taking those particular roles to be determined by the fact of their biological sex alone. The apparent "naturalness" of women's roles here must mean that they are seen as *not contrary* to women's natures; unlike being a slave, being a woman is not seen as "being in a condition imposed and sustained by force" (124). The obvious "arbitrariness and violence" (123) of enslavement is absent, or not obvious, in the case of women; thus the "standard" assumption, according to Williams, "that there was nothing arbitrary or coercive about the traditional arrangements" (ibid).

I've already spoken to the error of assuming that being "born a woman," in the relevant social sense of woman, is a biological *fait accompli*. Turning this around, we might also note that being born slave is just as much and in the same way a *fait accompli* as being born a woman, *given* the social order; many were born, rather than taken, into slavery in ancient Greece. Williams emphasizes that the free Greek males liked to distinguish themselves from barbarians, women, and slaves (122). But he wants to press the idea that being slave or not really could be seen as one's individual luck, i.e. the luck of the existing individual one actually is, while being a woman could not. Being a woman could not be seen to be arbitrary (even, he notes, if it was recognized as conventional), because it could not be thought to fall upon individuals who might have fared otherwise. But this is wrong: The existing sexed individual, male or female, might well imagine being born (or kidnapped into) other social worlds, where certain facts about oneself do not mean what they do in one's own.

Indeed, Williams is committed to the fact that a free woman could as readily imagine herself enslaved as a free man, for the contingent disaster of slavery could befall free persons of either sex. But so could a slave woman imagine herself free. She could imagine, for example, that she was born to a mother—her own, in fact—who had never been taken into slavery, and so could imagine she had been born a "woman," i.e. a free female and potential wife of a free man, rather than a "slave" or "slave woman." It is possible then to imagine oneself a woman when one is not, and to imagine oneself not a woman when one is. Such possibilities are imaginable *for females* within a social order with various roles and statuses for women (as they are imaginable by imagining a different social order). It is not, as Williams has it, that the test of imaginability or unimaginability (and hence the nonnecessity or necessity) of "woman" as a social identity variable over individuals rests on whether some Thales imagines this as a possibility *for him*. Or rather, this raises a different point about whose imagination counts here. The question of conceivability at issue has less to do with the imaginability of variations in role assignments among individuals, or within or between societies, than with the recognition of coercion and the credibility of evidence for it.

What shows that slavery is not natural to human beings is not theoretical argument about people's "natures," but the obvious fact that slavery requires coercion to subject them to it and keep them in it. If they were let to live otherwise, they would. The coercive subjection of some by others was taken for granted as the social and economic price of a certain way of life. Yet in the case of Greek slavery, subjection by force and, once subjected, exposure to violence was still something of which "any rational person would complain" (116) with reasons no one could deny. Everyone knew slaves were taken and kept by force. Everyone knew slaves were "answerable" with their bodies (108), variously liable to beating, branding, hard labor, rape and concubinage, disruption of ties of blood and affection, and sometimes torture. "It is not hard to say what is bad about the life of a slave, and slaves everywhere have said it" (112), Williams tells us; in ancient Greece it was said "frequently in drama and, certainly, in everyday life" (ibid.).

If "it was no secret to the Greeks . . . why it was unenviable bad luck to be in the power of another" (124), what then of women, their treatment and testimony? Williams says being a woman was "not seen, most of the time and in particular by men, as so bad. It was, for instance, less overtly coercive" (124). Here, "woman" clearly refers to females of a particular social status, for female slaves were obviously subject to all of the unenviable and brutal treatments above mentioned (perhaps with the exception of certain forms of hard labor). Compared with female slaves, the position of "women" would appear less overtly coercive. Yet slave and free often worked side by side in Greece, and surely there were trusted male slave domestics and workers who were neither secluded and confined within the household nor treated as sexual property of their owners, whereas "women" were both. It is also reasonable to think that women in private households, slave and free, were liable to sexual coercion and physical battery in ways many women are in "the home" today.

Reasonable speculation aside, Williams reminds us that complaints about the treatment of women are to be found in the literature of this culture, "almost every surviving word" of which was written by men (119). A woman in a fragment of Sophocles's complains that women are "nothing, are sold into marriage and moved around at their husband's will" (ibid.). It didn't take Sophocles to state the obvious. One wants to say: It is not hard to say what is bad about the life of a woman, and women everywhere have said it; if sometimes as *dramatis personae*, also "certainly, in everday life." If it is an obvious grief of slaves to answer with their bodies, so it is and has been the plight of females in many social stations. Is it possible that free men were more likely to be presented with the complaints of slaves than of wives? If the day-to-day continuance without violent revolt of tens of thousands of slaves in their vulnerable and often painful servitude did not give proof that their condition was unforced after all, why would it do so for women?

I don't disagree with Williams's claim (taken as a very rough generalization) that the Greeks saw being a woman as a necessary identity, and being a slave as not always or so clearly one. Nor am I suggesting that the conditions of slaves and women, or the Greeks' perceptions of them, were the same. My point is that the *evidence* for the involuntary, vulnerable, coercive nature of women's situation seems quite comparable, both in the forms of known treatment and of testimony, to that for slaves. The difference would not seem to be in the recognizability of an unchosen and unenviable situation of which any rational person could complain, but rather in its being *recognized*, in particular by those in a position to enforce that situation for others while remaining protected from it themselves.

What's in a Necessary Identity?

How, then, can some females' being women (or females' generally being various types of women) be *necessary* if the role or roles of women clearly involve subjection to men in ways of which women have often complained, and ways they have sometimes avoided or resisted?

The most successful part of Williams's account is his showing that Aristotle's saying that some people were slaves by nature could not make it be or seem so. It could not do so in the face of evidence manifest to those in as good a position to pronounce on the situation as Aristotle was: "The Greek world recognised the simple truth that slavery rested on coercion" (117). This recognition was hardly avoidable owing to the kind of institution Greek chattel slavery was, with its direct resort to war and capture, and its potential (and so imaginable, even if minor) threat to free people.

Williams's comparison between women and slaves then seems to come down to this. The Greeks could hardly fail to see that slaves were coerced into and within their lives as slaves, but the Greeks could not simply see that women were (comparably?) coerced into and within their lives as women. The latter remains puzzling. That a woman's life was that of subjection to the power, authority, and force of men, in general and in particular, whether they liked it or not, was one of the most obvious things about it. If male Greeks (perhaps not only free ones) proverbially were very glad not to be women, they knew very well why.

The "Aristotelian speciality" (126) of declaring certain social worlds consistent with a necessarily harmonious cosmic order—and providing the descriptions of things needed to preserve the claim of harmony—is particularly vulnerable to clear and common evidence of force, resistance, and strife. Either the order is not harmonious or the social world is out of whack. That was Williams's point about Aristotle on slavery. The next best blanket theoretical position justifying subordination of some by others is that the subordinated voluntarily serve. If one adds that it is in the nature of the subordinates to so comply, as Aristotle does in his claim that women's deliberative faculty is "without authority," this position naturalizes the subordination as well. But claims of voluntary servitude are similarly unstable in the face of opposition. Either sort of theoretical claim—"naturalness" or "voluntariness"—is poised for exhibition as flimsy wish-fulfillment or shabby ideology if complaints and struggles against subjection are not muted or strategically deflected.

Williams says men saw women's situation as "not so bad" and "less overtly coercive." There are two things to be looked at here: *what* men saw to be women's situation, and that it was *men's* view of it. On the first point, it's clear why women's roles being less bad and less coercive won't do here; any obvious need for force or restraint to sustain this role, or to contain individuals within it, will belie its inevitability in the order of things. The second point raises the question Whose recognition counts? The "Greek world" that knew what Aristotle tried not to admit seems to include both free and slave; free men's fears and reflections, as well as slave's testimonies, are invoked or alluded to by Williams. In the case of women it is different; it is *men's* estimate of women's situation that is appealed to, and it is not clear whether or how women's own testimonies count.

Well over two millennia after the Greeks, John Stuart Mill (Mill 1869) replied on behalf of women to both the arguments from nature and from voluntary submission. In one of many enduringly elegant ripostes, Mill responded to the second argument that it simply wasn't true that women accepted their roles. The proof was utterly straightforward: Once able to write and speak publicly, many women said they did not. Mill was right to notice that women's having a "public" voice in saying this is a matter of critical importance. A public voice is "louder," more audible or audible to more people, than private complaint. It is more durable and tangible too, able in some forms (for example, written ones) to persist as documentary evidence. More than this, a newly public voice of subjected people is itself already a change in the configuration of epistemic community, of who can say and claim to know. It may not by itself confer credibility, but it is an opening wedge.

Still, in Mill's time as in the time of the Greeks, women may say, but it's men who are the judges. Mill went on from this brief reply to an explanation of why many more women were understandably not likely to voice their complaints, much less "be collectively rebellious to the power of men" (443). He might, though, have explored another issue: the variety of ways in which what women say goes unheard or is easily discredited, and how women's resistance or rebellion fails to be noted as such. It is after all not just saying, but *being heard*, that constitutes having a voice. And it is those already authorized to enter and moot claims who, at least initially, decide whose claims count for what, or count at all. Theories that would naturalize or justify some people's subjection to others have to be supported by social arrangements that make truths about people's subordination and its alternatives hard to recognize, or easy to cover up. This includes making certain testimonies costly if not impossible, as Mill knew. It also includes making certain testimonies easily impeachable where they nonetheless emerge.

If the case of women's subordination appeared different to the men referred to as "Greeks" in Williams's discussion, perhaps appearances are the place to look. Instead of asking how females' being women could be necessary, especially with at least some coercive aspects showing and complained of, we might ask this: What does it take to make roles like this continue to *look necessary enough*, and not just or primarily to those assigned to the roles, but to those others in the business of shoring them up? I think the answer is far less complicated than the social apparatus that the answer requires. The key is: The more obvious the coercion required to sustain an identity (and keep people in it) is, the less necessary that identity (for those people) appears. In turn, the more visible the coercion is to everybody, and the more audible the complaints against it by those coerced, the more obvious the coercion is likely to be.

Whether people can "tell" an identity isn't necessary is not solely a question of whether there is coercion into and within it. It is also a function of how obvious the coercion is to all; this includes how deniable the coercion is by those who will appear as coercers if coercion cannot be denied. In general, the less force that must be exerted against a person's formed will and express intentions; the more shielded or secluded the arenas of force; the more routine and global the total system of enforcement and restraints; and—crucially, in the event that the others fail or do not apply—the more effectively silenced or presumptively discredited are the victims, the less obvious or more deniable coercion will be. These are the effects of the social processes that make and keep identities looking necessary. These identities need to be *naturalized, privatized,* or *normalized,* in some combination. Those who bear the identities must be *epistemically marginalized* or *unauthorized,* so that the former setup cannot be contradicted or contested by them. In the "ideal" case, it cannot even be pointed out. But there are no real ideal cases so long as identities are parts of a functioning social order in which identified and identifiers are ongoing participants. At the limit lies a situation of direct violence in which there are no subordinates, only victims, "petrified" objects of main force (Weil [1945] 1986, 185). Up to that point, it is a requirement of *interpersonal* relations that terms of recognition, however asymmetrical, be kept alive and in play (see Thomas 1995).

I believe this is the situation Williams is trying to bring out in saying that for the "Greeks" "woman" was a necessary identity. He wants to explain why they couldn't "tell." Williams wants to find the explanation of this in a certain kind of "fact" about what the "Greeks" thought, a concept they didn't have or a distinction they didn't draw. But there is no one fact (or even a few) that explains this, and the many relevant facts that do are not ones "about" people, or even a group of people, in the sense of properties those people or groups simply "have." The relevant facts are about relations of power and resistance, address and response, expression and recognition *between* people or groups.

Social identities—adult, woman, worker, shaman, master, warrior, uncle, wife—are socially salient means of identification and recognition of people by themselves and others. What are identified are interpersonally significant positions, standings, or roles characterized by powers and prerogatives, responsibilities, and exposure to expectations and claims. The structure of such facts as constitute identities is relational: A's are identified as B's by C's (themselves and/or others) in the context of certain institutions or practices, or to certain ends. Recognizable identities invite both predictions about and expectations of their bearers. The line between these may not be well defined, and the expectations include expressly normative ones, expectations about what certain people may, should, or must do and about the kinds of responsibility and answerability appropriate to them (Smiley 1992, 190, 240). We should look for the apparent necessity of identities, then, in many facts about who has recognized power over whom, how the power is expected to be exercised. The powers includes asymmetric or lopsided epistemic authority some have over others, and the muting or absence of "voice" of subordinates. These are facts about who gets to do what to whom, and who gets to talk about what gets done and is taken seriously by those with powers of authoritative judgment.

Necessary identities are created and maintained in complex social arrangments and their allied epistemic regimes. Necessary identities require a certain kind of social reality with a certain distribution of credibility; each fills gaps in the other. These together determine whether many things are likely to happen or not, and who will be in a position to credibly attest to what is going on. They set limits within which there can be interpretation of what undeniably takes place, of whether, for example, it is remarkable or typical, in need of explanation or not worth pointing out. The terminology of "necessity" is in one way unhappy for the kind of social determination this involves, for it is a matter of degree. In another way, it is perfectly apt; the "necessity" of identities refers to just how much certain understandings of some people's places are *needed* by some other people to legitimate the latter's treatment of the former. Identities are necessary to make treatments of some people look "matter of course" where those treatments would be extraordinary for some other people, especially for those delivering the treatment.

The relative "necessity" of some social identities consists not in the fact that some features of some people make those identities inevitable for them, but in the degree of difficulty in making plausible, imaginable, or even coherent claims that it *need not be that way* for those people. The greater the inevitability of this difficulty, the more "necessary" an identity is. How necessary an identity is, is less a question of its specific content (e.g. "woman" or "slave") than of the precise combination of real force and epistemic rigging that is required to sustain that difficulty. The situation of black slaves in the antebellum United States may in some respects be more like the situation of women in ancient Greece than like slaves there, for example. The situations of U.S. black slaves and ancient Greek free women include strictly private ownership and use, the relevance of bodies of a certain kind, and relatively complete epistemic disqualification, particularly in those matters relating to their own subjection and treatment. The necessity of certain identities is not, after all, for those who bear them, but for those who might otherwise have to account for the way they treat those people. The assumption of a necessity takes the place of certain justifications that might otherwise be required and sought, or experienced as missing (Judith Bradford, conversation). The distinction Williams tries to make can only be drawn within a more complex picture—or a picture of a more complex set of relations and effects—than he provides.

How to Make Identities (Seem) Necessary

It might truly be said that Plato wrote the book on necessary identities, or at least the first philosophically systematic one. Williams might have profited by paying as much attention to what that Greek had worked out in elaborate detail as to Aristotle's attempt at the quick way. With the same unnerving *sangfroid* that he displays in dissecting the breeding and other functions of his guardian class, Plato in the *Republic* gives a stunningly well-thought-out blueprint for a rigidly, hierarchically stratified society in which all stations are inexorably naturalized, everyone born to a lifelong place, every place already structured for its ordained occupants. Enormous thought has gone into a central problem of social engineering: completely coordinating a social and epistemic structure.

The rigidity of actual placements and controls, Plato is fully aware, must be precisely synchronized with an epistemic regime, one of the principal functions of which is to erase factors of human authority and design. Plato envisions a population imbued with widely disseminated "useful falsehoods" and an elite (or perhaps elites) possessing both truths and powers rigidly shielded lest anyone be in a position to see and say something that suggests alternatives either to the whole system or to anyone's places within it. Intentional totalitarian versions of this sort of thing tried within the actual world result in matching miserable cynicism and furtiveness to clumsy deceit and corruption. Where that fails as an equilibrium, there is terror, detention, disappearance, execution. The only really utopian thing about Plato's design is the promise that the requisite epistemic and material organization will be obtained without considerable, or even significantly remedial, violence. (Unless this is itself a useful lie.)

Identities identify people for certain activities or treatments. The necessity of identities has to do not with their prescriptive or permissive content, but with how firmly that content is kept in unquestioned, and preferably unquestionable, place. Several sorts of practices and processes shore up the necessity of identities. These occur at the intersection of patterns of relationship, social practices and institutions, their material conditions and environments, and distributions of credibility and authority. In real social worlds the propagation of identities is a complicated and always unstable accomplishment, requiring a variety of supports and, like all serviceable designs, a fair degree of redundancy.

Naturalizing identities involves producing and sustaining appearances of the spontaneous inevitability of certain places for certain people. Inevitability is best simulated by no-entry/no-exit identities. Since nothing denaturalizes situations quicker than evidence of coercion into them, the most effective implementation of naturalized identities is making them conditions of birth, ceasing at death. Individuals upon whom the identities are conferred simply "find" themselves in them from the point of self-consciousness, and others never know them otherwise. Spontaneity fits ill not only with abrupt induction or impressment, but with obvious signs of election or conferral, for what is decided or given might be rescinded or retracted. Physical features or marks, body-types or conditions, are the very best bases for assignment at birth. It is then as if the individual's identity had come into the world with the individual, due to some straightforward fact about her or him.

This naturalizing pattern fits many actual cases of gendered, racial, or ethnically based identities. Although it may be the optimal arrangement, other cases of subjected populations suggest that practices of physical marking (branding, shearing, tattooing, costuming) may sometimes substitute for naturally occurring physical features, or appear as needed indicators of too-subtle ones. Inevitability of identities will then be a question of making sure that appropriate candidates are indelibly separated out. In fact, it is common for this latter process to overlay the former, socially ramifying identities naturally attributed. This is not surprising, in that naturalizing is a process of making sure people know what marks to "look for" in others.

Marks of identity are only, as it were, the signifiers of possible modes of interaction, responsibilities, and treatments. The realities of what happens to people once marked may go differently, and may go well beyond the explicit, commonly recognized norms defining their status. It is a commonplace that subordinates are placed not only under the socially sanctioned authority or control of others, but are thereby in fact very often exposed to force or abuse. The treatments of subordinates that are best shielded from scrutiny are those confined to private spaces. "Private spaces" and contexts can include those that are literally enclosed or separated off from entry or inspection by all but a restricted group to whom those spaces "belong." *Privatization* can also be effected by customs, moral understandings, or laws that declare certain interactions outside legitimate or acceptable scrutiny, reaction, or public comment by others, even if those interactions take place in plain sight, or in places not private in the former sense. The privacy, in either sense, of interactions between ruled and rulers is a direct way to make blatant coercion and violence disappear either literally, behind walls, doors, and fences, or virtually, by disqualifying as improper or inappropriate intervention (or even report) by "outsiders."

Naturalizing and privatizing for the most part set promising conditions for coercive practices to proceed without some of the compunction or protest they might otherwise stir; they aim to keep some people and what happens to them outside the view of some authoritative community of mutual moral accounting. But they are pretty blunt instruments, and can never conceal all that they need to. An enormous role is left for patterns of practice that seem at first glance the inverse of ones that try to keep things private. Yet, in what is only a seeming contradiction, practices that *normalize* coercive dominance can not only be more effective than privatizing it, but can work in tandem with standards of privacy, each shoring up the other.

Certain patterns of behavior and relations are normalized when there are effective norms pertaining to them, but the norms *presume* these relations and patterns to exist as a threshold of application for the norms. Norms' (moral, legal, social) being premised on situations presupposed as standard and normal is ubiquitous, and not inherently a problem. It can be a problem, though, when the regulative function of norms tends to conceal their constitutive roles: when what norms tell us to do given the assumed conditions tends to deflect attention to why these conditions are assumed to obtain and whether they need or should obtain. It can be more problematic still when the norms purport to embody significant controls or restraints within areas of conduct they regulate, with the effect of making legitimate uncontrolled or unrestrained conduct beneath the threshold at which they apply.

In a clear example bearing on the kind of necessary identity "woman" can in some contexts be, Catharine MacKinnon jarringly reveals why rape law and its customary interpretation in American jurisprudence reveal "forced sex is paradigmatic," i.e. rendered or taken as given in law (MacKinnon 1987, 141). The law predefines spheres of consent by presumption ("little girls may not consent; wives must" (142)), a dividing practice that sets facts of coercion and women's testimonies out of play in many cases. The issue becomes not whether a person is coerced but what the law permits in the way of sexual access by certain categories of men to certain categories of women. In cases not so defined, the law adjudicates "the level of acceptable force starting just above the level set by what is seen as normal male sexual behavior," rather than at the victim's perceived point of coercion (143). In actual cases, what women typically need to prove is not just the aggression, threat, or control of assailants, but fairly violent application of force.

For such reasons MacKinnon claims, "Rape, from women's point of view, is not prohibited; it is regulated" (144). A lattice of law, custom, expectation, and the familiarity of what is pervasive and repeated, makes it so. If regulating force past a certain point can legitimize force up to that point, so can permitting coercive treatments make those who abstain from inflicting them appear admirable. If you may of course beat your slaves, you are a very kind mistress not to do it. When practices that otherwise would look bad are rendered normal in these ways for certain contexts or certain people in them, those who rebel against what "everyone" accepts appear as irrational freaks, malcontents, complainers, unstable deviants, or dangerous elements out of control.

Each of these social processes, just barely sketched, requires and constitutes a sort of "epistemic firewall" sealing off recognizable injuries and credible complaints. Often large portions of this firewall consist of physical confinements and exclusions, explicit barring from certain positions or places of authoritative speech, or disabling economic and intellectual conditions. Subordinates are often forbidden to speak and punished for "talking back." Some people are not allowed (or just unlikely) to be seen or heard on podiums and pulpits, or in classrooms, courtrooms, or councils. Some people are kept illiterate, unskilled, and undereducated. Some people and what happens to them are kept in their own spaces where others mostly do not go. But it is also necessary that some kinds of people are "known" going in to be liable to irrational discontents, manipulative complaints, incompetent assessments, childish exaggerations, dangerous willfuless, malicious ingratitude, wily deceit, or plain stupidity. The unnaturalness, exhibitionism, or abnormality of their claims or pleas or behavior itself shows, even "proves" their unreliability as judges and informants, the incredibility of their testimonies.

A reduced, circumscribed, or discredited status as knowers and claimers—being epistemically *marginalized* or *unauthorized*—is no small working part of the identities of those "necessarily" subordinate. In particular, what they are in a position to know better than anyone else—what it is like to be in their place—is one of the things they are presumptively disqualified from accurately reporting. It is not just that their views don't count; given what those people are, their views can't count. Women cry, manipulate, and complain. Slaves lie and run. Servants loaf and steal. Laborers are stupid. Natives are childish. No identity is so necessary as one that successfully precludes its bearer's confuting it. All the better if the means of enforcement of the identity actually induce or require in its bearers behavior that makes it impossible to deny.

Knowing Others' Places

In 1896 the Supreme Court of the United States found against Homer Plessy, an octoroon, who tested the Louisiana state law requiring "separate but equal" railway accommodations for whites and blacks. Justice Henry Billings Brown, writing for the majority, denied that separate accommodations were a "badge of inferiority" for colored people. Brown said "it is not by reason of anything found in the act, but solely because the colored race chooses to put that construction upon it" (*Plessy v. Ferguson*, 163 U.S. 537 [1896]). The opinion of those who wore that badge was a mere "construction," while the opinion of white justices was law.

A century later, a shocking videotape was broadcast across the United States that showed Rodney King, a black man, face down on the pavement being repeatedly hit and kicked by armed white policemen surrounding him. A white jury later failed to see that videotaped performance as an unnecessary application of force by officers of the Los Angeles Police Department. The jury "saw" what we all saw; somehow they were able to "unsee" what it was. In newspaper and magazine coverage following the incident and the verdict, African-Americans of every economic status and many occupations were quoted asserting the common occurrence of police harassment and undue force applied to blacks, and describing their own experiences and fears of this. Many white people do not seem to believe this form of mistreatment, or many other reported daily ones, are commonplace for black people.

In 1989, the *New York Times* reported that "[s]urveys have found that as many as one in four women report that men they were dating persisted in trying to force sex on them despite their pleading, crying, fighting him off or screaming. In one survey of women on 32 college campuses, 15 percent had experienced at least one rape, and 89 percent of the time it was by men the women knew. Half the rapes occurred during a date." Even so, "Despite the high proportion of women who have experienced forced sex, very few men admit to having been involved in such acts" (Goleman 1989).

The necessity of the identities of some of us, long ago as now, consists of many facts about our social arrangements and how we have learned to see ourselves and others in them. These contingent features of our social worlds make what some people know the condition under which others cannot speak or be heard. What those silenced others know is precisely what discredits them: It is itself the reason for their being prevented or discouraged from saying it. At the upper bound of effectiveness, necessary identities may seem to consist in just a simple fact or few about some people that cannot be denied, especially by them, and that renders them inevitably subject to others, who no longer need explain anything to anyone who counts.[1]

eight

Unnecessary Identities

Representational Practices and Moral Recognition

The human body is the best picture of the human soul.
> —Ludwig Wittgenstein, *Philosophical Investigations*

I guess this depends upon what picture of the human body you have in mind.
> —Catharine MacKinnon, "Not A Moral Issue"

Southern trees bear a strange fruit, blood on the leaves and blood at the
  root
Black body swinging in the Southern breeze, strange fruit hanging from the
  poplar trees.
Pastoral scenes of the gallant South, the bulging eyes and the twisted
  mouth,
Scent of magnolia sweet and fresh, and the sudden smell of burning flesh!
Here is a fruit for the crows to pluck, for the rain to gather, for the wind to
  suck, for the sun to rot, for a tree to drop
Here is a strange and bitter crop.
> —Lewis Allan, "Strange Fruit," recorded by Billie Holiday

One moral philosopher says, "The human form in others invokes deep-seated patterns of projection, identification, and sympathy" (Weston 1992, 49). Well, sometimes. Very often the human form in some people prompts in others indifference, suspicion, fear, aversion, contempt, xenophobia, and, more than occasionally, hatred and sadism. This can lead to disregard, ridicule, abuse, exclusion, subordination, subjugation, exploitation, violence, oppression, enslavement, and, more than occasionally, extermination of many whose human forms did not invoke identification or sympathy in some others. This happens not only between individuals, but conspicuously between "peoples" or cultures; and not only between peoples, cultures, or societies, but within them. In fact, negative or diminished recognition and response happen all the time to people who are identified with groups despised, devalued, or feared by some others. Why this happens, happens often, and happens when it does is an urgent matter for empirical investigations. What it is for this to happen—what characteristic forms moral misrecognition takes, how such patterns are expressed, and what moral toll they take— is one topic for an ethics about actual social life. The specific structures of perception and understanding, or misperception and misunderstanding, that constitute failures of mutual recognition is a central study for a socially critical moral epistemology.[1]

This essay is about one aspect of that, a study of the relation of representational practices to moral perceptions. I call it *moral graphics*. Some depictions are morally dubious or outright malignant, not (only) because of what is individually shown but because of the power of what is shown in the the context of certain practices of representation. Some picturing practices representationally "ensoul"—personify, subjectify— some people for others in morally disturbing or vicious ways, whether as "objects," as diminished subjects, or as disqualified (or peculiarly qualified) agents. Awareness of these images may also figure in distorted interactions between people, patterned in ways that transcend individual whims, tastes, blind spots, or biases.

The patterns of representation that interest me here express what Diana Meyers calls "culturally normative prejudice," commonplace stereotypic conceptions of social groups carried by "vivid figurations that turn up in widely disseminated stories and pictures" (Meyers 1994, 52). "Culturally entrenched figurations," Meyers notes, "are passed on without obliging anyone to formulate, accept, or reject repugnant negative propositions about any group's standing or self-congratulatory positive propositions about one's own" (Meyers 1994, 53). Like Meyers, I believe pervasive or salient patterns of representation of certain "kinds" of people are not only expressions, but are vehicles of moral prejudice of varied types.

Often the assumption that people with certain physical or behavioral characteristics *are* a (socially significant) kind, and what kind that kind is, is itself propagated, if not created, by these representational practices. Representational practices are among those that construct socially salient identities for people. These identities, once culturally commonplace, can start to look "necessary," as if the identity naturally befitted the people, rather than people's being fitted to it through many social facts and practices, including these representational ones. The practices condition our sense of which features of human beings are "identifying," and they confer specific interpretations and associations on identities constituted this way or by other means. While these practices can create honored and privileged identities, I am concerned here with the other kinds.

If some widespread and familiar practices of representation affect some people's morally significant perceptions of and interactions with other people, and if they can contribute to those perceptions' or interactions' going seriously wrong, they bear on fundamental questions for ethics. What allows us to take someone in particular to be deserving at all of the moral consideration due to people, whatever kind of consideration we might think that to be? What makes some of us take some of us to be worthy of lesser or different moral consideration than some others? These are questions about who various of us take to be "us" and who "them." They are questions about the constitution, not just the regulation, of a universe of moral kin. I want to look more closely here at one working part of those attitudes and habits of perception—such as racisms, ethnic chauvinisms, homophobias, or invidious sex, class, age, and other status distinctions—that erase or deform moral kinship among human beings.

The tendency in contemporary moral theory is to believe that problems of moral recognition can (or must) be met *within* a normative moral theory, either by constructive definitions of personhood, by formal requirements of universality or universalizability, or by substantive demands for impartial or equal consideration. I do not think these theoretical manouvers meet the problem I have in mind. Verbal definitions of personhood depend for their application on our being able to recognize the applications of their constitutent parts, being able to "see the same" in open-ended applications of the defining concepts. They require us to recognize, say, intelligence, rationality, self-consciousness, intentional behavior, or thought of certain kinds or complexities. Yet it is the very indisposition of some human beings to see quite the same—recognizably fully human—features in some (other) human beings that partly constitutes the problem in the first place. As for universalism, one universalizes predications over a domain; whatever isn't included within the domain will not be a possible substitution instance of a generalization, no matter how impeccably universal. Similarly, I can adopt a strategy of impartiality or substantive norms of equality with respect to those I morally consider, but this will not explain why I view them as eligible for this sort of moral consideration in the first place.

Ethical views that stress feeling as the wellspring of moral response may seem more promising in this regard. It may be true that how we "take" things and what we pay attention to depends on how things strike or interest us, that our perceptions are guided by primitive or immediate affective responses. But a less intellectualized view of morality does not itself solve problems of moral misrecognition. Morally directive and reactive feelings especially cannot be brute or blind surges of affect, whether any emotions or feelings are. Moral sentiments will have to discriminate, as our concepts do (and perhaps by means of them). And this will lead us back to asking how we have learned to feel *appropriately*, to feel the right things, at the right time, in the right proportion, toward the right objects; or for the case in point, how we may have learned otherwise.

So here I turn attention to some practices of representation that I believe show a way our perception of, and responsiveness to, individuals' humanity can be shaped, and so how specific patterns of morally significant nonperception or misperception are propagated or abetted. I will call these practices *stereo-graphy*, *porno-graphy*, and *necro-graphy*. I use these categories to highlight clear examples of inscriptions of (or on) human flesh that are morally charged in negative, even hideous, ways. Each of the practices I discuss may well have its positive analogue. Depiction of role models may be positive stereo-graphy, ritual practices of respect for the dead, positive necro-graphy. Some of those who distinguish erotic from pornographic depiction think the former does in the "right" way what the latter does harmfully or demeaningly.

Analysis of privileged or malicious constructions of social identity is standard fare in burgeoning literatures of cultural, literary, feminist, and ethnographic studies, and theories of race, postcolonialism, and sexuality. What is startling is how little attention has been paid to this at the center of moral philosophy "proper." By contrast, thousands of pages have been spent in this century alone at the center of moral philosophy on problems of egoism and bias resulting from individual self-interest, and on the nature of impartiality as a view free from invidious biases of any type. Worries about these prompt methodic intellectual remedies— generalization, universalization, role-taking, and other impartiality tests—for individuals to apply individually to their specifically moral reasoning in the event of moral deliberation.

Yet it is not at all clear that the circulation of socially systemic prejudice and its impacts on mutual recognition can be understood, much less remedied or extinguished, by focusing on what or how individuals think in discrete episodes of explicitly moral reflection. In fact, it is characteristic of prejudices that are truly "culturally normative" that the huge number of situations and encounters they structure, and morally deform, are often not experienced as problematic at all, neither dwelt nor deliberated upon, at least by those who are not on the losing end of them. The holders of the prejudice don't even notice its enactment, because it's normal; it feels like business as usual to them. That's what it means for a morally questionable pattern of relations to *be* culturally normative.

My objective here is limited, and my method is illustrative, not demonstrative. I hope only to make persuasive the claim that moral graphics and the politics of representation, which have scarcely been topics in moral philosophy at all, are among its most urgent issues.

A Body Is a Picture

When Wittgenstein remarked, "The human body is the best picture of the human soul" (Wittgenstein 1958, 178), he spoke of the "human soul," not in the sense of a metaphysical or supernatural entity, but in the sense of the personality that animates living human bodies. This is a remark about how we recognize so-called "mental" or "psychological" states in human beings, how we tell that people are understanding, suffering, hoping, intending, or grieving, or when they are angry, afraid, confident, or puzzled.[2] The states of the soul, in this sense, are those states and modulations of what we like to call people's "inner" lives. To recognize and respond to the full gamut, rich variety, and changing procession of these states is to take people in as human personalities, and not as objects, furniture, or (other) animals.

The remark reminds us of something we all know; we "tell" what is going on "in" others (when we can tell) by paying attention to how living human bodies look and what they do and say in particular settings. Some of what requires attention is obvious and striking: Wincing, writhing, screaming, whimpering, crying, and clutching at a wound are among the clearest expressions of pain. Some of what needs to be noticed is subtle, ephemeral, or ambiguous: eyes blinking or narrowing, lips tightening or curling, the complexion going rosy or pale might mean many different things, some of them expressive of personality (embarrassment, envy) and some of them not (indigestion, involuntary reflexes). And so, in fact, might wincing, crying, or screaming mean different things, personally expressive or not, depending on what else is going on or has led up to them. It might not be pain but surprise, grief, or hilarity that these displays show; or, one might be slicing onions or rehearsing a part. So it is not just behaviors and features that tell us what is going on with people, but combinations and configurations of behaviors and features, and not just these configurations, but their occurrence in certain circumstances. What matters for telling what others are experiencing, feeling, thinking, enjoying, or suffering are *whole familiar patterns* of clusters of features (of behavior and reaction, vocalization, posture and gesture, carriage, facial expression, utterance and inflection) in certain characteristic *settings* and *sequences* (Wittgenstein 1958, remarks 580–91; and 1970, remarks 238, 492, 533–34, for example). Any part of the whole configuration (a gesture, exclamation, look, or comment) might mean something quite different in a different combination or setting. Wittgenstein sometimes helpfully called the recurring patterns "physiognomies," reminding us of how such configurations of features, like familiar faces, have a distinctive "look," and appear "the same" in the midst of their own changing play of expressions and against many different backgrounds (Wittgenstein 1970, remarks 375–78, 513–14, 567–68). Facial expressions themselves ("looks"), of course, are among the most salient physiognomies that display what people are experiencing.

By speaking of a body as "picturing" a soul, Wittgenstein's remark reminds us of something else, which we may mostly forget. *What* these immensely variable but still recognizable patterns of features-in-context show (or "picture") about people is something we have had to *learn*. We learn from and are taught by others to recognize what states of others' souls are expressed in their comportment, gesture, visage, and expression; and others must know what subjective states our comportment, gesture, visage, and expression show, in order to teach us to name and describe our own psychological, emotional, or intentional states. As with other depictions—symbols, maps, diagrams, schematics, signs, and assertions—we have to grasp the code of recognition (what Wittgenstein called the "method of projection" or the "application" of a kind of picture) that connects certain displays with certain meanings, and so makes a picture show what it does.

It can be easy to forget that we must learn what the expressiveness of bodies tells us, because particular expressive styles, once familiar, have a way of seeming natural and inevitable. Yet the "language" of bodily expression (even when this includes verbal utterance) is notoriously variable in many respects, not only among cultures or societies, but within them. Expressions of respect, sadness, courtesy, anger, or shame may vary significantly and globally between cultures, but often also vary substantially among class or ethnic or age groups, or between males and females, within the same culture. Even where expressions are native to and spontaneous for human beings, such as smiles or certain reactions to pain, there are still specific meanings attached to variations on these displays and to the significance of the situations and interactions in which they occur. There are polite smiles, demure smiles, seductive smiles, angry smiles, greedy smiles, condescending smiles, leering smiles, and pained ones. But which smiles are such, in which contexts, is not the same everywhere, and is not something anyone is born knowing. It must be learned from others in a particular social setting. So "a body is a picture" reminds us that our physical persons in action and expression are the concrete signs, read under conventions we have learned and been taught, of the states of our psychological or "inner" lives.

Learning what people's behavior and expression shows about them will be learned in learning the relevant concepts ("angry," "convinced," "self-important," "curious,") and in learning what to expect of, and how to respond to, people in the states the concepts mark. Our forming articulate beliefs about the states of people's subjective lives are just some among the responses (in actions, words, or feelings) which constitute our recognition of their "human souls," their subjective lives and personalities.[3] We will not only or always say, but may show in other ways, whether and how we are taking other human beings in as people. Not only "He's suffering" or "Poor you!" but a hand to the shoulder or face full of concern, show when points are taken about how it is for others. Our recognition of others may show directly and simply, or its display may be subtle or complex.

But if there is something to get right here, in belief, reaction, or feeling, then there is also something to get wrong, and different ways to do so. One might fail to recognize, or might misrecognize, what certain expressions mean. Not to notice the inappropriateness of a certain smile or remark to a transaction, location, or relationship may result in comedy or misunderstanding, or it may be a dangerous error or a cruel slight. But interestingly different kinds of mistakes are possible here.

A mistake can result from temporary inattention, or it may mean that one is a neophyte, and an outsider, or an oaf. These sorts of incompetence may be occasional and unsystematic, or a function of simple unfamiliarity. Other failures of recognition are not like this. I might, for example, not notice someone's state because I do not feel obliged or moved to pay enough attention to that person to notice this. I might not pay attention to what another is expressing because I am sure I already know what I would see or hear. I might have a habit of noticing only certain things about some people no matter what is there to be noticed. Or, I might see what is there to be noticed, but count what I see differently in some people's cases than in others. (His sticking by his decision is reassuring firmness, hers is a hard edge.) Cases like these might reflect idiosyncratic insensibility or bias, even when the failure of recognition is persistent, and when those who fail to be perceived are people of certain kinds or categories. But what if such forms of nonrecognition or misperception *typically* befall people of certain "kinds," especially when the viewers are of certain other "kinds"? Is this likely to be a peculiar coincidence?

Stanley Cavell has strikingly said that part of the interest in recognizing how the body pictures the soul is that "the block to my vision of the other is not the other's body but my incapacity or unwillingness to interpret or judge it correctly, to draw the right connections ... I suffer a kind of blindness, ... a kind of illiteracy" (Cavell 1979, 368). If we perceive the soul by "reading" the body, and this is something we have learned from others, perhaps we have not learned accurately to recognize all that we could. Suppose we have not learned to recognize certain psychological or emotional states in people, or have learned a peculiar coding of them; therein will lie certain interpersonal impediments, certain disturbing and poignant predicaments. Or, we might not have learned to recognize in certain *kinds* of people things we know how to see in the cases of others, or have learned not to interpret them in similar ways, or have learned to pay attention only to certain things, or have learned not to bother.

It is even possible to have learned that certain attributions of subjectivity or personality apply only to certain kinds of people; it might even be part of some concepts to work this way. (Might just anyone be "manly," "demure," or "bitchy"?) Perhaps our intersubjective literacy is not just spotty but selective; this depends on our teachers and our "reading" materials. If it is selective in certain ways for some kinds of us with respect to whole categories of others, this is not a personal deficit. It is a social problem with moral dimensions and, sometimes, tragic ones. There is a significant disanalogy between the socially learned ability to read people and ordinary literacy, for we do not without injury or illness forget how to read in the latter case. Yet upsurges in interethnic conflict, for example, can involve an interposition of distorted and diminished perceptions of some people by others where all had before lived as if, and sometimes as, kin.

Wittgenstein reminded us that our concepts for psychological states are profoundly *parochial*, in a particular sense: Their acquisition rests on, and their primary site of application remains, the familiar configuration, expressions, and comportment of a living human body. I believe this is right, but I also fear that the application of such characterizations to others might be parochial in other ways with which Wittgenstein was not concerned. When Wittgenstein said "... only of a living human being and what resembles (behaves like) a living human being can one say: it has sensations; it sees; is blind; hears; is deaf; is conscious or unconscious" (Wittgenstein 1958, remark 281), he used only the most generic attributes of a subject of experience, and his point was a generic one about certain pernicious and incoherent Cartesian views about the "mind" or "soul." I suspect Wittgenstein was sanguine about the equivalence of "human forms" for these purposes, and I do not think we can be. Still, as a view about how we tell what is going on with others, or what they are going through, "a body is a picture" is ripe with possibilities. It tells us important things about where we must look, what we must see, and what we must already be familiar with, to recognize others as kindred human beings. For the same reasons, it can help us to notice some ways this can fail, or what can get in the way. The most important thing it can help us to notice is that what is in the way is *not*, in fact, some people's bodies.

Graphing Souls

I claim that the body's being the soul's picture is an insight of deep moral importance. But some will immediately object that this is exactly, even dangerously, wrong, that taking the body to picture the soul is the *mistake* at the root of many kinds of prejudice. When people respond, so this objection goes, to the blackness, the femaleness, the Semitic or wizened appearance, the physical deformity, or so on, *instead of to the person*, there prejudice gets its grip. People, it is often said, need to see "beneath" or "past" merely superficial physical characteristics; institutions, it is sometimes said in the same vein, need to be "color-blind," "sex-blind," and so on. The body must not be *allowed* to matter, and so to mislead.

The worry is quite right here, but the diagnosis, I am claiming, is quite wrong. It is true that if the living human body, rightly taken or read, permits the soul to be recognized, if it is by the correct reading of your body that the person you are is seen, then it is also possible for a body, misread, unread, or illegible to occlude or distort the state, even the presence, of a human personality. This does commit us, for example, to "the view that as we move away from the normal human form the possibility of ascribing, for example, pain in the normal sense is compromised" (Cockburn 1990, 78). But this should not lead us to try to see through, beneath, or beyond human bodies, for then there is nothing left to take rightly or wrongly.

We do need to look in another direction, though. We should look at *who* it is who is unable to decipher the humanity in the expressive display of a particular living human body. We should look around to see *which* is the "normal" human form, expression, or comportment for those viewers, deviations from which result in misreadings or illegibility. We should take a look, in other words, at which body is "the" body—the standard or canonical one—for the viewers in question; perhaps better, we should ask whose body they take this to be. Which bodies and comportments are normatively or paradigmatically human within certain points of view, and what puts or holds them in that status? And which bodies, in consequence, are thought by some to have that bad habit of "getting in the way" of their own souls' being perceived?

Instead of going "blind," let's look harder at *how* we see or don't, directing our attention to what shapes our perceptions of the animating personalities in the bodies we see. Remember that to see what's in a picture (or what it is a picture of) we have to be familiar with the code of recognition which makes the picture picture what it does, as it does. Anything might be (or be recruited to serve in or as) a picture of something else. The very same thing might serve, differently applied or read, as a picture of two quite different things; and two quite different things, as a picture of the same. For something actually to picture (to depict, exemplify, illustrate, express, represent) something to us, we must use or take (or learn to use or take) it *that* way. We must learn what it pictures and how it pictures that. So too with bodies' pictures of their souls; we must learn *how* bodies are made to picture, and so *what* they show.

There are two ways we can learn this. We can learn how a *body* of a certain form in a certain kind of expressive comportment is a picture of a certain kind of soul or the state of it. Or we can learn through the uses of *pictures* of bodies how to understand the pictured bodies as pictures of souls. In either case, we learn a map from bodily expressions to states of the person, or even from body-kinds to person-kinds; we are taught or prompted to make "correct" judgments or responses to what is represented, whether by a body directly or by some picture(s) of it. Thus, understanding what bodies picture, and how, is a question of being party to certain *representational practices*, whether in the medium of words or in other media. These practices involve both ways the body can be pictured to project the soul differently (or even to project a different kind of soul), and the ways bodies themselves can, by being made to look different or having their looks marked as different from some other bodies, picture differences in or of the soul. I now turn to three broad categories of representational practices, with illustrations of the forming and deforming power of these ways of "graphing" human bodies.

Stereo-Graphy, Porno-Graphy, Necro-Graphy

Stereo-graphy refers to body-pictures that fuse representation of a group of human beings to one kind of bodily configuration or style of expression and comportment, and so identify those human beings exclusively or peculiarly with a certain kind or version of soul. Body-pictures can only be stereo-graphs when they are read both as generalizing (such people/such souls) and differentiating (such souls vs. other souls); otherwise any such representation will just be of someone who happens to be shown some way. For body-pictures to be stereo-graphs they must be a part of some *system* of pictures which codes this equation by repetition or salience. Or, they must be pictures apt to trigger responses controlled by connections or codes which are part of the context in which the picture appears. Either way (or mixing both), for body-pictures to be stereo-graphs they must be, or be connected to, practices of representing certain people in certain ways, where these ways are consistently different from the ways *other* people are represented. The origins, entrenchment, and reproduction of these codes may be complex, but it is not hard to notice that innumerable representations work stereo-graphically. Although "positive" stereo-graphs are possible, I use here (as throughout) disturbing (and I hope disturbingly representative) examples.

George Orwell's description of Marrakech, 1939, acutely analyzes a familiar pattern of racial stereography, and ends up, troublingly, too vividly enacting it:

> When you walk through a town like this—200,000 inhabitants, of whom at least 20,000 own literally nothing except the rags they stand up in—when you see how the people live, and still more, how easily they die, it is always difficult to believe that you are walking among human beings. All colonial empires are in reality founded upon that

fact. The people have brown faces—besides they have so many of them! Are they really the same flesh as yourself? Do they even have names? Or are they merely a kind of undifferentiated brown stuff, about as individual as bees or coral insects? They arise out of the earth, they sweat and starve for a few years, and then they sink back into the nameless mounds of the graveyard and nobody notices that they are gone. And even the graves themselves soon fade back into the soil. (quoted in Said 1979, 251–52)

"The Arab" or "North African" graphed here is first telescoped into the most wretched, ragged 10 percent, whose "easy" (for whom?) and "unnoticed" (by whom?) deaths partake of the same effacement that is "the" life of "such" people. The loaded master trope is that of the live, indeed teeming, but unindividuated and soulless mass of the "lowest" forms of nonhuman life, in which repetition of individuals is "a mindless stutter" without meaning (Dillard 1985, 160–61). In fact, these people do have names, are not born of earth but of particular women who may have fiercely loved them, and are very likely mourned and missed when they die by others with whom they have sung and played as well as sweated and (perhaps) starved. This potent trope virtually "unsouls" those whose bodies are rendered, massed, in its terms; to see them so is not to see their humanness, or at any rate, their individual humanity.

Orwell's *picture*—for it is of course that, not people but a depiction of a people—is not strange to many of us. Edward Said, who quotes Orwell, points out that in contemporary Western "newsreels or newsphotos, the Arab is always shown in large numbers. No individuality, no personal characteristics or experiences. Most of these pictures represent mass rage and misery, or irrational (hence hopelessly eccentric) gestures" (Said 1979, 287). In another discussion, Said examines Albert Camus's continuing status as a "universalist" writer, representing "liberated existential humanity facing cosmic indifference and human cruelty with impudent stoicism" (Said 1994, 185). Said asks us to notice that novels like *L'Etranger* and *La Peste*, supposed "parables of the human condition" (ibid., 175) use the deaths of unnamed and unindividuated Algerian Arabs to stage French characters' dramas of conscience and individual responsibility in what is in fact a context of colonialism. Sometimes it is what is in the background of depictions, or what fails to appear at all, that is an important part of the message sent. Some human beings may figure as a kind of challenging or hostile landscape for others' specifically human pursuits of happiness, glory, or self-consciousness.

Many familiar subhumanizing tropes are exploitable in stereo-graphy. Groups of people are often graphed as animals, even if sometimes awesome and beautiful ones, as in one description of the figuration of Zulu warriors in nineteenth-century British accounts as "not real people, more like dangerous black game that made the hunt especially exhilirating" (Tilghman 1991, 106 quoting Robert Edgerton). People still called "primitive" or "tribal" are often imagined or actually depicted (in ethnographic accounts as well as flora-and-fauna-like natural-historical displays) suspended in a "nonhistorical time" (Clifford 1988, 202). This mode of presentation perhaps images their lives as Edenic, but it invariably represents them, in the familiar and morally telling phrase, as "simpler souls."

These examples involve bodies pictured, but *bodies themselves* may be styled so as to show forth a soul deemed appropriate. Feminist philosophers like Sandra Bartky notice how gender as a social norm in our society requires the production of a female body "which in gesture and appearance is recognizably feminine," i.e., of a certain size and configuration, with a specific gestural and postural repertoire, and which suggests itself as an ornamental surface (Bartky 1990, 65). In what Judith Butler calls this "surface politics of the body" (Butler 1990, 135) the cultural "law" of gender is produced on and through bodies (of men and women both) in a "repeated stylization . . . a set of repeated acts within a highly rigid regulatory frame that congeals over time to produce the appearance of a substance, of a natural sort of being" (ibid., 33). The socially required production of gender as a look and an act projects a socially specified kind of personality and identity: masculine or feminine, where this duality is not just a difference but a hierarchy. A body thus engendered pictures a certain kind of soul and its social places.

Pornography—by a simple definition, explicit sexual depictions intended to arouse the reader or viewer sexually—is increasingly being analyzed as stereo-graphy. Since in most (and the most publicly visible and widely disseminated) pornography the depicted are women, and the presumed viewer is a heterosexual man, it is important to ask whether and how pornography stereo-graphs women as a group for these men; whether, or in what circumstances, in Catharine MacKinnon's bracing statement, "Men treat women as who they see women as being. Pornography constructs who that is" (MacKinnon 1987, 148; see Kittay 1984; and see Collins 1990 on racial stereography in pornography). We should ask as well how pornography stereo-graphs women *for themselves*, particularly when it is embedded in a wider array of culturally prevalent depictions, a general practice of *porno-graphy*.

I don't think it accidental that recent treatments, mostly by women, of pornography in the United States as a politically loaded representational practice with implications for all women coincide with a surge in the availability and general visibility of (especially soft-core) pornography, and with a blurring of boundaries between this and ever more ubiquitous sexualized displays of (mostly) female bodies in fashion, arts, advertising, film, video, and so on. What form of soul is graphed for ones whose bodies are so repetitively, ubiquitously marked as anonymous and public sexual displays? Naomi Scheman remarks that "[w]omen's bodies may be interchangeable, but not by us. Rather our bodies establish the terms under which we'll be exchanged, they establish our worth, our identity" (Scheman 1993, 185). Pervasive pornographing leaves little doubt what the going terms are.

Novelist Milan Kundera's depiction in *The Unbearable Lightness of Being* of one female character's nightmare suggests a macabre image for this: Naked women march in formation, singing in "the joyful solidarity of the souless," having thrown off "that laughable conceit, that illusion of uniqueness" (Kundera 1984, 57). With Tereza's dream Kundera dramatizes her fear that women are sexually interchangeable, that she and other women are trapped in "a vast concentration camp of bodies, one like the next, with souls invisible" (ibid., 47). But Kundera's view of this is not exactly right. Being porno-graphed, being relentlessly, involuntarily, anonymously, and publicly "sexualized," is not being graphically *un*souled, but being *en*souled in a specific way. This way is not really (as the common phrase has it) as a "sexual object," but rather as a generically sexualized subject, one whose gestures and behaviors will necessarily be taken (no matter what that subject means by them) as expressive of its sex, and a presumed sexuality. Being taken this way confutes self-possession: a firm grasp on one's individual identity and confidence that one's comportment is self-expressive in ways reasonably under one's control. Kundera says Tereza longed to "be a body unlike other bodies, to find that the surface of her face reflected the crew of the soul charging up from below," but that "her sad, timid, self-effacing soul ... was ashamed to show itself" (ibid., 47). Yet Tereza's suffering was occasioned by her mother's contemptuous ridicule and her husband's tireless infidelity, that is, her terror that others she loved saw nothing in her face and body that was not repeatable, replaceable. Why does Kundera think Tereza's soul is hiding *from her*?

Sandra Bartky notes a shift in the contemporary American cultural regime of gender that may explain why porno-graphy has become a representational hot spot. "Normative femininity is coming more and more to be centered on woman's body—not its duties and obligations or even its capacity to bear children, but its sexuality, more precisely, its presumed heterosexuality and its appearance.... What was formerly the speciality of the aristocrat or courtesan is now the routine obligation of every woman, be she a grandmother or a barely pubescent girl" (Bartky 1990, 80).

There is, in fact, a kind of graphing that comes close to *unsouling* its objects representationally. In the post–World War II world, the (recurring) hideous *necro-graphy* of the death camp is instantly recognized. In Reska Weiss's harrowing description of concentration camp inmates from World War II: "[u]rine and excreta poured down the prisoners' legs, and by nightfall the excrement, which had frozen to our limbs, gave off its stench.... We were really no longer human beings in the accepted sense. Not even animals, but putrefying corpses moving on two legs" (Reska Weiss quoted in Hallie 1985). The representative body of the camp inmate, with skeletal form, shaved head, empty glazed eyes, blank face is surely not merely an accidental effect of administrative necessities, whether in Nazi Germany or contemporary Bosnia. It seems as well the production of a body signifying one "already dead," beyond hope, care, or relief, and yet frightening, even repellant, in its not-quite-deadness.

In recent postwar decades, a disturbingly similar pattern of imagery has become familiar to the point of everydayness, the iconography of "starving Africa." In affluent Western countries we have seen so many of these images—of the emaciated, listless, empty-eyed, (and especially where a child, usually naked) "African"—that they amount to a picture-type, an icon. Alongside pictures of violence, these images are parts of another iconography of the helpless and hopeless, a kind of people doomed one way or another, either by starvation, plagues, or political chaos. While images of starvation have evoked outpourings of concern and money, the effects of this repetitive imagery occlude the actors, African, European, and American, and the histories and political complicities, that figure in the explanations of why these particular actual people are starving or dying at this particular place and time. At least the concentration camp imagery unambiguously signals specifically moral monstrosity, not only the obscene fate of victims but the culpability of a particular set of perpetrators.

Stanley Cavell has said that "[t]he crucified body is our best picture of the unacknowledged human soul" (Cavell 1979, 420). The bodies of camp inmates seem to me better examples of that. Crucifixion, like other grisly forms of execution, murder, or postmortem mutilation (especially when these are practices, and they often are) suggests not an unrecognized soul, but a despised or reviled one. A deliberately mutilated body pictures a soul retro-graphed on its body as despicable or revolting—as one who deserved this. This grotesque practice of necro-graphy, inscribing the dead body with (or in) the display appropriate to the soul it was, has its positive counterpart in the burial preparations and rites of every human group. Both testify to how ineluctably human bodies attract soul-attributions; not only of the ones they have, but of ones they once did.

Body Graphics and Moral Philosophy

It's an old, apparently pre-Platonic, legacy of Western philosophy that (what is called, interestingly) "the" body is not the metaphysical, or epistemological, or moral point. It has been said that suspicion and derogation of the bodily goes so deep that Western philosophy might be termed "somatophobic" (Spelman 1988, 126–30). At any rate, bodies and what pertains to them are always on the lower or offending side of the formative dualisms of our philosophy, which we all instantly recognize—mind/body, culture/nature, active/passive, thinking/feeling, and so forth—whether we consider ourselves dualists or not. That is, these dualisms are still within our repertoires even if we resist or disdain them; it may not be easy to know how they continue to operate in shaping our sense of philosophical issues and questions, how they direct and limit our attention. I think they should not draw or deflect our attention away from looking at human bodies and how they are looked at.

Think of persons or personalities (the person-ness, or person-part of a living human being) as you like, and suppose if you want that human bodies are not themselves the point or target of moral concern. Still, human bodies are the primitive point of *perceptions* of who, what, and how another is, and so of that to which we have to respond morally. If that much is true, what we are able to see of persons *in* and *on human bodies* is morally fateful. Where human personality goes unseen or misseen, where "paranthrapoid identities" (Rubinstein 1975, 6) or inferior castes of soul are seen instead, sound principles regarding respect for persons, calculations of interpersonal utility, and habits of virtuous conduct toward persons will not avail.

It may be thought that a lot of this is about the negative impact of stereotypes, in the familiar sense, on human relations and that this is a familiar fact, and one of more sociological than philosophical interest.

As "familiar" as the existence of stereotypes may be, their circulation, persistence, and specific effects may not be well understood. This reminds us how important good psychology and sociology (and neuroscience, history, anthropology, etc.) are to moral philosophy. Despite the prevalence (and in many cases the outright malice) of many group stereotypes and the hurtful, hostile, even violent actions they appear to prompt or rationalize, they don't seem to have been of special interest to moral or other philosophers (with the conspicuous exception of philosophers of feminism, race, or sexuality). And this, all the more oddly, given the central preoccupation in contemporary moral theory with impartiality, fairness, and equality, with what they are and how to achieve them.

It is possible that many philosophers share the common idea that stereotypes are *false beliefs* of individuals, either hasty, grossly distorted, or simply erroneous *generalizations*. Yet these supposed generalizations are notoriously resistant to the impact of disconfirming instances. It also seems that these supposed generalizations are not typically extrapolations, hasty or otherwise, from observed instances. Stereotypes seem to circulate and become entrenched in the repertoires of many people and groups in the absence of many, or even, in the case of individuals' beliefs, in the absence of *any* observed instances that might provide a basis for forming beliefs about the behavior or characteristics of a stereotyped group. Stereotypes seem to organize fields of interpersonal experience rather than being discovered within them, rendering especially salient those instances that fit, while screening out or cordoning off ones that don't (Code 1991, 188–203).

That is, stereotypes seem to work on (or in) the perceptions which prompt and guide the formation of many beliefs; at least, this seems to me to be one place where they do their damage. That is why I have talked about *practices* of representation that may school us in perceiving certain patterns of human expression and comportment in particular ways or not at all. Moral philosophers don't have any special interest in people's particular false beliefs as such, but if there are social, even institutional, practices that systematically thwart the formation of morally relevant true beliefs, or conduce to the habitual formation of morally relevant false beliefs, this would be a central problem for moral epistemology, and doubly so. Moral epistemology as epistemology would need to accurately describe and explain these aspects of belief formation or inhibition. Moral epistemology as moral philosophy would need to subject the practices themselves, the conditions that permit and sustain them, and their effects on the formation of beliefs to moral critique.

I am not suggesting that representational practices such as the stereo-graphing, porno-graphing, or necro-graphing above discussed are the sole or even primary causes of moral misrecognition or mistreatment. I do assume that such practices have the meaning and impact they do because they support and are supported by other social practices and many facts about the structure of our social worlds. Our susceptibility to these representational dividing practices and their effects might also involve certain facts of human psychological function.

Some psychological studies suggest that propensities to "in-group, out-group bias" are startlingly easily triggered, at least within experi-mental situations, by nothing more, for example, than arbitrarily assign-ing unacquainted strangers to groups and putting the groups in competition (see Flanagan 1991, 310–11). Stanley Milgram's famous "obedience experiments" are known for their main finding: that experi-mental subjects proved alarmingly likely to administer what they believed were painful shocks to others (who were really confederates) at the order of an authority in an apparently trivial psychology experiment. But Milgram also found an "interesting" correlary: "many subjects harshly devalue the victim *as a consequence* of acting against him" (Mil-gram 1974, 10; see also 160–61).

Morally invidious representations might, then, be causative of morally discriminatory attitudes, actions, or practices, or they might be effects of these. They also might be symptomatic or expressive of prejudices prop-agated and sustained by other means. And surely these patterns of repre-sentation within cultures or groups render certain assumptions or associations familiar, making them seem unremarkable, even "natural," and providing a basis for rationalizations of conduct which conforms to them. These possibilities do not exclude each other, and I see no reason not to entertain all of them as hypotheses for investigation. Whether as cause, effect, or legitimizing support, there are multiple ways these pat-terns of depiction might figure in our social lives and our moral under-standings of them. I will suggest three.

The most obvious case for concern is when stereotypic identities pro-duce, signal, or license diminished moral *regard* or *consideration* for some people as objects of others' actions. Some may not recognize the pain, shame, suffering, or humiliation of others (or their pleasure, joy, pride, or self-respect), or may be unmoved or differently moved by its recognition there. The treatment of "diminished" subjects may involve lesser respect, concern, compassion, or reciprocity. In some cases this might involve paternalism toward others who are in fact capable of assessing their own goods and taking their own chances. In others it may be a question of cruelty, abuse, or neglect. While these two versions sound very different, even mutually exclusive, rationalizations of masters in actual histories of social domination sometimes reveal a curious oscillation between callous or arrogant disregard and self-congratulatory emphasis on paternalistically described "burdens." The diminished or aberrant treatment of diminished subjects may sometimes trail off toward what P. F. Strawson called the "objective" attitude, in which, as he memorably put it, some people are to be "managed or handled or cured or trained" (Strawson 1968, 79). As commonly, or more so, there may simply be a moral "status system," in which deserts are ranked and differentiated by "kind." The human record suggests the latter is more rule than exception.

Differential moral recognition works not only to set lesser standards of treatment for some, but to disqualify, or differently qualify, their moral agency. Paul Benson argues that "free agency" involves not only certain output by individuals but certain uptake by others. Philosophers usually try to identify free agency with some kinds of unimpeded executive *control* over our actions. Some stress intrapsychic conditions (in which the action originates from some "part" of us that is "really" us), others, the absence of certain kinds of external coercion (in which someone else is the spring). Actions arising in appropriate ways are "really one's own," rather than alien or forced. Benson argues persuasively that a necessary condition for free agency is a capacity for "normative self-disclosure" (Benson 1990, 53), the ability to reveal normatively significant features of one's agency (e.g. one's character, motives, attitudes, intentions, and values) in what one does. A necessary dimension of free agency is one's ability to make oneself present to others as an agent of value in ways that one intends and others can recognize "in the context of potential normative assessments of what we do" (ibid., 55).

Perhaps I can't "present" myself in and through my actions because I am *unable* to appreciate others' standards of assessment or the way they will be applied to me, because I am a child or I am cognitively impaired, for example. (Or, because someone literally forces me to do something which does not represent or express my own intentions, values, or desires.) But my incapacity or diminished capacity to present myself to some others might be another kind of problem, involving my marginal or oppressed or simply different social position. I may fail to understand or find it difficult to grasp fully standards or concerns in certain social arenas in which I have little experience, or have not been encouraged or allowed to learn. Or, I may appreciate, but still resist, certain normative expectations at a cost of being persistently misread or illegible in various regions of my differentiated social worlds. I know how "they" understand people "like" me, but I don't intend to put myself forward in "their" terms for me. Or, I may find that attempts to express confidence, sincerity, indignation, friendliness, or pride are invariably or largely unrecognized or misrecognized by many others in people like me, especially in certain contexts by certain other "kinds" of people.

Benson's point is that I might fail to qualify as a free agent because I lack certain capacities on my own part, or because some among my social worlds preclude coherent intentional expression or reception of who I am. These aspects of free agency are fundamentally *relational*; their successful exercise requires reception and appropriate recognition. If I am perceived as less than standardly human, as parahuman, or as differently human, my free agency may be fundamentally compromised in my interactions with those others who so see (or mis-see) me. Deformed moral perceptions, then, infiltrate the status of human beings as both moral agents and moral patients.

The examples of morally pernicious effects just mentioned presuppose that some people act *from* stereotypic perceptions or preconceptions. Another important but unsettlingly different sort of problem is suggested by psychologist Claude Steele. The results of Steele's experiments over the last four years, described by Steele in an interview with journalist Ethan Watters, include black Stanford undergraduates performing as well as whites on a difficult verbal skills test when they think they are simply solving problems, but performing significantly worse when they are told the test measures intellectual potential. Steele also found negative effect on the performance of women students who believe a math test shows gender differences, and negative impact on white men taking a math test who believe that Asians outperform whites on that exam. Steele construes these results as showing "stereotype vulnerability," vulnerability to changes in one's behavior or performance that result, not from believing a stereotype, but from having to "contend" with the fact that there is one (Watters 1995).

The remarkable suggestion in this research is that stereotypes may work directly in situations and interactions to alter behavior and perception, not through beliefs that embody or affirm them, but rather through beliefs *that* the stereotypes exist. If this is true, all that is required for these impacts to happen spontaneously is that people be aware that stereotypes concerning those like them are in effect, so that they modify their behavior in attempts to confront, deflect, compensate for, or disprove the stereotypes, or in other ways behave in anticipation of a stereotype-constrained response from others.

To make people aware of their existence as common knowledge, in turn, all stereotypes have to do is *circulate* sufficiently for it to be common knowledge, at least to those stereotyped, that, and how, they are stereotyped. The effect is that those who know they are stereotyped will not act similarly in similar situations to those not stereotyped. And the effect of this, presumably, is that stereotype-sensitive modifications of behavior themselves produce or elicit different effects or responses. If it is also true that stereotypes *do* condition responses to stereotyped people *by others*, a peculiar and perhaps interminable spiral of (at least initially) stereotype-driven interactions may ensue. The stereotypes propel, as it were, stressed and peculiar interactions where there might otherwise have been unproblematic ones, or at least ones not problematic in these ways. All that is needed to propagate these effects is *efficient circulation* of stereotypes. And the forms of graphing I have been discussing are surely one of the most effective means, especially if such graphs are repetitively insinuated through popular and mass media.

Stereotype vulnerability also explains a peculiar difficulty with the oft-repeated injunction, in moral philosophy as in ordinary life, to "put yourself in someone else's shoes," or practice "role reversal" as a test of impartiality. It is one thing to imagine myself in a situation like the one someone else is in; it is another to imagine (much less inhabit) the complete epistemic "set" of people whose lifetime social experience, unlike my own, includes the (perhaps acute) awareness of what others may typically be expected to have learned to assume (annoyingly or disastrously) about them, and the many implications of those assumptions. When some men say, as I have many times heard, that *they* wouldn't mind sexual catcalls from women, they are probably absolutely right. They wouldn't. They've never been women. When many white men and women say *they'd* feel demeaned and patronized by knowing that they'd been assisted in getting their jobs by an affirmative action program, they might be right. But why do they imagine the experiences of social life that frame their understanding are ones that all others share?

Conclusion: Getting the Picture

Anyone might have idiosyncratic biases concerning left-handed people, Minnesotans, or history teachers. These biases are apt to be remarkable, and are likely to be remarked as such. Biases that are *culture, community*, or *group* wide, tend to be unremarkable as such for those whose biases they are. How do body-pictures functioning as soul-images become pervasive to the point of being widely unremarkable, and so, culturally normative? Which bodies, and which pictures (in the broad sense) of them serve as standards for recognizing the humanity in human beings, and which deviations from the standard become standardized as representative of what is lesser or other than the fully, or naturally, or normally human? These are questions of moral graphics as a central study for moral philosophy. Included in this study are investigations of moral philosophy's *own* repetitive figurations of agency, autonomy, integrity, and responsibility. Can moral psychology and epistemology afford *not* to speak to the power of invidious identifications, the "scaling of bodies" (Young 1990, 122–55) which yields a gradient of moral worth, and the incessant circulation of imagery that supports several kinds of traffic in bodies?[4]

part four

Testing Sight Lines

nine

Peripheral Visions, Critical Practice

I said I would "combat" the other man,—but wouldn't I give him *reasons*? Certainly; but how far do they go? At the end of reasons comes *persuasion*. (Think what happens when missionaries convert natives.)

—Ludwig Wittgenstein, *On Certainty*

What both American slavery and sexism show is that it is possible for there to be some form of moral affirmation in the very context of oppression, that the oppression could not, in fact, succeed in the absence of some form of moral affirmation.

—Laurence Mordekhai Thomas, "Power, Trust, and Evil"

Throughout these chapters I have defended a view of morality as culturally situated and socially sustained practices of responsibility that are taught and defended as "how to live." Morality inheres in those ways we acknowledge and constrain each other that show that we are responsible for certain things to certain others. In learning morality, we learn who we are, to whom we are connected, and what matters enough to care about and care for. We learn this by learning our places in a system of assigning, accepting, and deflecting responsibility for things open to human care and effort.

Initially, others teach us to take responsibility for ourselves as bearers of particular identities and actors in various relationships that are defined by certain values. Later some people are in positions to demand that we do so, and some of us are in positions to demand it of some of them. So this system provides us with a medium for expressing our identities, relationships, and values through our senses of responsibility, and it requires of us that we do so. We collectively sustain our moral practices by continuing to account to each other in the terms and standards they furnish. When we cease to do so, or begin to do so differently, moral practices and the understandings they express have changed. Our practices of responsibility are themselves always open to evaluation and revision, but terms of criticism must themselves be seated in some established or freshly configured understandings that are shared. For these responsibility-placing understandings are where in the world morality is to be found. I have called this way of identifying morality an *expressive-collaborative conception.*

Mutual moral accounting must use shared terms that allow us to make sense of ourselves to each other. Terms are shared when they are mutually recognized as being in force between us. Our recognition of certain terms as authoritative secures some degree of mutual intelligibility in our expectations and interactions, and some degree of mutual intelligibility in moral terms defines a "we" for moral purposes. Moral terms in force need not be terms that equally favor or protect all of us who share them, nor need we all have had a hand or a voice in their being the terms in force. And it is characteristic of actual moral orders that not everyone is accountable to the same people, for the same things, in the same ways. It is precisely in understanding what we are apt to be held to account for, what sorts of account we will be expected to give, and to whom, that we demonstrate our competence in our particular form of moral life. In this way we show we are one of "us." This, I have tried to show in chapters 5–8 above, may be a better or worse thing depending on which moral community it is we are a member of, and which member of it we are. Often moral communities nest within each other and overlap each other, and so do people's senses of their own and others' identities and responsibilities. When very disparate moral communities collide, people may literally not know who is who and what is what unless or until some moral understandings are shared. These understandings may be fragile and temporary bridges, or they may settle into firm common ground.

As we negotiate the placing of tasks, burdens, expectations, and complaints among us, the flow of mutual accounting sustains or reconfigures our moral understandings (see chapters 3 and 4). Moral understandings include shared norms, principles, maxims, and guidelines, but such moral "standards," in the usual sense, are just one small if essential part of what we must share. We must also, for example, understand when and to whom standards apply, by whom and in what cases they may be credibly invoked, what they require or leave to the discretion of particular people in actual situations, and what assessments and costs attach to their fulfillment or disregard. We need to understand enough to know when we can trust someone and whom we can trust to take or fulfill responsibilities. In actual moral orders understanding what applies to oneself and to others usually involves appreciating positions, roles, relationships, identities, and institutions where different standards apply or standards apply differently.

The single most important claim of this book is that a lot of what we need in order to understand specifically moral judgments or principles goes beyond specifically moral matters. We need to understand a *social world*. Practical reason is not pure. Morality is not a distinct module within human cognition or social worlds, and moral understandings are not modular (see chapter 1). This is important because the intricate mesh of moral and social worlds has deep implications for how morality can be investigated, what moral justification can be, what force moral criticism may be expected to have, and what is entailed in seeing to it that others believe as we do. Yet the structure of social worlds, people's actual places in them, the understandings that hold the places in place, and how people are parties to these understandings are not plain to see, and are not even in our own cases packaged for ready "reflective" access.

The fabrics of social worlds through which moral understandings are woven are the works of many hands down generations meeting different strains and circumstances. Fabrics of distinct origin, or torn ones, may be joined through artful redesign or makeshift patchwork; elegance of design or appearance does not guarantee strength or durability. Moralities, like the social lives from which they are not separable, are collective more by accretion and concurrence than by concerted effort or design. They are collective works sustained by their reproduction in many activities of many people who are only sometimes aware that they are sustaining something at the level of "society" or "morality." Most often, if people are trying to sustain anything in engaging in practices of responsibility it is a kind of relationship, or something or someone they care about, or their sense of who they are. The result of their trying to do this in ways that make sense to themselves and those others to whom they suppose they are accountable is nonetheless a collective product: a specific form of moral-social life.

As I have it, then, morality is a dimension of actual social lives that inheres in a society's ways of reproducing its members' senses of responsibility.[1] But any view that identifies morality with the specific and contingent social being of moral cultures is suspected by many moral philosophers and others of having missed the real question about morality, the question about how morality is entitled to its authority over us (see Korsgaard 1996, 9–10 on "the normative question"). In every time and place human beings will learn and be taught—be "socialized" in—a "right" way of going on, the objection goes, but that way is just something they happen to have learned, whereas morality is about the way it is *really* right to go on.[2] If local moral beliefs are firmly inculcated, people will of course experience their moral arrangements as authoritative, but morality *really is* normative; it rightfully commands us. There are "positive" moralities or "mores," which are local and customary ways of judging conduct, and there is morality, i.e. what is "really," "truly," or "universally" right or valid.[3]

The objection against my kind of historically and culturally situated, real-time, naturalized view of morality is that on it there is something morality *can't do*. Morality must provide a basis for *genuine* justification and criticism, either within or "across" cultures. But actual socially embedded practices of responsibility can't do that. So moral practices embedded in societies at specific places and times cannot be real morality. The *real* thing with *rightful* authority must be something that transcends times, places, and cultures. Sometimes what is said to be real morality is a moral reality independent of human belief and judgment; sometimes real morality is identified with "universal" standards of conduct or judgment.

The roots of the demand for "real" morality, as opposed to "mere" mores and lifeways that people learn at certain times and places, go deep. I am not sanguine that I can persuade those whose demands on moral justification and criticism are so rooted that I have a better idea. But I am obliged to make clear what my idea is, to provide a view of moral justification, criticism, and correction fitted to the expressive-collaborative conception I have elaborated. To preview my view succinctly: The only thing that corrects or refutes a morality on moral grounds is another, better justified, morality that shows the first one is wrong. What is involved in justifying a morality, however, is no one thing and no simple ones. In the first part of this chapter I argue that we are able to engage in confident moral judgment and responsible moral criticism of our own and others' ways of living on the view that morality is an improvable practice inhering in particular lifeways. Then I return to how it is we might do that within an expressive-collaborative view on which morality is not socially modular.

What Is It We Can't Do?

The idea that what people in fact learn isn't "really" what morality is, or what moral philosophy is about—that morality is something or somewhere else—seems to be a view widely held by philosophers. Alan Gewirth in a recent paper provides a clear example of the standard line of argument that leads to a distinction between merely positive and real—"normative"—morality. If there are, as indeed there are, conflicts within and between positive moralities, then *if* any of these is really right or wrong, even better or worse, than another, there must be some standard or principle to decide this that is not just another one of those (Gewirth 1994, 26).[4] Not to have recourse to a normative morality transcending merely local mores "makes it impossible to present rationally grounded moral criticisms, in a non-question-begging way, of the positive moralities of other cultures or societies" (Gewirth 1994, 29).

The problem Gewirth presents us with is that societies, or groups within them, can go on in ways that are horrifying, cruel, callous, or unjust to some, or many, of their members or others. He means us to see that in the face of their immorality, there is nothing we can say if all we have are our moral standards to combat theirs; or rather, there is nothing we can say that is "rationally grounded" and "non-question-begging."

Obviously, Gewirth isn't thinking of the many cases of unjust or ill treatment that are defended with reasons that are demonstrably empirically false. In fact, I believe there is almost always a considerable mass of manifestly factually disconfirmable beliefs supporting particularly unjust and or brutal social orders, especially beliefs about the ways those treated unjustly or brutally are "different" from those whom one could not get away with treating so. I do not mean by this that vicious orders exist because of factual errors; I mean that they characteristically require the circulation of erroneous beliefs to ensure that certain things aren't seen and certain questions aren't put that might threaten their stability or existence; or at least that certain descriptions of what is seen aren't credible or that answers to certain questions are not available. I have argued in chapter 7 that epistemic rigging is central to coercive regimes, indeed, to any moral order wherever its supposedly trust-based understandings won't stand scrutiny, and studied the circulation of recognition-defeating stereotypes in chapter 8. One cannot overestimate the role of epistemic and discursive manipulation in understanding how flawed, even vicious, moral orders are reproduced.

Let us suppose, though, the appropriate test cases here are ones where our condemnation of their moral beliefs is rooted in our confidence in the truth of our own moral beliefs. Why must our moral beliefs *inevitably* fail to be rationally grounded? This could only be because it is in the nature of all actual moral beliefs to have too little grounding or the wrong kind of it. How do we know *in advance* that we are going to beg the question? It must be because whatever we believe is known in advance to have only so much or the very same kind of justification as whatever they believe. But now this argument itself seems to be begging the question, because this argument is supposed to *show* that a moral standard that is another one of those situated and local ones can't be rationally grounded, or more rationally grounded than another, in a non-question-begging way. But this is what the argument seems to assume about "positive moralities." It simply ignores precisely the possibility that if a particular moral standard or system can be held morally wrong or defective, it is because *another particular* standard or system (sometimes a correction of the first one) is better justified and reveals that the first is in error.

Central to the idea, or rather ideal—itself an evaluative standard—of objectivity is that good judgment must be made on bases and from positions that are reliable for the kinds of judgment in question. The idea of objectivity is that of "the best position to judge," one such that there is no other epistemic position which would be an improved one (Blackburn 1996). We attribute objectivity comparatively and by degrees; one judgment is more objective than another when the position issuing in the first judgment is freed from the known defects or distracting biases of the position issuing in the other. To say a judgment is (more) objective is always to pay it this compliment: It is from the (comparatively) best epistemic position we know of. In the case of judging moral views the standards for assessing reliability of positions and so objectivity of judgment might well include *moral* standards.

When a moral standard is held to be defective because a better justified one inconsistent with it is available or imaginable, the standards appealed to in comparative assessments can include ones that are parts of, or very like parts of, the defective system, or they might be more general epistemic standards of empirical plausibility, or logical or practical consistency. To say that some moral view is defective if there's another, better justified one that shows it to be so, it is important to emphasize, does *not* imply that the other, better justified one must be *admitted* by holders of the defective view to be better. It might fail to command their assent. They might be ignorant or misinformed, or they might be fanatical, corrupt, irrational, or too desperately or self-interestedly wedded to certain assumptions to give them up. If others of us can see and justify by our best lights a better view, then their view is worse.

If the standards that figure in the invidious comparison include moral ones *not* native to, or even very like, those in the system criticized as defective, then if those criticized do not concur, we will judge that part of the problem is their failure to grasp some of the right moral standards or perhaps to possess some of the right concepts. In this latter case, though, we do well to be more cautious in drawing conclusions about what it is that believers under our critical scrutiny do not "see," and why they do not see it. There may not be enough shared background beliefs of different sorts to get from where they are to our "here." In that case, though, we might be similarly unable to get "there." We might not see some things that they do.

Perhaps we can bolster our confidence by demonstrating to our satisfaction that our account of matters provides an error theory of theirs, that our account shows not only that they are mistaken and where, but why they are stalled on, or have veered off, the path to better views. This can indeed be a good justificatory strategy in principle (see Taylor 1993). The history of these error theories of other cultures in our own, however, is in many respects not a pretty one, epistemically or morally. So this, too, must surely be a part of *our* best considered account; we need error theories of our error theories. It is fortunate that work in feminist, race, postcolonial, sexuality, and cultural studies has begun to provide these, for a critical view of our moral life cannot do without them. At any rate, cases of wholesale, rather than retail, cultural critique call for special caution and care, for both moral and epistemic reasons I return to shortly. And of course an entirely distinct moral determination is involved in deciding whether we ought to "make" them see what they do not or cannot.[5]

Now the question of what it is we "can't" do with the best justified moral standards and epistemic norms that we have may be made clearer. The fact that our best justified moral judgments and standards are not accepted by others on our grounds for them does *not* unjustify us in holding them. Unless others' criticism, duly considered in the light of everything we have reason to think we know, gives us a reason to doubt our good reasons, we remain where alone we can stand: on the justification we find cogent from our best position of judgment.

For related reasons, it also does not follow from our moral views' failing to convince some other people that we can't make justified judgments on the correctness of the views of those other people. We certainly can evaluate their evaluations, as they can ours, from the only position available: the one that for all we (or they) know is best. If some evaluations are right, others that contradict them must be wrong. When moral cultures are very disparate, establishing contradictions is often not a straightforward matter. And of course, our evaluations are fallible. We may be wrong in our confidence, or vain about our epistemic prowess or moral enlightenment. We can surely be unwise, unreasonable, irresponsible, arrogant, or malevolent in making these judgments in certain contexts or to certain ends. It is our task to try to be sure it is not so. We bear heavy empirical and hermeneutical burdens in making sure we really know what it is that we presume to judge. None of these pitfalls is utterly different in kind from ones involved in judging the conduct of others among "us." Ethics of judging and blaming are fundamental parts of our moral understandings, lying in the same plane as judgments of what we "do"; they too are doings (see Baier 1993).

The genuine issue here is this. We *can* be better or worse justified in our own moral beliefs, and we *can* make justified judgments on others' moral practices and beliefs. What we *can't* do is assume that our judgments ought to have *authority* for them, much less that it is a test of our or anybody else's moral beliefs that they achieve *universal* authority. And we certainly *can't* presume that the strength of our justification to us warrants our seeing to it that they believe as we do. Precisely to the extent that those judged do not share enough of our moral assumptions, factual beliefs, epistemic standards, and social worlds, we cannot to that extent expect their assent. In some cases we will in that way have begged their questions, although not simply so. In many others we will have gotten to places of moral belief to which they do not have reasons to go or have reasons not to go. To expect their assent would be to expect them to be irrational or subservient, to judge as we tell them and not as they think best to do. The issue here is not different from what it is with beliefs generally: people may not be able to concur in some beliefs if they do not share enough of certain other beliefs. A difference comes in the way moral beliefs are, at least broadly, action-guiding. But this means *our* beliefs guide *us*; it need not mean we are guided to see that they are guided by our beliefs. Let's take a closer look at the "missionary" position.

Shouldn't we try to persuade them? After all, *ex hypothesi*, we are persuading them to partake of our very best justified and most soberly considered judgments. There might be no harm in trying to convince or persuade them. What, though, and how much would this involve? How persistent should we be? After all, we believe they will be better off—we might suppose, *much* better off—once persuaded. Well, we believe this, but often they do not. There is an inevitable element of conflict here that can easily express itself manipulatively or coercively. In cases of contact between dramatically disparate forms of moral-social-cultural life, as conquerors, missionaries, and colonial administrators have always known, you do not only or mostly strive to convince people, if you are determined to get them to see that they must judge as you judge, especially in rather short order (say, a generation or two). You must change their lives.

You must freely cut and retailor their social fabric, or replace their ways whole cloth. You must not only give them a life in which your judgments make sense to them, but one in which their formerly familiar judgments no longer make sense to them; it is best if they are simply forgotten. Jesuit missionaries to North America in the seventeenth century saw early that "not much ought to be hoped for from the Savages as long as they are wanderers," (Kenton, 1925, 50), United States and Canadian governments banned native peoples' Sun Dances and potlatches in the nineteenth century (Nabokov 1991, 217), and twentieth-century British colonial officials in Africa would not acknowledge indigenous political organization through which women enjoyed independence, solidarity, and authority (Nzegwu 1995). They really, after all, cannot judge as we judge if they do not live as we live.

This is not only what we have *seen* to happen, it is what *has* to happen if morality is not socially modular. These are the stakes in deliberate, global moral conversion, or in radical moral surgery, and perhaps even attempts at "persuasion" that will not be turned. If we are required to act on *reasonably* justified judgments, and this applies to acting on judgments that people ought to be converted to better ways of life, are we sure we have a reasonable justification of *that* judgment? While there is nothing in the way of our evaluating others' very different moral views, it is difficult to see how our being well justified in our moral beliefs could support the conclusion that we are justified in *compelling* others to believe as we do. Even "persuading," most so in situations where the persuaders possess significant material advantages and superior power, is apt to be, if not a slippery slope, a steeply inclined one. Should you lose your grip, you're apt to fall quite a distance downward, into disrespect, bribery, or manipulation, if not cultural domination or worse.

In pointing out this very real danger, I do not imply that we have no obligations to protect and assist vulnerable people in other societies. There are cases in which we are obliged to assist and protect people from the aggression of those who live very differently from us, but who do so at the expense of some among them who do not want to live that way with them. These unwilling others, though, to whom we may owe assistance may also not want to live our way with us, or live our way at all. They may well want to live a corrected version of their way, which might be more like—or might just be in most other respects—the way of those who hurt or oppress them. They may be willing to split differences with their aggressors or oppressors that make better sense by their lights than they do by ours.

One thing we can do in such cases is to offer them the choice to live our way with us, as the Canadian and more recently the U.S. governments have done in extending political asylum to women escaping subjection to forms of female circumcision (Dugger 1996). I believe we are obliged to offer this, when they seek it. It is not, however, clear what we can offer to everyone who would seek a refuge from serious mistreatment. This suggests we are obliged to think of ways to avoid their needing a refuge, ways to change the situations from which they flee. It is very difficult, though, to decide what policies allow us to avoid complicity in others' oppressive and injuring practices without our own actions' being forced "surgeries" of a different, cultural kind (Glover 1995, 126). I don't pretend to answer these questions. I do not believe there are formulaic or general answers to them. I do think that in discussions of judgment "across" groups with significantly different moral ways of life, we do well to pay attention to where (from what vantage point and with what interests) and why (with what motives and to what ends) one group needs to judge morally another's actions or standards. Often we might do better to focus on what *we* really owe according to *our* values to others who do not live as we live. More than assistance or intervention in what they do, for example, we may owe them changes in our own way of life.

I have argued that we *can* be justified in holding to less-than-universally authoritative standards (including moral standards of universal scope) and in bringing those standards to bear in forming our judgments of how others live. But the presumption lies against wholesale corrective expeditions and radical moral surgeries. These have not been found, in the history of the human race, to have been prompted by or answerable to epistemic or moral visions that stand up well to a longer and wider view. Often in fact, ways of life, and many people who lived them, were crushed. Even if those who crushed them had a better morality, that still leaves them at least one reason short in justifying what they did.

What We Can Do, and Must

Gewirth's familiar argument expresses a real worry: How can we think of actual human moralities as proper standards of judgment; they are, after all, so flawed, so bad. It is possible, however, to do worse by ignoring them. Laurence Thomas identifies the costly error in assuming that deplorable social structures like U.S. slavery have no "moral floor," that these orders simply fall outside human interactions based in trust and responsibility (Thomas 1995, 161). Thomas defends the uneasy truth that this is not so. He reminds us of relations of several kinds bound by trust in both directions between slaves and masters, and contrasts this situation with the disappearance of such relations between Jews and their Nazi murderers. As long as human beings are ongoing participants in a social order, and not simply objects of direct violence and slaughter, *there is a moral order there*, as mutual understandings and bases of trust and expectations are being kept alive and in play. There exists a lattice of these understandings thick enough to support common life. It is precisely the job of moral criticism to examine human social arrangements, to find their moral floors, and to discover how so often they have made out of the basic human goods of trust and responsibility something sad, paradoxical, twisted, or mutilated. A crucial part of this same study is seeing how participants are unable to see the perversity of their order; or usually more to the point, what parts of an order have as their purpose or effect that this is not to be seen, and if seen, is not to be spoken, and if spoken, is to be ignored and discredited.

If morality is not socially modular, then to understand morality—what it is—requires understanding how it is seated and reproduced in actual human societies. Only then do we understand what moral justification and criticism can look like, and what makes moral change in better or worse directions possible. If it is characteristic of human societies (including our own) that moral standards, statuses, and distributions of responsibility work *through* social differences, rather than in spite of them, then to understand morality—what it is—is to see how morality works, and works better or worse, in just this way. If it is commonplace that the most obvious moral failings of human societies—cruelty, injustice, exploitation, oppression—are effected through their systems of social difference, then to mount effective moral criticism of these arrangements requires finding out precisely how relations of trust and responsibility can be manipulated and deformed into something ugly and dangerous, in just this way. Critical moral ethnography is then an especially urgent task of moral philosophy (see Rorty 1989; Thomas 1993; Shrage 1994; Addelson 1994; Moody-Adams 1997).

If, on the other hand, the complex skein of roles, relations, or statuses is made to look incidental to what morality is really about, or really like, almost all the matter of human moral relations thereby disappears as the object of moral theorizing (see chapter 2 on the "pure core" of moral knowledge). Yet ethics is supposed to be the project of understanding what morality is, how it goes on, and what modes of justification and evaluation are possible to it and appropriate for it. It defeats this purpose to partition off flawed practices, even oppressive, unjust, and exploitative ones, as *just* immoral, and to set them aside as "merely" something else. Real human moral systems are for the most part like this—imbalanced, one-eyed, mystifying, rigged. We avoid this painful issue at great cost. If we avert our eyes from these shabby spectacles—many of them quite everyday, many occurring (yes) right around us—we will not learn how a moral floor is set so low or so uneven, and *kept* there. We miss our chance to learn what makes that floor collapse, or how it can be jacked up or leveled. We don't get to see how certain incoherences, the distinct sight lines at different levels, the impossibility of anyone's seeing into all places from some place, present essential materials for criticism. This is the ultimate, disastrous effect of legacies of ideality and purity in moral inquiry: Its subject largely disappears.

We might instead accept that practical deliberation, evaluation, and criticism are always "from here," where "we" are, for some here and some we. Moral judgment, like any judgment, proceeds from a situation in which some terms and standards of judgment are given. We can always reflect on, and sometimes correct, given moral concepts and judgments or their applications, but we can do this only from the standpoint of some others. The others cannot be other than those of a particular historical time at a specific cultural place; we have to hope our own moral floor is indeed higher ground, and must try to see to it that it is. It's not different from the realization that there aren't "foundations" of knowledge; it is another, and distinctively complicated, case of it. This is not to give up on questions of justification but to take a different view of it, one that is consistent with a naturalized, but reflexively and socially critical, epistemology. If naturalized epistemologies have advice to offer, any "we" must begin with some of what it believes are its best-entrenched, most durable, powerful, and fruitful insights, and see where they lead and what may be learned from them. It is possible that one will learn that some of them were less durable, powerful, and fruitful than one hoped, or useful in different or more disturbing ways than one believed.

There's no sense, then, in continuing to try to back up to our standards one more time and get it right by getting to the ones that will stand on their own. The wish to find standards that stand on their own is unfulfillable. It is we who must stand on, and stand up for, them. If we can't keep backing up, or come to a justificatory full stop, we must help ourselves to lateral and forward views. What should we look at, and what should we be looking for?

A difference between our moral and some of our other equipments, is that moral understandings not only are made available through shared living and thinking, but are understandings *of* that particular shared life. What one learns through socialization to the moral order is "the *structure of social space* and *how best to navigate one's way through it*" (Churchland 1989, 300). More precisely, one learns this structure as a worthy and weighty structure, and one's way within it as a proper or binding way. However precisely this sense of gravity or dignity, depth or demand, of moral responsibility is installed (and no doubt much of it inheres in feelings and attitudes shaped to produce, among other things, that sense), moral understandings are understandings of how we live as "how to live."

What our (or others') best, deepest, and most fruitful moral insights are supposedly best and fruitful for, are producing forms of living that sustain certain goods. These forms of living acquire their authority (as distinct from, but not opposed to, what other powers hold them in place) by its being and seeming worthwhile to live like that. What is in question here are the general contours of a shared life; not anything one person does now, but a set of practices that keep people mutually accountable and important things accounted for. Is it worthwhile to live as we, or as others, do? Is how some of us live "how to live?"

I want to say, initially with utterly deceptive simplicity, that if this is what we are trying to find out, the relevant questions about moral understandings are three. What is *this* way of life (the one actually made possible, perhaps in some respects necessary, by these existing patterns of "socialization"—the ways we keep on learning to live)? What good *comes* of this way of life (what of value does it make available, and what foreclose)? What can be *said* for it, considering that it is a way of life that requires this specific pattern of pressures and inducements to reproduce itself? Crudely: One question is about what we *are* doing in a specific form of moral life; another is about what we *get* from it; the last is about its price, and the currencies in which we *pay* for it. I think of these questions as the operative ones in assessing the *habitability* of a particular form of moral-social life, or, usually more fruitfully, in assessing some significant aspect of that form.

As much as I do believe these are the appropriate questions for moral criticism in philosophy and life, I believe there are enormous complications in pursuing answers to these questions. It is these complications, not the avoiding of them, that make the subject interesting, and set its tasks. Here I point out two complications which show burdens that moral inquiry bears, but also places where it can get a firm grip. The first has to do with a way we are always in the midst of things in the project of moral justification. The second has to do with the way that none of us is ever right in the midst of all that needs to be looked at.

The three questions I have suggested for morally assaying aspects of moral forms of life might seem nicely distinct and clearly ordered in logical priority. It might seem we cannot *assess* a moral way of life evaluatively (questions two and three) without knowing first what that way is (question one). But this is not so. If the characterization of *what* it is we are doing is to be material for assessments of what morally we "get" and "pay," the evaluative measures to be applied will have to shape the characterization of what we are doing. That is, it is what we are doing "morally" or doing in terms of some basic goods for (or in) human beings that we need to get clear on. This does not mean that the attempt to understand a form of moral life is not an intensive empirical investigation. Still, the relevant characterization of what we are doing is already going to have to be selected and framed, in light of many facts, in some moral terms; it cannot be a bare description of facts. We discover what we are doing in moral terms by tracking goods and the distributions of responsibility that are the conditions of our enjoying them.

In addition, whether we can distinguish and order, and how we can understand, the second and third questions will depend on the nature of the moral conceptions and standards we have it in mind to apply. What can be seen as a good outcome with "costs" to be subtracted within one kind of evaluative perspective can appear in another as a moral misuse or abuse of things of deep importance, or as a colossal missed point. This corresponds to the familiar element of cross-purposes found in many consequentialist and deontological contests: If you start with weighing up, you can't give the right role to certain kinds of ultimate or fundamental requirements or prohibitions, and vice versa. We will have to start from some moral perspective to know whether we are going to be talking about benefits and costs, or about tolerability and limiting conditions, or excellences and flaws, or reverence and defilements. More complex still, part of what we are testing is whether lives are more worthy lived in some of these terms rather than others. In this way, we start in the midst of, and continue to move back and forth among the three questions, finding the fulfillments or absence of values in a lot of facts, seeing what facts matter in terms of some values, seeing some kinds of values as placing limiting conditions on other kinds.

This explains why it can seem easy to make comparisons between different ways of living in which a particular aspect stands out as singularly attractive or abominable, yet holistic moral comparisons are stubbornly elusive. Even if we know human sacrifice is terrible and the equal dignity of persons is an inspiration, this hardly enables us to say without further ado whether it is better to be "a" citizen of a Western democracy in the twentieth century or "an" Aztec in an ancient society.

But now, which citizen, which member of an Aztec community should we ask about? The questions ask what is it to live as we do, and what is of value in this life, considering what we undergo to achieve and sustain it. The life to which the questions are put, however, is our common life, or the shared way of living of some group. This means that answers are determined by what it is *like to be us*, or them. Here is the second complication. If it is the rule, rather than the exception, that the moral lives of societies are organized around differentiated roles, statuses, and positions within them, then while there may be some things it is like to be us or them typically, there will be many cases where there is something distinct that it is like to be *some* of us, or some among them.

We have now to disturb the assumption that there are "societies" (or groups) having "a morality," and that if you ask them, and they answer you sincerely, you can find out what it is. This assumes two things. It assumes, first, that "they" know what their form of life is. This might seem obvious, for it is *their* life, and we are asking about the standards they follow that give it its practical structure, that issue in "how they live." Surely, they know how they live? Yet it is not safe to assume that people typically know much of what they are really doing, and it is certainly doubtful that they know what and all that they are collectively doing in reproducing their form of life. Second, to the extent that people do and must know a good deal about how they live at some level (they are competent navigators of their social space, and they have to know how to do that) can we assume that what all people in that society (have to) know or do is the same? If differentiated moral-social lives are the rule, we cannot assume this. At the intersection of these two shaky assumptions lies this question: Is it likely that people typically understand what the way they live does to, with, and for *other* people, very differently placed, within their own societies? This is the shakiest bet of all. Yet its shakiness is one of the most tractable and fruitful places for moral inquiry to begin.

I spoke in an earlier discussion of enhancing "transparency" as an essential critical technique in testing the habitability of forms of moral life and what we think we know about them, especially from within them (chapter 3). To the extent that moral understandings are shared, they create mutual intelligibility of certain kinds. They coordinate people's expectations of others' beliefs, perceptions, judgments, actions, and responses, creating a kind of *equilibrium* between them. This does not mean everyone does what everyone else expects, but rather that the expectations (and so reactions to their being fulfilled or not) are recognized in common, and (often) as common. These expectations are expressed and further coordinated in the practices of responsibility in which this moral life consists.

The equilibrium is *reflective* to the extent that parties to it can make it, and its sustaining conditions and typical consequences, a subject of explicit consideration. This consideration consists of people's looking at what they are actually doing. Transparency is the state in which we can "see through" intervening media to what is really there. In the case of moral life, transparency consists of seeing how we live, both through and in spite of our moral understandings and practices of responsibility. In seeking transparency, people are looking at what they think they value and care about, at the mutual understandings they believe organize their practices of responsibility around these things, and at their places in the order that results. They are looking at what it requires to keep those understandings and practices stable and to reproduce them, and at what results for them, and is demanded of them, in doing this. The object of this reflection is to check if things are as we think, if they are good in ways we think, if there are ways they could be better. We try to see through the haze of habitual assumptions and our comfortable or uncomfortable familiarity with them in order to see what is actually going on.

What is going on, though, is never just something one person is doing or experiencing now, and is never fully visible from any one spot in the going order. First, there are parts of a working moral-social order that can be seen only or only reliably by people at particular places. There can be parts of social orders that are never seen by some people in those orders, even if those very parts are conditions of those people's living as they do. Feminist and other critical literatures show how often this is a function, or a facet, of exclusion or privilege, a social-structural matter of who does not get to be, or does not have to be, familiar with certain precincts of "our" life.

These studies teach us that exclusions are never symmetrical ("they don't know us, we don't know them"), and that while those more advantageously placed invariably think of themselves as having the most "informed" or "educated" or "sophisticated" views, part of their privilege is relief from familiarity with the less advantaged positions that make theirs possible. Many poor people, for example, actually know many specific things about how rich people live (including specific details of intimate corners of their personal lives): They are nannies, maids, cooks, cleaners, gardeners, drivers, groomers, "help," "service," or "labor," the "outsiders within" of whom Patricia Collins writes (Collins 1990; also Romero 1992). Rich people know very little about how poor people live, although they might think they do. Knowing what it is like to be "us," severally and corporately, is a massive inquiry that can only proceed by progressive addition and comparison of many accounts. More than being furnished with some facts, inquiry into how we live must be empirically saturated by candid, reflectively tested, and mutually corrected reports and observations of experiences at, and of, different positions within forms of moral-social life.

Second, there is the interesting situation in which understandings about us widely shared among us are not for the most part true of us. These understandings, including moral ones, may not even be believed true of us by many of us, if behavior counts an an expression of belief. Examples of these familiar but not obviously true assumptions in our society might be statements like "It's natural for people to be basically self-interested." "For us, life is not cheap." "People in our society are treated as individuals." Like "We don't eat peas with our fingers," these understandings seem to lead an ambiguous life, teetering between empirical generalizations and evaluative stances. Saying these are norms misleadingly expressed as facts does not quite capture their function, either.[6]

I think the story to be told here is about the many and surprising ways norms supply shared reference points and create intelligibility. Part of this story seems to be that norms exist to coordinate expectations and judgments, but not only or even necessarily the expectation that people will comply with or conform to them. An expressive-collaborative view warns us that morality is not *simply* about guiding action (see chapters 3 and 4 above). Another part of the story about norms is that people can recognize and reproduce the order they participate in under descriptions that they know others share, even if those dominant descriptions or shared stories do not characterize what most of these people are doing most of the time, or even what most people could be doing.

Norms, normative practices, and normative identities that are dominant—that are widely acknowledged or frequently invoked with solemnity or authority—may really be idealizations of specific positions of social prestige that nonetheless dominate shared understandings of how "we" live (Addelson 1994; Scheman 1993; and chapter 6 above). These are among the phenomena of actual moral orders and how they represent and reproduce themselves that disappear if we assume in moral theorizing that morality consists of action-guiding rules valid for all. There may instead be a core of dominant understandings that are widely repeated but differently grasped from different positions, and which in turn cover over many different understandings of relations of trust and responsibility that people actually enact in their different, daily lives.

Some exercises in rendering social arrangements transparent may produce reassuring and rewarding results, but given the differentiation and epistemic complexity of actual moral orders, they may also uncover incongruities and trouble understandings. They may reveal that only some select practices or domains of our society actually approximate "our" norms and ideals, or that only some kinds of people, or people in certain statuses, are "eligible" to see themselves and be seen by others in terms of our most esteemed values and representative identities. It may come clearer that few people are able to enjoy some of those goods that are "our" premier achievement, while others bear disproportionate burdens in supplying the conditions for an enjoyment of these goods that they will never share. Further, many of the differences of position within practices of responsibility that are said to be natural, naturally appropriate, or inevitable may be revealed as orchestrated. Different positions, and exclusions and disqualifications from them, may be revealed as produced in part by the very arrangements they supposedly justify.

All significant differentials in power are critical hot spots in social-moral orders, marked out as sites for transparency testing. This methodological maxim does not smuggle in an egalitarian moral premise. I am not claiming relations in which some people have authority or power over others, or social systems constructed around distinct statuses with different prerogatives and responsibilities, or all uses of coercion, are intrinsically bad or necessarily wrong. Authority, perhaps even authority with some rightful powers to coerce, is a basic feature of human society, and not an eliminable one, so far as I can see. For many people the least controversial case is that of adults who must tend and teach children; for some others it may be the case of those with standing to enforce laws protecting persons in a reasonably just system of which the laws are a just part. Even licit authority, however, may be abused or be abusive; and obviously many claims to authority, or to the right to use force, are without ground. It requires moral standards to decide whether specific power differentials or exercises of power are morally insupportable, rather than benign. Where particular differences of power or authority are morally wrong, it may be because they invite cruelty or allow abuse, or because they render people vulnerable to exploitation; it need not be because they embody inequalities.[7]

The maxim of paying special attention to power differentials instead reflects something we already know about social-moral arrangements and their shared and sustaining understandings. We know that powers of several types (coercive, manipulative, and productive) in various linked dimensions (economic, political, social, discursive, and cultural) can allow some people to rig both the arrangements and the perceptions of them, and so to obscure what's really happening to whom and why. It is this fund of knowledge that needs to be enlarged and theoretically articulated in general accounts and specific studies of *different relative moral positions in differentiated social lives.*

Transparency is potentially effective in altering the indefensible arrangements it exposes, in part, because it turns up lies (Williams 1985, 101) and occasions embarrassment (Lovibond 1983, 158), perhaps in both those who live well and those at whose expense they live that way. It is potentially transformative because in uncovering lies and precipitating embarrassment it tears or shreds the understandings in which we have trusted, the moral medium we have been given initially by others to live within, and must to some extent eventually have made our own. When the understandings are torn, or torn away, *then* there really are "just" habits and ways of going on, not anything we can say coherently for their worthwhileness, and so for the way we live as "how to live."

For this reason, it is those most favored by actual differentiated and hierarchical orders who have most to lose in seeing unexpected or unflattering images of themselves mirrored back to them by means of others' experiences. It is they who are most likely to have identified "how to live" with how "we"—that is, they—live. And it is they who are most likely to find themselves with, as Annette Baier puts it, "unpaid debts" and bad moral credit, with a sense of the worthwhileness of their lives that has relied for its availability and stability on "forces to which it gives no moral recognition" (Baier 1994, 8). More concretely, it is other people to whom they have given no, or inadequate, or second-rate, recognition.

It will usually not have completely escaped those unrecognized or less recognized that they are so. Whether they are, or think they are, able to change an order that neglects or exploits them will depend as much on the powers they have or can get, as on their awareness that it is not so good to live as they live.[8] Even within some of these orders, those least advantaged often still have a stake in some forms of satisfaction and pride in fulfilling their responsibilities and being trustworthy—given how they are forced to live. Under propitious circumstances, those less advantaged may find the decay or rending of prior trust relations allows them newly to trust themselves to pursue differently formed identities and relationships, and to trust each other in newly formed social alliances and political solidarities.

Philosophers recognize that pure coherence methods in ethics as elsewhere—methods that turn only on preserving consistency among beliefs—are endangered by the possibility that the beliefs selected for mutual consistency may just be false. Achievements of transparency do use the force of inconsistency—among beliefs, among actions, and between beliefs and actions—to put pressure on rigged and deceptive equilibria of moral understandings. But exercises in transparency, when guided by the awareness that there are different relative moral positions and that attendant differentials of power are under suspicion, do a great deal more than press toward coherence among available beliefs. They open gates for the flow of hidden experiences, excluded testimonies, submerged perceptions, and subjugated knowledges. Through these we learn anew how we live, what may be said for and against it, and what is felt about it; through this in turn relations of trust are buttressed, collapse, are renegotiated, or are newly forged. If "reflective equilibria" that sustain moral life are, as I have suggested, not simply within but *between* people, then a regulative ideal of transparency which organizes practices of criticism demands both "balance" and "refinement," to use Michael DePaul's terms for a fortified method of moral inquiry (DePaul 1993). On a fully interpersonal view, though, the balance to be struck or kept is among different people's understandings and the kinds of trust they support; the refinement to be sought is the resetting, perhaps the re-creation, of whole systems of reciprocal and shared assumptions, attitudes, feelings, and practices.

It might seem, finally, that the critical strategy of transparency is of use only within societies sharing some form of moral-social life with a presumption in favor of continuing to do so. For it is upon people in this situation with these commitments that the pressures of inconsistencies, incongruities, "unpaid debts," and trusts undermined or betrayed will impinge. That is to say, one might think that transparency does its work only within societies, not between them.

This suspicion rests, however, on a false assumption that is abetted by the very trope of moral judgment and criticism "across" cultures. This may fit instances of "judgment at a distance," when we make up our minds about them (or they theirs about us), perhaps just to clarify what we really think. (Remember, though, that even in these cases "global" comparative judgments between moral cultures are very precarious, for reasons already stated, and anyway not often useful. (See Williams 1985, 162–65, on the "relativism of distance.") But this trope does not fit many actions and interactions between differently cultured peoples, not even actions at a distance, including those collective actions of societies that have impacts on the lives and fates of others.

For in cases where there is contact (and more so where there are some ongoing or intermittent arrangements to which peoples are party, ones where peoples are not simply objects of main force and direct violence), some moral understandings, however fragmentary, tentative, dimly intelligible, and roughly aligned, will have started to come into play. There are then thin strands of a moral order *there*, thickening and interweaving as contact continues. A moral floor is forming and being tested. Parts of this may fall through straightaway, but if the contact continues, some parts will bear the weight of the understandings that support whatever arrangements take hold. Where those who are initially parties cannot find, in the perfectly appropriate phrase, "common ground," especially where material advantages and power are very unbalanced, the floor may fall, unevenly, into relations of domination punctuated by violence, or stepwise or by leaps into conquest and subjugation, cultural extirpation, and genocide. We really ought to look at, and not just imagine the various things that actually happen when missionaries and other new arrivals meet residents, a topic ripe for moral ethnography.

Even in less dramatic encounters, the pressures created by insistent, empirically steeped examination of what arrangements really obtain when peoples act upon each other or interact with each other may be effective. This can include, for example, attention to ways corporate practices and immigration policies that shape some people's lives perilously or miserably are the conditions for others' enjoyments of freedom, comfort, and personal autonomy (for example, see Enloe 1990). The opacities of intergroup relations are there, whether we look within or without, and moral philosophy must look in both places. Most societies of any size or complexity today are themselves best thought of as networks of overlapping cultures and intercultures whose moral discourses are not seamless and homogeneous.

Dark Glasses

It seems that either there is a transcendent point of view outside cultures and histories that lays its demands upon us, or that we need good guides within moral and social life to scrutinize our own and each others' moral cultures, enhance our understanding of what they are and how they work, and apply whatever materials are available to measure their worth against our best available views of what is valuable. At the close of the twentieth century, there no longer seem to be any widely convincing versions of a transcendent standpoint, if we understand that term not to mean a standpoint that transcends someplace we are now, but one that transcends any place we might actually happen to be. At least there are not any widely convincing secular versions of such a standpoint, and a nonsecular one will not serve interpersonal understandings in culturally variegated societies or between them. No one can stand uncontentiously on a particular set of intuitively self-evident judgments or a constitutive feature of moral judgments generally, or what or whom they address; one can't ascend or prescind to the viewpoint of pure practical reason, can't simply stipulate the transcendental pragmatic presuppositions of human discourse, can't simulate the point of view of the universe, or see with God's eyes; and one can't get anywhere being a spectator so impartial that he or she doesn't privilege any evaluative standpoint over another.

If morality is an actual practice of human social life, with many varieties and always with its internal fractures, its dim or rigged understandings, its opportunities for false consciousness and true callousness, its unstable and emergent moral "bridge" discourses when significantly different lifeways meet or collide within or between societies, then this practice (or these practices) is what moral criticism, in and outside of philosophy, is really about. It asks when such practices stand scrutiny, when they are worth reproducing. The catch is that there is no one to scrutinize and assess moral practices but us— either we who enact them or others who do something else. Moral criticism is not only about actual practices of moral judgment, but must itself proceed from some of them. The desired destination is an account of the actual conditions— possibilities and limitations—under which human beings can, and should, claim to have made *sound* judgments of this kind. This account needs to consider what difference it makes which of us scrutinize and assess which—and whose—moral practices. This sets an agenda for moral criticism to lead or guide us in slow, often puzzling, and sometimes painful and costly tasks of mutual correction.

Corrections are needed to build or retrieve reflective confidence that the moral orders we participate in and so reproduce do not deaden our imaginations about human beings, human possibilities, and the goods of shared lives. If we need this, it is because we need justified confidence that our moral understandings and lifeways do not render us parochial, ethnocentric, domineering, or cruel with respect to others; that they do not leave us complicit in our own subjection, alienation, exploitation, and oppression; that the ways we live now are not simply empty, deluded, stupid, or pointless. It is something we already know too well about human beings everywhere that they may need to test their confidence in or complacency about just such things at those points where they least feel that need.[9]

I have tried to show that the distinction between "real" morality and "mere" lifeways does not serve us if it tries to evade the fact that all moral valuations are "from here," for some we, and some here. These distinctions can leave their proponents simply standing on what requires being stood up for, pretending their moral foundations are in order and forgoing the task of asking what moral justification and correction might really be like. I mean what *real* moral justification and correction is like, the kind that leads to a grasp of how we actually live, or might; that is clear-headed and strong-hearted, does not need to avert its eyes from its own reflection, and does not simply choose to cover over or crush what, to it, is strange.[10]

notes

Chapter One

1. G. E. Moore's *Principia Ethica* (Moore 1903) is an outstanding example of undisturbed and unexamined assurance. In the preface to *Five Types of Ethical Theory* (Broad 1930), C. D. Broad fairly boasts of his "exceptionally narrow" range of experience. The reflective equilibrium approaches of Rawls 1971 and Daniels 1979 explicitly begin from "our" moral intuitions and Hare 1981 from our linguistic ones about moral concepts. Following Mill and Sidgwick (see chapter 2), D. W. Ross (1930, 39–41), and John Rawls (1971, 50) align their theories with the "educated," while David Brink (1989, 96–97) enters a brief for expertise and Shelly Kagan (1989, 15) for moral theory's (and so the moral theorists') "freedom." Thomas Nagel says philosophical ideas are "sensitive to individual temperament, and to wishes," but does not mention social or cultural location (Nagel 1986, 10). These few prominent examples are not exceptional; it would be easier to list moral philosophers in the twentieth century who worried about their socially situated epistemic vantage points than to list those who did not.
2. The distinction between "knowing that" and "knowing how" is not new. In a fresh approach through cognitive science, DesAutels (1995) explores the links between "low-level embodied" and "high-level cognitive" theories.
3. On empirically committed and naturalist approaches see Flanagan 1991 and May, Friedman, and Clark 1996. On cross-cultural study of morality, see Shweder 1991, Miller and Bersoff 1995, and Wainryb and Turiel 1995.
4. Annette Baier's uses of a "minimal condition of adequacy" on moral theories—that they not condemn the activities and relations on which the forms of life they prescribe depend—are instructive lessons in this kind of critical technique. See Baier 1987, 1993, and 1995.
5. The handy phrase "who gets to do what to whom," which I use throughout these chapters, is adapted from Catharine MacKinnon's characterization of gender as "a social status based on who is permitted to do what to whom" (MacKinnon 1987, 8).
6. My view that morality is fundamentally about revealing what we take responsibility for is profoundly indebted to Cavell 1979. Robert Goodin's work on responsibility and vulnerability (Goodin 1985) provides a backdrop for my own version of an ethics of responsibility in chapter 4. It is

from feminist philosophers, however, that I have learned how to look at distributions and enforcements of responsibility as a key to understanding and critically assessing the role of power in structuring moral forms of life. See especially Addelson 1991 and 1994; Baier 1995; Calhoun 1988 and 1989; Mann 1994; and Tronto 1993 in this regard.

7. Cp. Bernard Williams, "There is no reason why moral philosophy, or again something in some respects broader, in some respects narrower, called 'value theory', should yield any interesting self-contained theory at all" (Williams 1972, xxi). But for Williams (in the same paragraph), "It is merely that one's initial responsibilities should be to moral phenomena, as grasped in one's own experience and imagination, and, at the more theoretical level, to the demands of *other* parts of philosophy—in particular the philosophy of mind" (ibid.). Reservations about "one's own experience and imagination" are at the heart of my critical perspective; this is what makes it a feminist one, as I explain below.

8. Two samplers of "anti-theory" are Clarke and Simpson 1989 and Hauerwas and MacIntyre 1983. Anscombe 1958 is a root of defection from code-like theory, and papers collected in Foot 1978 are important for the revival of the virtue tradition as an alternative.

9. The variety of views more or less indebted to Aristotle's idea of "perception" of what is fitting in particular cases includes Nussbaum 1986 and 1990, MacDowell 1979 and 1994, Wiggins 1978, Dancy 1983 and 1993, McNaughton 1988. Jonsen and Toulmin 1988 resuscitate medieval and early modern traditions of casuistry. Cognitive science approaches to skilled moral perception include Churchland 1989 and 1996, Clark 1996, DesAutels 1996, Dennett 1988, Dreyfus 1990. See also Blum 1994.

10. Jaggar 1991 is the best compact summary of sources and directions of feminist ethics. Tong 1993 provides a basic overview as does Cole 1993 in the context of feminist philosophy as a whole. Collections include Held 1995; Cole and Coultrap-McQuin 1992; Card 1991; Code, Mullett, and Overall 1988; Hanen and Nielsen 1987; and Kittay and Meyers 1987.

11. Recent theory on gender is extensive. On the crucial insight that gender is about hierarchical power relations, not about "differences," see MacKinnon 1987, especially chapter 2. On how the powers gender distributes differ among and between men and women otherwise differently placed in society (by race, class, etc.), see Lugones and Spelman 1983; Moraga and Anzaldua 1983; hooks 1984; Spelman 1988; Anzaldua 1990; Collins 1990. On gender as a set of norms which produce what they purport to regulate, see Butler 1990. On social and textual constructions of gender in and outside feminism, see Donna Haraway's "Gender for a Marxist Dictionary: The Sexual Politics of a Word," in Haraway 1991. Jaggar 1983 provides thorough analysis of gender in the structure of liberal, Marxist, and some feminist political frameworks. Young 1990 explores interactions of gender with other systems of privilege within a comprehensive theory of justice.

Chapter Two

1. All quotations from Sidgwick that follow are from the seventh edition of *The Methods*.

2. Moral theory is likened to a certain picure of scientific theory, a covering-law model. It's not without irony that the prestige of a covering-law model

in moral philosophy continues to survive its contestation or repudiation in contemporary philosophy of science. I thank Jim Nelson for emphasizing this point.

3. The nomological, logical priority, and codifiability assumptions are constitutive of the structure that defines code-like theories. Contemporary dispute about the reality or intelligibility of moral dilemmas shows that systematic unity, in the strong sense in which it rules out mutually incompatible results of application, is arguable even among some who hold the code-like ideal in common, so Sidgwick's fundamental postulate is not uncontested within the theoretical project. See Gowans 1987 on the dilemmas debate.

4. One variation on this would be the fairly common view that universality or universalizability is constitutive of normative points of view as moral ones, i.e. that for a view (including a code-like normative theory) to be a moral view it must be held true for anyone if held true for oneself.

5. See Sidgwick's concluding chapter, "The Mutual Relations of the Three Methods," pp. 496ff., and Schneewind, "Sidgwick and the Dualism of Practical Reason," in Schneewind 1977, chapter 13.

6. Sidgwick has never been simply forgotten in discussion of the fundamentals of moral philosophy (see Anscombe 1958 and Rawls 1971, *passim*), and seems to be enjoying more attention of late (in addition to Williams 1985 and Jonsen and Toulmin 1988, see Gibbard 1990, MacIntyre 1990, Brink 1994, and Williams 1995). Some of these discussions go to content, and some to method, but none, I think, locates Sidgwick as squarely at the discursive foundations of twentieth-century theory as I claim.

7. I thank the audience at a colloquium of the Graduate Center of the City University of New York for discussion of this paper that sharpened my sense of the stakes for moral philosophy in defending or rejecting a theoretical-juridical model. I am grateful to the late Marx Wartofsky for his interest in the paper. Graduate seminars at Fordham University and Washington University provided a medium for refining this interpretation of Sidgwick.

Chapter Three

1. Gilligan 1982 is the best known source of such a view. Held 1995 collects work spurred by Gilligan. For systematic developments of care ethics, see Noddings 1984; Ruddick 1984; Held 1993; Manning 1992; Tronto 1993; and Bowden 1997. Critical responses to Gilligan or care ethics include Card 1990; Grimshaw 1986; Houston 1987; Hoagland 1991; Larrabee 1993; Michele Moody-Adams 1991; and Friedman 1993. On race and class concerns, see Harding 1987 and Stack 1993. See Whitbeck 1983 on responsibility and Baier 1995 on trust.

2. On strong objectivity and on socially marginal standpoints as resources, see Harding 1993. On criteria of objectivity in application to communities, see Longino 1993a, 1993b. On situated knowledge and "material-semiotic" technologies, see Haraway 1991. On the need for inquiry into the nature and effects of bias, see Antony 1993. On complexities of evaluation on a holistic view, see Nelson 1993. On empirical study of the social organization of knowledge, and on micronegotiations in epistemic communities, see Addelson 1993 and Potter 1993.

3. Rawls 1971 is the original for the reflective equilibrium view, although it is rooted in Sidgwick's approach to rectifying "commonsense morality" (see

chapter 2 of this book). Sidgwick in turn thought it was what Aristotle had done. Some interesting later developments are Daniels 1979; and DePaul 1993. For the more culturally situated and interpersonal cast of Rawls's later views, see Rawls 1993.

4. For an illustration of the difference in structure and outcome between a deductivist model and a narrative one when applied to a particular case in medical ethics, see my discussion of Carlos and Consuelo in Walker 1993, 35–36.

5. Sawicki 1991, chapter 5, discusses disarticulation of Enlightenment ideals from some practices and rearticulating them in terms of others, within a Foucauldian framework. Mann 1994 analyzes the coming apart of liberal conceptions of agency under rapid mutations of certain gendered roles and expectations.

6. A contemporary collection that illustrates this way of framing moral epistemology is Sinnott-Armstrong and Timmons 1996. A version of this chapter appears in that volume.

7. See Korsgaard 1996, lectures 2 and 3, for a view of "reflective endorsement" strategies of moral justification that sees these in essentially a first-person way; but see also lecture 4 for a way others give us reasons just by "being someone." This move is too quick; as I discuss below in part three, recognition depends on the kind of someone you are. Compare also Scanlon 1982, 128, on "what morality is about."

8. Thanks to the following people who commented on earlier drafts of this chapter: Malia Brink, Marilyn Friedman, Christopher Gowans, John Greco, Alison Jaggar, Diana Meyers, Hilde Nelson, Jim Nelson, Walter Sinnott-Armstrong, and Iris Young. Special thanks to Susan Walsh for perfect workspace when I was in transit while working on this piece.

Chapter Four

1. Two proposals for responsibility ethics other than Robert Goodin's (discussed below) are Jonas 1984 and Whitbeck 1983. Psychologist Carol Gilligan's theory of an ethics of responsibility in relationships (or "care ethic"), allegedly more characteristic of female respondents in her studies, sparked extended debate. See Gilligan 1982 and, for the debate, Kittay and Meyers 1987, Larrabee 1993, and Held 1995.

2. Goodin's view also includes a principle of collective responsibility and one specifying individual responsibilities in the collective case. I don't discuss this important aspect of Goodin's views here. See Goodin 1985, chapter 5, and Goodin 1995, especially chapter 2.

3. John Kilner (Kilner 1984) found results surprising to a Western audience in a study of values guiding decision-making in cases of scarce life-saving medical resources among the Akamba people of Kenya. It was common to favor saving lives of adult or older people rather than small children, and childless male adults rather than those with children. Many also thought it better to give half treatment to each of two dying patients, even where half treatment is insufficient, rather than provide one patient with full treatment. Kilner found more education correlated with less egalitarian thinking.

4. Philips 1994 argues against the "constancy assumption" and for the shifting value of moral considerations precisely with respect to duties to rescue.

5. Recent work on "human capabilities" opens up the vista of questions about

normative standards for "human" functioning (Nussbaum and Glover 1995).

6. Gordon 1994 is a thorough discussion of the shifting perceptions, political stakes, and social fortunes of single mothers and their dependent children in the context of twentieth-century U.S. welfare legislation. Gordon illustrates how a dominant social consensus on responsibility for young children is transformed under the impacts of economic, political, immigration, and other social trends and activist movements. At any time, standard practices and accepted institutions remain surrounded by a penumbra of alternative visions and possibilities. See also Kathryn Addelson's story about how Margaret Sanger's movement for "birth control" as a political agenda for working class women and men was domesticated into the personal responsibility (and opportunity) of "family planning" for the middle classes, in Addelson 1994. Okin 1989 is a thorough critique within a liberal political framework of existing divisions of labor and responsibility in families. Nelson 1997 contains diverse analyses of "normative" families and their alternatives.

7. See May 1992 for a provocative analysis of responsibility through moral negligence even where one has not directly caused harm.

8. The problem of "moral luck" (Statman 1993) is an interesting study in this regard, as several philosophers present different views of "our" concept of responsibility, based on what is said, thought, done, or felt by "us." My own earlier view (Walker 1991) is included in Statman.

9. Special thanks to Jim Nelson for making me worry about whether we have more responsibilities than we think. I read Peter Unger's fascinating and disturbing book on this issue, *Living High and Letting Die* (New York: Oxford University Press, 1996), when my own was already in press, so I was unable to consider it here.

Chapter Five

1. Care ethics has been defended and developed by Gilligan 1982; Noddings 1984; Baier 1987; Held 1987 and 1993; Ruddick 1989; Manning 1992; and Tronto 1993. Whitbeck 1984 and Bishop 1987 emphasize responsiveness to particular others in specific relationships. Others who argue for a responsibility ethics, although not necessarily one so particularistic and contextual as that sketched here, include Goodin 1985 and Jonas 1984. My formulation of the key idea of responsibility ethics is modelled on Goodin's "vulnerability principle." See chapter 4 for my fuller discussion.

2. See Williams 1973b, 1981a, and 1981b, and Stocker 1976, on the dis-integration claim. Objections to consequentialist morality on the ground that it insufficiently respects, or even violates, the distinctness of persons and the importance to them of their individual lives are also found in Rawls 1971; Nozick 1974; Nagel 1979; and Scheffler 1982.

3. That moral responsibility is not limited by and to what a person herself controls, and that integrity has much to do with accepting this, is discussed in Card 1996 and Walker 1991.

4. Such characterizations figure in a nonfeminist philosophical literature on integrity. Calhoun 1995 discusses Taylor 1985, McFall 1987, and Blustein 1991, as well as Williams 1973b, 1981a, 1981b. Kekes 1983 might be added to this group. Benjamin 1990 recognizes the need for change and compromise in a realistic pursuit of integrity, but still sees the subject of in-

tegrity as a whole life. Gaita 1981 speaks instead of "due influence" of the past, not incompatible with my account here.

5. This is Lee Quinby's description of the self-understanding expressed by Maxine Hong Kingston's *The Woman Warrior* (Quinby 1991, 136).

6. Morgan 1987 is one powerful original discussion of double-binding, invisibility, and "moral madness" of women. I urge more reserve in assuming that rigged terms of intelligibility for women and others actually commonly corrupt or disintegrate agency. I emphasize instead the first two problems. There is also something in between: see Mann 1994, 54–61, on "surd" behavior, an inability to make both complete and coherent sense of what one is doing at a given time under mutations and misalignments of social practices and assumptions.

7. Neisser and Fivush 1994 contains varied discussions of the nature and production of storytelling constraints. Kathryn Addelson strikingly illustrates narrative pressure from authorities and authoritative discourses throughout Addelson 1994.

8. Mann 1994 analyzes the female counterpart of the male liberal citizen-peer as a "subsumed nurturer," and explicitly connects this position to being unable to act "in one's own name."

9. This chapter began life as a little paper on selves and narratives at the conference "Moral Agency and the Fragmented Self" at the University of Dayton in 1990. I am grateful to that audience and particularly to my commentator "Tess" Tessier for early discussion of these issues. I thank the following people whose reactions to or comments on earlier versions of this essay helped me see what I was trying to do or hadn't done: Simon Blackburn, Judith Bradford, Paul Lauritzen, Diana Meyers, and especially Hilde Nelson. Thanks to Joel Anderson for telling me about the Rev. Shields and giving me a copy of the NPR transcript. I'm grateful to Cheshire Calhoun for private communication about the strong similarity as well as difference in emphasis between our views; I can't say she would agree with how I have represented that here.

Chapter Six

1. I thank Iris Young for pressing me to make my point clear here, and for supplying some distinctinctions needed to do it.

2. Addelson also criticizes Diana Meyers's theory of personal autonomy in Meyers 1989. See Meyers 1994 for her more recent views.

3. In an earlier essay Williams said the desire to stay alive won't do even as a minimal categorical desire "once the question has come up and requires an answer in calculative terms" (Williams 1973a, 99). This amounts to saying that if you are at some point not sufficiently propelled to live unless you can give yourself a reason, then you are going to have to give yourself a reason in order to go on. But then this *is* a special, rather than a general, kind of case.

4. On the possible pointlessness of chronicling, and a meaningless way of appropriating all the stuff of one's own life, see the strange but true tale of the Rev. Shields in chapter 5 above.

5. For a related discussion see Flanagan 1990.

6. There's a curious passage in which Taylor remarks that there is "something like" but "not quite" an "a priori unity of a human life through its whole

extent," and this because of "imaginable" cultural variations (Taylor 1989, 51). Taylor's own remarks about failing, though, are enough to show that narrative unity of lives is very far from universally and necessarily true.

7. Two other detailed Kantian accounts of the architecture of autonomous subjectivity that deserve close analysis are those of Herman 1993 and Korsgaard 1996.

Chapter Seven

1. Thanks to the audience at a Vassar College Philosopher's Holiday in February, 1996, who helped me to focus the issues, and to Judith Bradford, whose understanding of epistemological Chinese boxes is my touchstone.

Chapter Eight

1. Frye 1983 is a classic feminist analysis of arrogant perception of women by men; Meyers 1997 is a more recent feminist discussion of moral perception.

2. For Wittgenstein the view is about more than this; the grammar of psychological concepts tells us what kind of thing psychological states are. For my purposes here, which do not include controversies in the philosophy of mind, I only adapt some of Wittgenstein's insights into the ascription of psychological states to other people.

3. *Investigations*, page 178. See Peter Winch, "Eine Einstellung zur Seele," *Proceedings of the Aristotelian Society* (1980–81): 1–15, for a classic discussion of this. See also B. R. Tilghman, *Wittgenstein, Ethics and Aesthetics* (Albany: State University of New York Press, 1991) and David Cockburn, *Other Human Beings* (New York: St. Martin's Press, 1990) for discussions of this approach to philosophy of mind and its fundamentally ethical import.

4. This chapter was "reincarnated" several times, yet even now the picture it gives is not as effective as I would like it to be. For many improvements I have been able to make, I thank members of my feminist reading group—Pat Mann, Kate Mehuron, Lee Quinby; and audiences when the paper was given at the philosophy departments of Washington University and Fordham University, and the Department of Art History at the State University of New York at Stony Brook. Special thanks to comments by Brian Davies, Chris Gowans, and John Greco, and discussion with Judith Bradford, that helped me sort out different kinds of recognition problems.

Chapter Nine

1. Other philosophers who have characterized morality as a kind of social artifact in recent literature are Williams 1985; Philips 1994; and Greenspan 1995.

2. Churchland 1989, 301 and Flanagan 1996 identify this objection as a central one aimed at naturalistic approaches to morality. DePaul 1993, chapter 1, discusses the use of this objection in the work of R. M. Hare, Peter Singer, Richard Brandt, Kai Nielsen, and David Lyons against a reflective equilibrium method that begins from a set of actual moral beliefs assumed to be well considered.

3. Some influential statements of the idea that true or real moral judgments

must be universal are Donagan 1977; Gewirth 1978; Nagel 1970; Hare 1963; Baier 1958. I don't mean to imply that these are not different views, nor that the differences among them are negligible. The variations on this view suggest rather that the association between real morality and universality is strong and common, and so has been worked out in many ways.

4. Gewirth acknowledges that this argument is insufficient to show that there actually *are* such (real) standards. He supplements this argument by defending the universal validity of a single moral principle, the Principle of Generic Consistency.

5. Gibbard 1990, parts three and four, provides fresh and searching discussion of the status of claims to objectivity, the burdens and limits of coherence, and the possibilities for shared lives under conditions of moral disagreement.

6. Millikan 1996 discusses representations that are at once "descriptive" and "directive."

7. I thank Michael Byron for pointing out to me the need to make this point clearer.

8. Okin 1994, 36–37, cites a recent study by Wainryb and Turiel of women's and girls' perceptions of sex inequality in hierarchical patriarchal families among Druze Arabs in Israel: "While almost 80 percent of the women and girls judged that it was unfair for a husband to dictate his wife's choices, at the same time 93 percent of them said that the wife should acquiese. . . . The women were quite prepared to acknowledge that this situation in which they had no choice but to live was unjust."

9. Williams 1985 presents "confidence" in a way of life as an alternative to knowledge of moral reality.

10. Thanks to Hilde Lindemann Nelson for help with this chapter in earlier drafts. A work-in-progress group at the Ethics Center of the University of South Florida gave these ideas a lively discussion that helped me see how slight are the distinctions I have made here in the face of many problems of moral difference within and between societies. Thanks to members Peter French, Peggy DesAutels, Michael Byron, Mitch Haney, and Mark Woods. Michael Byron provided numerous detailed suggestions on style and substance for which I am grateful. Very special thanks to Peggy DesAutels for searching comments in the final days of revising that led to significant improvements. No one above-mentioned should be assumed to share any of the views herein.

bibliography

Addelson, Kathryn Pyne. 1991. *Impure Thoughts*. Philadelphia: Temple University Press.

Addelson, Kathryn Pyne. 1993. "Knowers/Doers and Their Moral Problems." In *Feminist Epistemologies*. Ed. Linda Alcoff and Elizabeth Potter. New York: Routledge.

Addelson, Kathryn Pyne. 1994. *Moral Passages*. New York: Routledge.

Anscombe, G. E. M. 1958."Modern Moral Philosophy." *Philosophy* 33: 1–19.

Antony, Louise. 1993. "Quine as Feminist: The Radical Import of Naturalized Epistemology." In *A Mind of One's Own*. Ed. Louise Antony and Charlotte Witt. Boulder, Colo.: Westview Press.

Anzaldúa, Gloria. 1990. *Making Face, Making Soul*. San Francisco: Aunt Lute Foundation Books.

Baier, Annette. 1985. "What Do Women Want in a Moral Theory?" *Nous* 19: 53–63.

Baier, Annette. 1986. "Trust and Anti-Trust." *Ethics* 96: 321–60.

Baier, Annette. 1987. "The Need for More Than Justice." In *Science, Morality and Feminist Theory*. Ed. Marsha Hanen and Kai Nielsen. Calgary: University of Calgary Press.

Baier, Annette. 1993. "Moralism and Cruelty: Reflections on Hume and Kant." *Ethics* 103: 436–57.

Baier, Annette. 1995. *Moral Prejudices*. Cambridge, Mass.: Harvard University Press.

Baier, Kurt. 1958. *The Moral Point of View*. New York: Random House.

Bartky, Sandra. 1990. "Foucault, Femininity, and the Modernization of Patriarchal Power." In *Femininity and Domination*. New York: Routledge.

Baumrind, Diana. 1993. "Sex Differences in Moral Reasoning: Response to Walker's (1984) Conclusion That There Are None." In *An Ethic of Care*. Ed. Mary Jeanne Larrabee. New York: Routledge.

Benhabib, Seyla. 1987. "The Generalized and the Concrete Other." In *Women and Moral Theory*. Ed. Eva Kitty and Diana Meyers. Totowa, N.J.: Rowman and Littlefield.

Benjamin, Martin. 1990. *Splitting the Difference*. Lawrence: University Press of Kansas.

Benson, Paul. 1990. "Feminist Second Thoughts on Free Agency." *Hypatia* 5: 47–64.

Bishop, Sharon. 1987. "Connections and Guilt." *Hypatia* 2: 7–23.

Blackburn, Simon. 1993. *Essays in Quasi-Realism*. New York: Oxford University Press.

Blackburn, Simon. 1996. "Securing the Nots: Moral Epistemology for the Quasi-Realist." In *Moral Knowledge? New Readings in Moral Epistemology*. Ed. Walter Sinnott-Armstrong and Mark Timmons. New York: Oxford University Press.

Blum, Larry. 1980. *Friendship, Altruism, and Morality*. London: Routledge and Kegan Paul.

Blum, Larry. 1994. *Moral Perception and Particularity*. New York: Cambridge University Press.

Blustein, Jeffrey. 1991. *Care and Commitment: Taking the Personal Point of View*. New York: Oxford University Press.

Bok, Sissela. 1995. *Common Values*. Columbia: University of Missouri Press.

Bowden, Peta. 1997. *Caring: An Investigation in Gender-Sensitive Ethics*. New York: Routledge.

Brink, David. 1989. *Moral Realism and the Foundations of Ethics*. New York: Cambridge University Press.

Brink, David. 1994. "Common Sense and First Principles in Sidgwick's *Methods*." In *Cultural Pluralism and Moral Knowledge*. Ed. Ellen Frankel Paul, Fred D. Miller, Jr., and Jeffrey Paul. New York: Cambridge University Press.

Broad, C. D. 1930. *Five Types of Ethical Theory*. London: Routledge and Kegan Paul.

Bruner, Jerome. 1994. "The 'Remembered' Self." In *The Remembering Self*. Ed. Ulric Neisser and Robyn Fivush. Cambridge: Cambridge University Press.

Butler, Judith. 1990. *Gender Trouble*. New York: Routledge.

Calhoun, Cheshire. 1988. "Justice, Care, Gender Bias." *Journal of Philosophy* 85: 451–63.

Calhoun, Cheshire. 1989. "Responsibility and Reproach," *Ethics* 99: 389–406.

Calhoun, Cheshire. 1995. "Standing for Something." *Journal of Philosophy* 92: 235–60.

Card, Claudia. 1990. "Gender and Moral Luck." In *Identity, Character, and Morality*. Ed. Owen Flanagan and Amelie Rorty. Cambridge, Mass.: MIT Press.

Card, Claudia. 1991. *Feminist Ethics*. Lawrence: University Press of Kansas.

Card, Claudia, ed. 1996. *The Unnatural Lottery*. Philadelphia: Temple University Press.

Cavell, Stanley. 1979. *The Claim of Reason*. New York: Oxford University Press.

Churchland, Paul. 1989. *A Neurocomputational Perspective*. Cambridge, Mass.: MIT Press.

Churchland, Paul. 1996. "The Neural Representation of the Social World." In *Mind and Morals: Essays on Cognitive Science and Ethics*. Ed. Larry May, Marilyn Friedman, and Andy Clark. Cambridge, Mass.: MIT Press.

Clark, Andy. 1996. "Connectionism, Moral Cognition, and Collaborative Problem Solving." In *Mind and Morals: Essays on Cognitive Science and Ethics*.

Ed. Larry May, Marilyn Friedman, and Andy Clark. Cambridge, Mass.: MIT Press.

Clarke, Stanley, and Evan Simpson, eds. 1989. *Anti-Theory in Ethics and Moral Conservatism*. Albany: State University of New York Press.

Clifford, James. 1988. *The Predicament of Culture*. Cambridge, Mass.: Harvard University Press.

Cockburn, David. 1990. *Other Human Beings*. New York: St. Martin's Press.

Code, Lorraine, Sheila Mullett, and Christine Overall, eds. 1988. *Feminist Perspectives: Philosophical Essays on Method and Morals*. Toronto: University of Toronto Press.

Code, Lorraine. 1991. *What Can She Know?* Ithaca: Cornell University Press.

Cole, Eve Browning. 1993. *Philosophy and Feminist Criticism*. New York: Paragon House.

Cole, Eve Browning, and Susan Coultrap-McQuin, eds. 1992. *Explorations in Feminist Ethics: Theory and Practice*. Bloomington: Indiana University Press.

Collins, Patricia Hill. 1990. *Black Feminist Thought*. New York: Routledge.

Conly, Sarah. 1983. "Utilitarianism and Integrity." *Monist* 66: 298–311.

Dancy, Jonathan. 1983."Ethical Particularism and Morally Relevant Properties," *Mind* 92: 530–47.

Dancy, Jonathan. 1993. *Moral Reasons*. Cambridge: Basil Blackwell.

Daniels, Norman. 1979. "Wide Reflective Equilibrium and Theory Acceptance in Ethics." *Journal of Philosophy* 76: 256–82.

Davion, Victoria. 1991. "Integrity and Radical Change." In *Feminist Ethics*. Ed. Claudia Card. Lawrence: University Press of Kansas.

DePaul, Michael. 1993. *Balance and Refinement*. New York: Routledge.

DesAutels, Peggy. 1995."Moral Perceiving: Bridging Cognitive Science and Moral Philosophy." Dissertation, unpublished.

DesAutels, Peggy. 1996. "Gestalt Shifts in Moral Perception." In *Mind and Morals: Essays on Cognitive Science and Ethics*. Ed. Larry May, Marilyn Friedman, and Andy Clark. Cambridge, Mass.: MIT Press.

Dennett, Daniel. 1988. "The Moral First Aid Manual." *The Tanner Lectures on Human Values*, Vol. 8. Ed. Sterling M. McMurrin. Salt Lake City: University of Utah Press.

Dillard, Annie. 1985. *Pilgrim at Tinker Creek*. New York: Harper & Row.

Dillon, Robin. 1992. "Care and Respect." In *Explorations in Feminist Ethics: Theory and Practice*. Ed. Eve Browning Cole and Susan Coultrap-McQuin. Bloomington: Indiana University Press.

Donagan, Alan. 1977. *The Theory of Morality*. Chicago: University of Chicago Press.

Dreyfus, Hubert, and Stuart Dreyfus. 1990. "What Is Morality? A Phenomenology of the Development of Ethical Expertise." In *Universalism vs. Communitarianism: Contemporary Debate in Ethics*. Ed. Douglas Rasmussen. Cambridge, Mass.: MIT Press.

Dugger, Celia. 1996. "U.S. Grants Asylum to Woman Fleeing Genital Mutilation Rite." *New York Times*, June 14.

Enloe, Cynthia. 1990. *Bananas, Beaches and Bases*. Berkeley and Los Angeles: University of California Press.

Feinberg, Joel. 1970. *Doing and Deserving*. Princeton, N.J.: Princeton University Press.

Fivush, Robyn. 1994. "Constructing the Self in Parent-Child Conversations." In *The Remembering Self*. Ed. Ulric Neisser and Robyn Fivush. Cambridge: Cambridge University Press.

Flanagan, Owen. 1990. "Identity and Strong and Weak Evaluation." In *Identity, Character, and Morality*. Ed. Owen Flanagan and Amelie Rorty. Cambridge, Mass.: MIT Press.

Flanagan, Owen. 1991. *Varieties of Moral Personality*. Cambridge, Mass.: Harvard University Press.

Flanagan, Owen. 1996. "Ethics Naturalized: Ethics as Human Ecology." In *Mind and Morals*. Ed. Larry May, Marilyn Friedman, and Andy Clark. Cambridge, Mass.: MIT Press.

Foot, Philippa. 1978. *Virtues and Vices*. Berkeley and Los Angeles: University of California Press.

Foucault, Michel. 1979. *Discipline and Punish*. Trans. Alan Sheridan. New York: Vintage Books.

Fraser, Nancy. 1989. *Unruly Practices*. New York: Routledge.

French, Peter. 1992. *Responsibility Matters*. Lawrence: University Press of Kansas.

Friedman, Marilyn. 1993. *What Are Friends For?* Ithaca: Cornell University Press.

Frye, Marilyn. 1983. *The Politics of Reality*. Trumansberg, N.Y.: The Crossing Press.

Frye, Marilyn. 1992. "White Woman/White Feminist: The Meaning of White." In *Willful Virgin: Essays in Feminist Theory*. Freedom, Calif.: The Crossing Press.

Gaita, Raimond. 1981. "Integrity." *Proceedings of the Aristotelian Society*, Supplementary Volume 55: 161–76.

Gates, Henry Louis, ed. 1987. *The Classic Slave Narratives*. New York: Penguin Books.

Geertz, Clifford. 1983. *Local Knowledge*. New York: Basic Books.

Gewirth, Alan. 1978. *Reason and Morality*. Chicago: University of Chicago Press.

Gewirth, Alan. 1994. "Is Cultural Pluralism Relevant to Moral Knowledge?" In *Cultural Pluralism and Moral Knowledge*. Ed. Ellen Frankel Paul, Fred D. Miller, and Jeffrey Paul. New York: Cambridge University Press.

Gibbard, Allan. 1990. *Wise Choices, Apt Feelings*. Cambridge, Mass.: Harvard University Press.

Gilligan, Carol. 1982. *In A Different Voice*. Cambridge, Mass.: Harvard University Press.

Glover, Jonathan. 1995. "The Research Programme of Development Ethics." In *Women, Culture, and Development*. Ed. Martha Nussbaum and Jonathan Glover. New York: Oxford University Press.

Goleman, Daniel. 1989. "When the Rapist Is Not a Stranger." *New York Times*, August 29.

Goodin, Robert. 1985. *Protecting the Vulnerable.* Chicago: University of Chicago Press.

Goodin, Robert. 1995. *Utilitarianism as a Public Philosophy.* New York: Cambridge University Press.

Gordon, Linda. 1994. *Pitied but Not Entitled: Single Mothers and the History of Welfare, 1890–1935.* Cambridge, Mass.: Harvard University Press.

Gowans, Christopher W. 1987. *Moral Dilemmas.* New York: Oxford University Press.

Greenspan, Patricia. 1995. *Practical Guilt.* New York: Oxford University Press.

Grimshaw, Jean. 1986. *Philosophy and Feminist Thinking.* Minneapolis: University of Minnesota Press.

Hallie, Philip. 1985. "From Cruelty to Goodness." In *Virtue and Vice in Everyday Life*, 1st edition. Ed. Christina Hoff Sommers. San Diego: Harcourt Brace Jovanovich.

Hanen, Marsha, and Kai Nielsen, eds. 1987. *Science, Morality and Feminist Theory.* Calgary: University of Calgary Press.

Haraway, Donna. 1991. *Simians, Cyborgs, and Women.* New York: Routledge.

Harding, Sandra. 1987. "The Curious Coincidence of Feminine and African Moralities." In *Women and Moral Theory.* Ed. Eva Kittay and Diana Meyers. Totowa, N.J.: Rowman and Littlefield.

Harding, Sandra. 1993. "Rethinking Standpoint Epistemology: What Is Strong Objectivity?" In *Feminist Epistemologies.* Ed. Linda Alcoff and Elizabeth Potter. New York: Routledge.

Hare, R. M. 1981. *Moral Thinking.* New York: Oxford University Press.

Hare, R. M. 1963. *Freedom and Reason.* Oxford: Oxford University Press.

Hauerwas, Stanley, and Alasdair MacIntyre, eds. 1983. *Revisions.* Notre Dame, Ind.: University of Notre Dame Press.

Heath, Shirley Brice. 1982. "What No Bedtime Story Means: Narrative Skills at Home and School." *Language in Society* 11: 49-76.

Held, Virginia. 1987. "Feminism and Moral Theory." In *Women and Moral Theory.* Ed. Eva Kittay and Diana Meyers. Totowa, N.J.: Rowman and Littlefield.

Held, Virginia. 1993. *Feminist Morality.* Chicago: University of Chicago Press.

Held, Virginia, ed. 1995. *Justice and Care: Essential Readings in Feminist Ethics.* Boulder, Colo.: Westview Press.

Herman, Barbara. 1983. "Integrity and Impartiality." *Monist* 66: 233–50.

Herman, Barbara. 1993. *The Practice of Moral Judgment.* Cambridge, Mass.: Harvard University Press.

Hoagland, Sarah Lucia. 1988. *Lesbian Ethics.* Palo Alto, Calif.: Institute of Lesbian Studies.

Hoagland, Sarah Lucia. 1991. "Some Thoughts about 'Caring.'" In *Feminist Ethics.* Ed. Claudia Card. Lawrence: University Press of Kansas.

hooks, bell. 1984. *Feminist Theory: From Margin to Center.* Boston: South End Press.

hooks, bell. 1994. *Outlaw Culture.* New York: Routledge.

Houston, Barbara. 1987. "Rescuing Womanly Virtues: Some Dangers of Moral

Reclamation." In *Science, Morality and Feminist Theory*. Ed. Marsha Hanen
  and Kai Nielsen. Calgary: University of Calgary Press.
Jaggar, Alison. 1983. *Feminist Politics and Human Nature*. Totowa, N.J.: Row-
  man and Allanheld.
Jaggar, Alison. 1991. "Feminist Ethics: Projects, Problems, Prospects." In *Femi-
  nist Ethics*. Ed. Claudia Card. Lawrence: University Press of Kansas.
Jaggar, Alison. 1995. "Toward a Feminist Conception of Moral Reasoning." In
  Morality and Social Justice: Point/Counterpoint. Ed. James Sterba, Alison
  Jaggar, et al. Lanham, Md.: Rowman and Littlefield.
Jonas, Hans. 1984. *The Imperative of Responsibility*. Chicago: University of
  Chicago Press.
Jonsen, Albert, and Steven Toulmin. 1988. *The Abuse of Casuistry*. Berkeley
  and Los Angeles: University of California Press.
Kagan, Shelly. 1989. *The Limits of Morality*. New York: Oxford University Press.
Kekes, John. 1983. "Constancy and Purity." *Mind* 92: 499–519.
Kenton, Edna, ed. 1925. *The Jesuit Relations and Allied Documents: Travels
  and Explorations of the Jesuit Missionaries in North America (1610–1791)*.
  New York: Albert & Charles Boni.
Kilner, John. 1984. "Who Shall Be Saved? An African Answer." *Hastings Cen-
  ter Report* 14: 18–22.
Kittay, Eva Feder. 1984. "Pornography and the Erotics of Domination." In *Be-
  yond Domination*. Ed. Carol C. Gould. Totowa, N.J.: Rowman and Allan-
  held.
Kittay, Eva, and Diana Meyers, eds. 1987. *Women and Moral Theory*. Totowa,
  N.J.: Rowman and Littlefield.
Kitto, H. D. F. 1957. *The Greeks*. Baltimore: Penguin Books.
Korsgaard, Christine. 1996. *The Sources of Normativity*. New York: Cam-
  bridge University Press.
Kundera, Milan. 1984. *The Unbearable Lightness of Being*. New York: Harper
  & Row.
Larrabee, Mary Jeanne, ed. 1993. *An Ethic of Care*. New York: Routledge.
Longino, Helen. 1993a. "Subjects, Power and Knowledge: Description and Pre-
  scription in Feminist Philosophies of Science." In *Feminist Epistemologies*.
  Ed. Linda Alcoff and Elizabeth Potter. New York: Routledge.
Longino, Helen. 1993b. "Essential Tensions—Phase Two: Feminist, Philosophi-
  cal, and Social Studies of Science." In *A Mind of One's Own*, Louise Antony
  and Charlotte Witt. Ed. Boulder, Colo.: Westview Press.
Lovibond, Sabina. 1983. *Realism and Imagination in Ethics*. Minneapolis: Uni-
  versity of Minnesota Press.
Lugones, Maria. 1990. "Hispaneando y Lesbiando: On Sarah Hoagland's *Les-
  bian Ethics*." *Hypatia* 5: 138–46.
Lugones, Maria. 1991. "On the Logic of Feminist Pluralism." In *Feminist
  Ethics*. Ed. Claudia Card. Lawrence: University Press of Kansas.
Lugones, Maria, and Elizabeth Spelman. 1983. "Have We Got a Theory for
  You: Feminist Theory, Cultural Imperialism, and the Demand for 'The
  Woman's Voice,'" *Hypatia, A Special Issue of Women's Studies International
  Forum* 6: 573–81.

MacDowell, John. 1979. "Virtue and Reason." *Monist* 62: 331–50.

MacDowell, John. 1994. *Mind and World*. Cambridge, Mass.: Harvard University Press.

MacIntyre, Alasdair. 1981. *After Virtue*. Notre Dame, Ind.: University of Notre Dame Press.

MacIntyre, Alasdair. 1988. *Whose Justice? Which Rationality?* Notre Dame, Ind.: University of Notre Dame Press.

MacIntyre, Alasdair. 1990. *Three Rival Versions of Moral Inquiry*. Notre Dame, Ind.: University of Notre Dame Press.

MacKinnon, Catharine. 1987. *Feminism Unmodified*. Cambridge, Mass.: Harvard University Press.

Mann, Patricia. 1994. *Micro-Politics*. Minneapolis: University of Minnesota Press.

Manning, Rita. 1992. *Speaking from the Heart*. Lanham, Md.: Rowman and Littlefield.

May, Larry. 1992. *Sharing Responsibility*. Chicago: University of Chicago Press.

May, Larry, Marilyn Friedman, and Andy Clark, eds. 1996. *Mind and Morals*. Cambridge, Mass.: MIT Press.

McFall, Lynn. 1987. "Integrity." *Ethics* 98: 5–20.

McNaughton, David. 1988. *Moral Vision*. New York: Basil Blackwell.

Meyers, Diana. 1989. *Self, Society, and Personal Choice*. New York: Columbia University Press.

Meyers, Diana. 1994. *Subjection and Subjectivity*. New York: Routledge.

Meyers, Diana. 1997. "Emotion and Heterodox Moral Perception: An Essay in Moral Social Psychology." In *Feminists Rethink the Self*. Ed. Diana Tietjens Meyers. Boulder, Colo.: Westview Press.

Milgram, Stanley. 1974. *Obedience to Authority*. New York: Harper and Row.

Mill, John Stuart. 1969. *The Subjection of Women* [1869]. London: Oxford University Press.

Miller, Joan G., and David M Bersoff. 1995. "Development in the Context of Everyday Family Relationships: Culture, Interpersonal Morality, and Adaptation." In *Morality in Everyday Life*. Ed. Melanie Killen and Daniel Hart. New York: Cambridge University Press.

Miller, Peggy. 1994. "Narrative Practices in Self-Construction." In *The Remembering Self*. Ed. Ulric Neisser and Robyn Fivush. Cambridge: Cambridge University Press.

Millikan, Ruth. 1996. "Pushmi-pullyu Representations." In *Mind and Morals*. Ed. Larry May, Marilyn Friedman, and Andy Clark. Cambridge, Mass.: MIT Press.

Moody-Adams, Michele. 1991. "Gender and the Complexity of Moral Voices." In *Feminist Ethics*. Ed. Claudia Card. Lawrence: University Press of Kansas.

Moody-Adams, Michele. 1997. *Morality, Culture, and Philosophy: Fieldwork in Familiar Places*. Cambridge, Mass.: Harvard University Press.

Moore, G. E. 1903. *Principia Ethica*. Cambridge: Cambridge University Press.

Moraga, Cherríe, and Gloria Anzaldúa, eds. 1983. *This Bridge Called My Back*. New York: Kitchen Table Press.

Morgan, Kathryn Pauly. 1987. "Women and Moral Madness." In *Science, Morality, and Feminist Theory*. Ed. Marsha Hanen and Kai Nielsen. Calgary: University of Calgary Press.

Nabokov, Peter, ed. 1991. *Native American Testimony*. New York: Penguin Books.

Nagel, Thomas. 1970. *The Possibility of Altruism*. Princeton, N.J.: Princeton University Press.

Nagel, Thomas. 1979. *Mortal Questions*. New York: Cambridge University Press.

Nagel, Thomas. 1986. *The View from Nowhere*. New York: Oxford University Press.

National Public Radio. 1994. "Former Teacher Keeps Track of His Days Minute by Minute." Transcript, Morning Edition, January 27.

Neisser, Ulrich, and Robyn Fivush, ed. 1994. *The Remembering Self*. Cambridge: Cambridge University Press.

Nelson, Hilde Lindemann. 1995. "Resistance and Insubordination." *Hypatia* 10: 23–40.

Nelson, Hilde Lindemann, ed. 1997. *Feminism and Families*. New York: Routledge.

Nelson, Lynn Hankinson. 1993. "Epistemological Communities." In *Feminist Epistemologies*. Ed. Linda Alcoff and Elizabeth Potter. New York: Routledge.

New York Times. 1992. "Jurors Hear Evidence and Turn It Into Stories," May 12.

Noddings, Nel. 1984. *Caring*. Berkeley and Los Angeles: University of California Press.

Nozick, Robert. 1974. *Anarchy, State, and Utopia*. New York: Basic Books.

Nussbaum, Martha. 1986. *The Fragility of Goodness*. New York: Cambridge University Press.

Nussbaum, Martha. 1990. *Love's Knowledge: Essays on Philosophy and Literature*. New York: Oxford University Press.

Nussbaum, Martha. 1995. "Human Capabilities, Female Human Beings." In *Women, Culture, and Development*. Ed. Martha Nussbaum and Jonathan Glover. New York: Oxford University Press.

Nussbaum, Martha, and Jonathan Glover, eds. 1995. *Women, Culture, and Development*. New York: Oxford University Press.

Nzegwu, Nkiru. 1995. "Recovering Igbo Traditions: A Case for Indigenous Women's Organizations in Development." In *Women, Culture, and Development*. Ed. Martha Nussbaum and Jonathan Glover. New York: Oxford University Press.

Okin, Susan. 1989. *Justice, Gender, and the Family*. New York: Basic Books.

Okin, Susan Miller. 1994. "Political Liberalism, Justice, and Gender." *Ethics* 105: 23–43.

Patterson, Orlando. 1982. *Slavery and Social Death*. Cambridge, Mass.: Harvard University Press.

Philips, Michael. 1994. *Between Universalism and Skepticism*. New York: Oxford University Press.

Plato. *The Republic*.

Potter, Elizabeth. 1993. "Gender and Epistemic Negotiation." In *Feminist Epistemologies*. Ed. Linda Alcoff and Elizabeth Potter. New York: Routledge.

Quinby, Lee. 1991. *Freedom, Foucault, and the Subject of America*. Boston: Northeastern University Press.

Rawls, John. 1971. *A Theory of Justice*. Cambridge, Mass.: Harvard University Press.

Rawls, John. 1980. "Kantian Constructivism in Moral Theory." *Journal of Philosophy* 77: 515–72.

Rawls, John. 1993. *Political Liberalism*. New York: Columbia University Press.

Rich, Adrienne. 1979. "Women and Honor: Some Notes on Lying." In *Lies, Secrets, and Silence*. New York: Norton.

Romero, Mary. 1992. *Maid in the U.S.A.* New York: Routledge.

Rorty, Richard. 1989. *Contingency, Irony, and Solidarity*. New York: Cambridge University Press.

Rorty, Richard. 1991. "Feminism and Pragmatism." *Radical Philosophy* 59: 3–14.

Ross, D. W. 1930. *The Right and the Good*. Oxford: Oxford University Press.

Rubenstein, Richard L. 1975. *The Cunning of History: The Holocaust and The American Future*. New York: Harper & Row.

Rubin, David. 1986. *Autobiographical Memory*. Cambridge: Cambridge University Press.

Ruddick, Sara. 1989. *Maternal Thinking*. New York: Ballantine Books.

Said, Edward. 1979. *Orientalism*. New York: Vintage Books.

Said, Edward. 1994. *Culture and Imperialism*. New York: Vintage Books.

Sandel, Michael. 1982. *Liberalism and the Limits of Justice*. New York: Cambridge University Press.

Sawicki, Jana. 1982. *Disciplining Foucault*. New York: Routledge.

Scanlon, T. M. 1982. "Contractualism and Utilitarianism." In *Utilitarianism and Beyond*. Ed. Amartya Sen and Bernard Williams. New York: Cambridge University Press.

Scheffler, Samuel. 1982. *The Rejection of Consequentialism*. New York: Oxford University Press.

Scheman, Naomi. 1993. *Engenderings*. New York: Routledge.

Schneewind, J. B. 1977. *Sidgwick's Ethics and Victorian Moral Philosophy*. Oxford: Oxford University Press.

Schneewind, J. B. 1984. "The Divine Corporation and the History of Ethics." In *Philosophy in History*. Ed. Richard Rorty, J. B. Schneewind, and Quentin Skinner. New York: Cambridge University Press.

Shrage, Laurie. 1994. *Moral Dilemmas of Feminism*. New York: Routledge.

Shweder, Richard. 1991. *Thinking Through Cultures*. Cambridge, Mass.: Harvard University Press.

Sidgwick, Henry. 1981. *The Methods of Ethics*, Seventh Edition [1907]. Indianapolis: Hackett.

Sinnott-Armstrong, Walter, and Mark Timmons, eds. 1996. *Moral Knowledge? New Readings in Moral Epistemology*. New York: Oxford University Press.

Skillen, Anthony. 1978. *Ruling Illusions*. Atlantic Highlands, N.J.: Humanities Press.

Smiley, Marion. 1992. *Moral Responsibility and the Boundaries of Community*. Chicago: University of Chicago Press.

Smith, Sidonie, and Julia Watson, eds. 1996. *Getting a Life*. Minneapolis: University of Minnesota Press.

Spelman, Elizabeth V. 1988. *Inessential Woman*. Boston: Beacon Press.

Stack, Carol. 1993. "The Culture of Gender: Women and Men of Color." In *An Ethic of Care*. Ed. Jeanne Larrabee. New York: Routledge.

Statman, Daniel, ed. 1993. *Moral Luck*. Albany: State University of New York Press.

Stocker, Michael. 1976. "The Schizophrenia of Modern Ethical Theories." *Journal of Philosophy* 73: 453–466.

Stocker, Michael. 1990. *Plural and Conflicting Values*. New York: Oxford University Press.

Strawson, Peter. 1968. "Freedom and Resentment." In *Studies in the Philosophy of Thought and Action*. Ed. Peter Strawson. New York: Oxford University Press.

Taylor, Charles. 1989. *Sources of the Self*. Cambridge, Mass.: Harvard University Press.

Taylor, Charles. 1993. "Explanation and Practical Reasoning." In *The Quality of Life*. Ed. Martha Nussbaum and Amartya Sen. New York: Oxford University Press.

Taylor, Charles. 1995. "A Most Peculiar Institution." In *World, Mind, and Ethics: Essays on the Ethical Philosophy of Bernard Williams*. Ed. J. E. J. Altham and Ross Harrison. New York: Cambridge University Press.

Taylor, Gabriele. 1985. *Pride, Shame, and Guilt: Emotions of Self-Assessment*. New York: Oxford University Press.

Thomas, Laurence Mordekhai. 1993. *Vessels of Evil: American Slavery and the Holocaust*. Philadelphia: Temple University Press.

Thomas, Laurence Mordekhai. 1995. "Power, Trust, and Evil." In *Overcoming Racism and Sexism*. Ed. Linda Bell and David Blumenfeld. Lanham, Md.: Rowman and Littlefield.

Tilghman, B. R. 1991. *Wittgenstein, Ethics and Aesthetics*. Albany: State University of New York Press.

Tong, Rosemary. 1993. *Feminine and Feminist Ethics*. Belmont, Calif.: Wadsworth.

Tronto, Joan. 1993. *Moral Boundaries*. New York: Routledge.

Wainryb, Cecilia, and Elliot Turiel. 1995. "Diversity in Social Development: Between or Within Cultures?" In *Morality in Everyday Life*. Ed. Melanie Killen and Daniel Hart. New York: Cambridge University Press.

Walker, Margaret Urban. 1987. "Moral Particularity." *Metaphilosophy* 18: 171–85.

Walker, Margaret Urban. 1989a. "What Does the Different Voice Say? Gilligan's Women and Moral Philosophy," *Journal of Value Inquiry* 23: 123–34.

Walker, Margaret Urban. 1989b. "Moral Understandings: Alternative 'Epistemology' for a Feminist Ethics," *Hypatia* 4: 15–28.

Walker, Margaret Urban. 1991. "Moral Luck and the Virtues of Impure Agency." *Metaphilosophy* 22: 14–27. Reprinted in Daniel Statman, ed. 1993. *Moral Luck*. Albany: State University of New York Press.

Walker, Margaret Urban. 1992. "Feminism, Ethics, and the Question of Theory." *Hypatia* 7: 23–38.

Walker, Margaret Urban. 1993. "Keeping Moral Space Open: New Images of Ethics Consulting." *Hastings Center Report* 23: 33–40.

Walzer, Michael. 1983. *Spheres of Justice*. New York: Basic Books.

Walzer, Michael. 1993. "Objectivity and Social Meaning." In *The Quality of Life*. Ed. Martha C. Nussbaum and Amartya Sen. New York: Oxford University Press.

Walzer, Michael. 1994. *Thick and Thin*. Notre Dame, Ind.: University of Notre Dame Press.

Watters, Ethan. 1995. "Claude Steele Has Scores to Settle," *New York Times Magazine*, September 17.

Weil, Simone. 1986. "The *Iliad* or The Poem of Force [1945]." In *Simone Weil: An Anthology*. Ed. Sian Miles. New York: Weidenfeld & Nicolson.

Weston, Anthony. 1992. *Toward Better Problems*. Philadelphia: Temple University Press.

Whitbeck, Caroline. 1983. "A Different Reality: Feminist Ontology." In *Beyond Domination*. Ed. Carol C. Gould. Totowa, N.J.: Rowman and Allanheld.

Wiggins, David. 1978. "Deliberation and Practical Reason." In *Practical Reasoning*. Ed. Joseph Raz. Oxford: Oxford University Press.

Williams, Bernard. 1972. *Morality*. New York: Cambridge University Press.

Williams, Bernard. 1973a. "The Makropulos Case: Reflections on the Tedium of Immortality." In *Problems of the Self*. Cambridge: Cambridge University Press.

Williams, Bernard. 1973b. *Utilitarianism For and Against*. With J. J. C. Smart. New York: Cambridge University Press.

Williams, Bernard. 1981a. "Persons, Character and Morality." In *Moral Luck*. Cambridge: Cambridge University Press.

Williams, Bernard. 1981b. "Moral Luck." In *Moral Luck*. Cambridge: Cambridge University Press.

Williams, Bernard. 1985. *Ethics and the Limits of Philosophy*. Cambridge, Mass.: Harvard University Press.

Williams, Bernard. 1993. *Shame and Necessity*. Berkeley and Los Angeles: University of California Press.

Williams, Bernard. 1995. "The Point of View of the Universe: Sidgwick and the Ambitions of Ethics." In *Making Sense of Humanity and Other Philosophical Papers, 1982–1993*. New York: Cambridge University Press.

Wilson, Catherine. 1993. "On Some Alleged Limitations to Moral Endeavor." *Journal of Philosophy* 90: 275–89.

Wittgenstein, Ludwig. 1958. *Philosophical Investigations*. Trans. G. E. M. Anscombe. New York: Macmillan.

Wittgenstein, Ludwig. 1970. *Zettel*. Trans. G. E. M. Anscombe and G. H. von Wright. Berkeley and Los Angeles: University of California Press.

Young, Iris M. 1990. *Justice and the Politics of Difference*. Princeton, N.J.: Princeton University Press.

index

DATE DUE

GAYLORD			PRINTED IN U.S.A